Edward Hancox lives in Shropshire in the United Kingdom with his wife and a small, noisy child but spends as much time as he can in Iceland. Music – especially contemporary Icelandic music – is his other passion. He writes about both subjects for various magazines and websites, including *Iceland Review*, *Atlantica*, and the *Reykjavík Grapevine*, and on his blog, icelanddefrosted.com.

Edward enjoys growing plants which, not unlike himself, are tall and thin. He has had particular success with bamboo and rhubarb. It is not possible to grow bamboo in Iceland, but rhubarb is surprisingly prevalent.

ICELAND
DEFROSTED

EDWARD HANCOX

SilverWood

Published in 2013 by the author
using SilverWood Books Empowered Publishing®

SilverWood Books
30 Queen Charlotte Street, Bristol, BS1 4HJ
www.silverwoodbooks.co.uk

Some passages of this work by the author have previously been
published online by *Iceland Review*. They have been reproduced
here with their kind agreement. Passages from RN Stewart,
Rivers of Iceland, (Icelandic Tourist Board, 1950) have been kindly
reproduced with permission from Kjartan Lárusson,
on behalf of ITB/Úrval Útsýn.

ISBN 978-1-78132-108-9 (paperback)
ISBN 978-1-78132-109-6 (ebook)

British Library Cataloguing in Publication Data
A CIP catalogue record for this book is available from the British Library

Set in Sabon by SilverWood Books
Printed on responsibly sourced paper

Dedicated to my two girls, Nichola and Lily

Contents

Map of Iceland

1	A Stone's Throw	9
2	Hot Pots and Hot Dogs	18
3	The Beautiful South	42
4	Hopelandic	67
5	Urban Puffin Patrol	87
6	Great Find, Huh?	101
7	Lord of the Arctic	120
8	A Feast with the Huldufólk	136
9	A Plump of Hook-Nosed Sea Pigs	161
10	A Creative Bunch	189
11	Dauðalogn	210
12	Sea Monsters of the West Fjords	230
13	Blink and Save	258

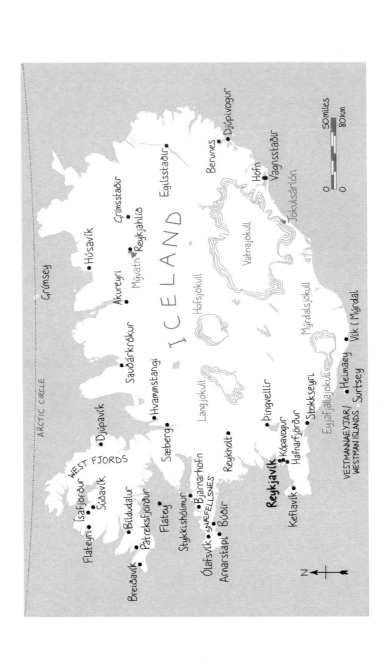

Chapter 1

A Stone's Throw

I have always enjoyed winter so much more than summer, so it's perhaps no surprise I was drawn to Iceland. I'd rather put on my biggest, warmest coat and go out for a stroll in that silent new world of a fresh snowfall than battle with insects, sun creams and sandwiches that actually include sand. I prefer the crisp frosts and deep blue skies of mid-winter to the semi-warm, wasp-infested flat lemonade of an English summer.

To begin with I was fooled by the name, too, and by thoughts of polar bears and penguins, Eskimos (no offence intended, Inuit people) in igloos, darkness for eleven months of the year, Santa Claus' workshop surrounded by reindeer, deep snow year round and the Northern Lights arching over frozen landscapes. Like a puffin to a shoal of sand eels, I was drawn in. Of course some of these stereotypical perceptions of Iceland are far from the truth and I can now prove that they're misguided, comical even. I will endeavour to do this over the coming pages. I'm still searching for those Northern Lights, though.

Iceland is actually one of the United Kingdom's neighbours and is only a stone's throw at 1123 miles away (if you can find a half decent stone-thrower) over the rough and chilly North Atlantic. Flights take a mere two hours and a bit from Glasgow to Keflavík, Iceland's main international airport. Yet it is rarely mentioned in the British media, save in connection with volcanic eruptions, subsequent ash clouds, financial blunders and the Icelandic princess of pop, Björk. More of all of them later.

Oh, and the Eurovision Song Contest, don't forget that – although 'Euro' and 'song' both seemed to have been somewhat stretched in meaning. Since when does wailing with a heavy metal soundtrack constitute a song? Eurovision, since you brought it up, is huge in Iceland. I'm not really sure why. Parties are planned around it, friends and family sit themselves in front of the screen, lapping up the skewed results and painful renditions. I have grown to dread the night; the UK entry, despite our impressive pop heritage, is consistently awful and, not having many political allies, we often come fairly low in the rankings. This is of much amusement to my Icelandic pals, who feel it necessary to boast about their success via text messages or even drunken phone calls. I usually just laugh it off.

I once took an Icelandic friend home to the UK to meet my family. I spent the next hour cringing as Einar patiently explained that he didn't live in an igloo and had seen British TV. In fact, he has a soft spot for *Dad's Army* and Everton Football Club. On the same trip, my Icelandic pal was treated to a whirlwind tour of everything that I considered to be stereotypically 'British'. The best of British, if you like. It started with a Test match at Edgbaston. England vs. South Africa. I spent most of the game explaining the rules (Duckworth–Lewis method, anyone?), but sun and beer improved the day no end. This was followed – in no particular order – by fish and chips, a rainy day in Llandudno, tikka masala, a Friday night in a Shropshire market town, shopping, real ale, a steam engine, and roast beef. Throughout this tour, family and friends asked increasingly though unintentionally ignorant questions about Iceland. ('Do you only eat fish?' cropped up a lot.) Despite the Icelandic tourist board's best efforts, the majority of British people, like my friends and family, seem to still be in the dark about Iceland. And we are a neighbouring country. I dread to think what more distant countries think of the place. Perhaps Iceland should play more cricket.

This doesn't seem to work both ways. Icelanders generally speak excellent English, and are generally knowledgeable about British culture. The Icelanders I have met are only too clued-up on which football team has drawn Manchester United in the Cup, and many have an encyclopaedic knowledge of British comedy. I was initially stunned to learn that even some of the smaller English football clubs draw Icelandic supporters, and that David Walliams and Matt Lucas catchphrases – 'I want that one' being a particular favourite – have caught on in this remote land. They are aware of British politics; please see the Gordon Brown hate campaign of 2009. You could probably catch an Icelander out, though, if you really wanted to. You could ask them to pronounce Leominster or Worcester, or to try some pork scratchings. Actually, best not. They can outdo us in the pronunciation stakes and with food-that-shouldn't-really-be-food every time.

As for Icelandic influence around the world: Their music has a massive hold on pop culture; you can't turn on the TV these days without hearing Sigur Rós. They have football players in the English Premier League; even Wolverhampton Wanderers has one. And they own some of the UK's leading high street shops, including a stake in the eponymous Iceland frozen-foods chain.

The trip to Llandudno in North Wales, by the way, was a day not to be forgotten. Einar and I were accompanied by my wife, Nichola, and we set off in my car. My car, I should add, is several years old and has seen better times. I am no mechanic and, as I have no interest in vehicles, I pay it little attention other than ensuring it is legal and goes when required to do so. We decided to take a route over the scenic Welsh hills, thereby showing Einar another aspect of Great Britain that is not industrial wasteland or Big Ben and the Houses of Parliament. Einar and I had known each other for a good few years at this point, and any politeness had given way to a sturdy friendship that could take a bit of ribbing. Einar considers himself an excellent driver, as do the majority of Icelanders, and frequently gave me tips on how he thought my driving skills could be improved. On reaching the Snowdonia National Park, my car started making some pretty awful noises, and despite us trying to block these out by turning up the radio and talking loudly, the rattle became louder and louder until it was unbearable. Various lights flashed up on the dashboard and I was forced to pull over. Being a man, I knew what had to be done here. I stepped outside and opened the bonnet, looked inside and scratched around, pulling some things and pushing others. After making a few 'hmm' noises and silently cursing myself for having zero mechanical prowess, I got back in the car.

'Have you sorted it out, Ed?' Einar asked.

'Yep, I think so,' I bluffed, before starting the car to the same rattle, only this time accompanied by an impressive plume of smoke from the exhaust.

I drove on, in silence. Einar was silent too. He was obviously contemplating his next move, which turned out to be a corker.

'Have you checked the oil?' he said.

I hadn't. I know I should have, but I hadn't. What followed was embarrassing for me, but highly amusing for everyone else. Einar pointed out that one of the flashing lights was shaped like an oil can, and that this was not coincidental. He then asked me to pull over, sent me off red-faced to a garage, refilled the engine with oil, and completely solved the problem. I'm sure that he repeats the story with regularity at dinner parties all over Reykjavík. I never want to mention it again.

The story doesn't end there though. On arrival at Llandudno, we did all the touristy-type things: the pier, the teddy-bear grab machines that never quite grip, the promenade, poor-quality ice cream from a van, got wet, the Great Orme, the trams, the whole caboodle. I then decided that we should have fish and chips for dinner. Could anything be more quintessentially British than eating fish and chips at the seaside? The sea close by, the salt in the air and the remnants of the beach still in your shoes – fish and chips are the only thing to be eaten in such situations. The only thing missing was red-spotted handkerchiefs on our heads. I know a great fish and chip shop in Llandudno near the tram station, called – groan – Fish Tram Chips, and we set off for it. It is award-winning and serves beer, and the best ever mushy peas too. We arrived and, breaking with tradition, sat in the restaurant half of the premises. We were handed menus and started to browse them. To my surprise, and Einar's pride, the menu proudly declared the cod to be 'fresh from Iceland'.

Iceland is a European country. In some respects anyway. One particular nod to Europe is the Icelander's love of coffee (*kaffi*). This does not extend to a fancy, overly fussy connoisseurship of beans and blends, just an acceptance that without coffee, Iceland would fall. Everywhere you go, the dark, strong, scalding brew is served. Every morning, at bars across Reykjavík, coffee is consumed in an almost religious manner. Men, either feeling worse for wear from the previous evening, or gearing themselves up for work, or both, enter in silence, pick up a copy of the daily newspaper (*Fréttablaðið* or similar) and wait for the waitress to bring a flask of coffee. That's right, a flask. None of your London-style overpriced thimblefuls here, or your American-style mocha-frappuccino-espresso-grande-to-go either. A flask. In silence, in semi-darkness, the coffee is consumed. Ready for the day, the chap sets off, only to be replaced by another, who will repeat the ritual. Filling stations around the country almost count fuel as a secondary commodity; coffee is the real reason they are there. Older Icelanders still drink coffee in a unique fashion. Rather than sweeten it by dropping sugar into the cup, they place the sugar cube in their mouths and drink the coffee through it. The younger generation have ditched this habit, but the name of Björk's first band – the Sugarcubes – is thought to have come from this practice.

It's often been said that Iceland should have been

named Greenland, and vice-versa. I'm not a great believer in this logic. Not only because the name 'Iceland' is bound to prevent it becoming the next Ibiza (I'm not being selfish, I just want it to myself), but because it does have some sense and history to it. When the first settlers arrived in Iceland in 874 – Ingólfur Arnarson and those chaps – it must have seemed pretty icy, particularly with all those huge glaciers all over the place. Glaciers still cover 11% of Iceland's surface, among them Europe's largest – Vatnajökull – which occupies 8100 square kilometres. Perhaps it was a harsh winter too. Others have suggested that Flóki Vilgerðarson – a Norwegian Viking (forget those images of horned hats and tossing a chewed meat bone over your shoulder, this is serious now) – named Iceland after seeing an ice-bound fjord from the top of a mountain. If it was Jökulsárlón that Mr. Vilgerðarson (because you would call him 'Mister') saw, then I can vouch for him. That glacial lagoon is chock full of calved icebergs.

I'm also sure that there must be green and fertile areas of Greenland too. Though I have never been there, Kangerlussuaq looks pretty green and lush to me, unless the photos have been doctored to attract visitors. Interestingly, there is a theory that Greenland was so named to do just that. Erik the Red (or, more accurately, Erik the Ginger) was an early Icelander credited with discovering and naming Greenland. Erik had no qualms about committing murder and manslaughter. At one point he became an 'outlaw', following several bloody murders, and set off on a voyage to pass the time during his three-year exile. During this little enforced holiday, Erik landed on the southern tip of what is now Greenland. After his return to Iceland, in a move that would now be called 'promoting the USP' and have marketing managers proud, Erik boasted about 'Greenland' in an attempt to attract visitors to the world's largest island. Perhaps it's Greenland's emblem of a fierce polar bear showing his tongue, or simply that Erik's words fell on deaf ears, but Greenland is today one of the most under-populated countries on the globe. Out of Iceland and Greenland I know which I prefer.

I have no cultural, familial or historical links to Iceland, but somehow I am repeatedly drawn there; it is some kind of silent beckoning. This interest has cost me thousands of hard-earned English pounds, and some strange looks from friends and family. It has turned from a passion into an obsession. I frequently think of it as an addiction, and I'm always looking for the next hit. A book or film about Iceland will quell my longing for a while, but I'll soon be found looking at the Icelandair website for deals, or trying to blag a ticket to this year's Iceland Airwaves music festival. An Icelandic beer also helps some, although experience tells me that too much is counter-productive. Music by Sigur Rós, articles in *Iceland Review* and films by Baltasar Kormákur might keep me going for a while, but the yearning doesn't really stop until the plane banks over Keflavík and I can see the red, blue and green roofs of Reykjavík in the distance, framed by the snow-covered peaks of Esja. Maybe writing this book is an attempt to keep those memories alive for a little longer.

I love the tingle of excitement I get when telling people that I'm going to Iceland, when queuing at airports behind people wearing huge backpacks and mountaineers' boots. I love the constant interest that my travels bring – 'But what's it like? Really?' It still feels like going on an adventure, like somewhere different. I like going somewhere that isn't on the holiday circuit but is just three hours from where I live. Iceland might be getting more popular – tourist numbers rise each year; certain volcanoes have inadvertently raised its profile, as has the influence of Icelandic popular culture on the mainstream; and Ben Stiller and Tom Cruise, Jake Gyllenhaal and Russell Crowe have all been spotted carousing the bars of Reykjavík – but it still feels different. It's certainly not Costa-del-Anywhere, and I'm grateful for that. In a way, it feels like 'my' special place, if that isn't too solipsistic. If I could bottle this feeling, I would. Instead, I've tried to distil it into this book.

Chapter 2

Hot Pots and Hot Dogs

The standing joke about Anchorage, Alaska could easily be applied to Reykjavík: that Reykjavík is a great city 'because Iceland is only half an hour away'. There is an element of truth to this – in that, unless you travel out of the city, you'll never experience the real Iceland. Reykjavík certainly isn't representative of Iceland as a whole, but that doesn't make it any less enjoyable.

In fact, I find that it adds to the thrill, to the buzz of the place. It feels like a frontier, like some amazing adventure is about to happen. Seeing the peaks of Esja – and sometimes Snæfellsjökull as well – from the city, reminds you that you are not that far away from nature, from the harsh, cold and often barren environment, or even an Arctic fox. The Northern Lights might even flash overhead, if you are very, very lucky. 4x4 vehicles roll through the streets, their tyres clogged with lava chips, and small planes fly out to far-flung places such as Egilsstaðir, Grímsey, Gjögur and even Greenland. The sense of excitement is palpable.

Reykjavík is home to approximately 120,000 people, or a third of the population of the country. This is roughly the same as Chester in the UK. If you include the suburbs of Reykjavík, the population tops 200,000, which leaves only approximately 100,000 living elsewhere. This is partly what makes the city special: it feels close-knit. There is a restaurant in Reykjavík that keeps a running total of the country's population on its wall: Hamborgarafabrikkan ('Hamburger Factory') promises to celebrate the birth of every new Icelander (motto: 'We are not so many, but we are working on it!'). Everyone kind of knows everyone, and if they don't, they have a friend who does. Secondly, the city is easily navigated on foot, which makes it compact and cute in the same way that your mother used to say that 'the best things always come in small packages'.

The real heart of the city, though, is kept well hidden from most casual visitors. You could quite easily spend a day there and not find it. I didn't even find it on the first weekend I spent in Reykjavík, and I don't think you'd find it on one of those all-inclusive tours that cost thousands of pounds. Sure, you get to do all the tourist stuff: the excursions, the museums, the square, the shops, the stuffed puffins and the ornamental Vikings. But until you find the heart of Reykjavík, you will feel like a complete outsider.

I'm not talking geographically, clearly. Although you would be forgiven for thinking that the downtown quarter known as 101 Reykjavik is the city's heart. It can certainly feel like the capital of hipster-ism. I am in no way a hipster (I actually like the stuffed puffins) and I used to think that the immigration officers at Keflavík Airport were not just checking your passport but also whether you were cool enough to enter. I've not seen anyone get turned back, but I bet it's happened.

No, the heart of Reykjavík is the Icelanders themselves. Specifically, Icelanders in relaxation mode. Icelanders can come across as a little aloof and uncommunicative;

they know this and even play along. So you need to seek them out at the places they go to wind down.

I had seen glimpses of it a few times, before I caught on fully. On the first occasion, it was in the hot pots of Laugardalslaug, a Reykjavík swimming pool. The entire city of Reykjavík is powered by geothermal energy – the largest such system in the world – and has been using naturally warmed water to heat its buildings and homes ever since 1930; now even some of its pavements (sidewalks, American cousins) are heated. Happily, geothermal energy also gives rise to hot pots and public swimming pools as a rather excellent by-product, and you can find these all over the city.

Hot pots come in two varieties: natural hot pots – pools – fed by hot streams or underground springs, and the more urban ones at swimming pools that look like big blue spiral-sided Jacuzzis. The urban ones, like those at Laugardalslaug, generally accommodate up to ten people and range in temperature from lukewarm to super hot. They are cheap to get into; you just pay for a locker, basically, and then you can bathe in the naturally heated tubs for as long as you want, or until you wither like a Christmas prune. If you go, try not to be typically 'English' about the whole thing. Yes, you will have to get changed in front of others – there are signs explaining exactly which body parts need to be scrubbed prior to entry (don't be embarrassed or shy, and do observe the 'Athugið!' – 'Please Note!' – signs, or face the wrath of any nearby Icelander); and you may have to walk across ice to get to the tubs, but don't hoot or scream – that will blow your cover straight away.

To Icelanders a hot pot is the equivalent of an English

pub or an American sports event. It's where people come to relax, talk, gossip, or just get away from it all. Sure, you do get those octogenarians who swim in the pools for miles at the pace of a manatee, but those are a constant across the world. It's not really about that. It's about choosing a hot tub that won't cook your insides while your hair freezes to your head. Immerse yourself, relax and just see what happens. People's frosty exterior suddenly slips away, and you will find yourself a target for idle banter and searching questions alike. Businesspeople make deals in hot pots, friends make plans in them, hangovers are cured in them, rumours are born and jokes cracked. It's a great idea, and should be exported across the world, I think; perhaps in the same way as saunas from Finland, or pubs from Ireland. Maybe not, then.

The best hot pots are the ones on the roof at Sundhöllin, the oldest pool in the city. The pool was designed by the renowned Icelandic architect Guðjón Samúelsson and built in 1937. Its white building is tucked away behind the iconic church Hallgrímskirkja. I have spent hours in the rooftop hot pots here, looking out over the city, at the colourful houses, sparse pine trees and snow-capped mountains beyond, while my body is bathed by the naturally heated water and my ears are chilled by the winter air. Bliss. Just watch out for your hair freezing, though.

If you can't find the heart of Reykjavík in a hot pot, you could probably find it on a night out. It'll be elusive, though, so I'll give you a few tips. Most tourists hit the town at around 8pm, just like they would back home. This is way, way too early. Most Icelanders won't even be thinking about going out, and will still be at home. The streets will be empty and the bars will only contain other tourists, looking at their watches and grumbling to themselves that they have been misled by the Iceland tourist board. Beer is still a novelty for Icelanders and this, coupled with high prices in bars, means a different attitude to it. All alcohol was prohibited in Iceland in 1915, although this became more relaxed with some alcoholic drinks – including wines and spirits – being made legal over time. Strong beer (over 2.25% alcohol by volume), however, was prohibited until an astonishingly recent 1989, when legalisation of all alcohol came into line with other European countries. 'Beer Day' is still very much celebrated on 1st March every year.

The Icelanders clearly had some catching up to do, and some say that they are still trying now. Icelanders will often start drinking at home, with friends. This is cheaper, as drinks are bought from the state-run liquor shops (see the queues on Friday and Saturday for evidence of this), and generally means you can fit more drinking hours into the night. These shops still serve bottles of wine and spirits in plain brown paper bags, just like the ones alcoholics use in American movies. After eating and drinking until the time an average Englishman has drunk himself to a standstill, Icelanders hit the town. This is usually between midnight and 1am. And it is absolute mayhem. Clubs are full to the brim, with queues of more people trying to get in. Everywhere is playing music, and beats spill from doorways as you pass. Boy meets girl. Boy meets boy. Girl meets girl. I've had a few big nights out in my time, as every man should have, but Reykjavík is something else. A night out here is serious stuff, not least on your wallet. This is the beating heart of the city, and it will go on until 5 or 6am. And at that point you need to go for a *pylsa* (hot dog) – the best tip ever given to me. This is an Icelandic habit; after drinking it works perfectly and *pylsur* are often consumed one after another. Try to forget that the sausage is a mix of lamb, pork and beef; just cover it with 'the works' (*ein með öllu*), a myriad of multi-coloured sauces and diced raw and fried onions. It is the perfect after-drink food any time of the night. Or day.

The biggest night of the year, though, is New Year's Eve. Every Icelander knows this, and if you have read *101 Reykjavik* by Hallgrímur Helgason you'll know this too. Helgason has a knack of describing Reykjavík life in high definition. I've been in Reykjavík for a New Year's Eve, and it was the best New Year's I've ever had. Although, to be fair, previous competition had only included damp squibs of parties in England, empty promises of friends getting together, counting down to another year with the TV set to Jools Holland and his *Hootenanny* (a what exactly?), and Auld Lang Synes with strangers and people I probably wouldn't see for another year.

My friend Einar and his wife Klara had invited Nichola and me to spend New Year's in Reykjavík and we couldn't wait. On 31st December, we boarded the plane to Keflavík with undisguised excitement, jumping up and down in our seats like little children. This child-like state of mind was only reinforced when we touched down at Keflavík to find it covered in a sprinkling of snow, and the entire ground staff engaged in a snowball fight. Iceland seemed exactly as it should be on 31st December: cold and dark, with snow spiralling to the ground. It might have been me, or too many miniatures on the plane, but there was something else too. A tangible sense of excitement and anticipation for the night's celebration. Everyone knew it was coming, and everyone was counting the hours.

Einar collected us from the airport – at that time I still lacked the courage to drive on the 'wrong' side of the road – and transported us speedily into the suburbs of Reykjavík. Later that day, we sat down to a feast prepared by Klara and, chef for the night, Einar. Well, he had put an apron on and flitted around a bit, but no one was fooled. We ate a carpaccio of lamb with cranberries, fresh lobster, fillet of beef and an insanely good dessert that seemed to contain equal parts fresh fruit, chocolate and cream. The food was so delicious; it put the usual New Year Chinese takeaway at home to complete shame. Actually, maybe I've been a little harsh on Einar here. He did cook the steaks, after all, and in a style more associated with Antipodeans than Icelanders. The barbeque. This is a huge deal in Iceland, and the madness of nipping out into Arctic weather to turn a steak is offset by grabbing an extra cold beer while you are out there. The beer in Iceland is excellent, by the way, although we were sticking mainly to wine and, dangerously, champagne and cognac. It keeps the cold away, I suppose.

Speaking of Arctic weather, it is usual on New Year's Eve for everyone to attend huge organised bonfires in their local neighbourhood. This spreads the party out, and incorporates everyone. Or it would have, if the snow had not turned to torrential rain and howling wind. The authorities decided that it would be too dangerous to go ahead with the bonfires. This health-and-safety-based decision seemed sensible, but we attended the rescheduled bonfire a couple of nights later and found that the fire had been built on a steep slope and consisted of cylindrical wooden pallets. Occasionally a burning pallet would break free and roll towards the crowd, in quite an alarming fashion.

Equally alarming, but certainly non-negotiable, is the Icelandic tradition of fireworks on New Year's Eve. They start at about 7pm and peak at midnight. Just before midnight, we all donned our outdoor gear and headed out into the wind and rain. It was cold, but only around minus 3 degrees Celsius. I was handed a battery of fireworks and we began to simultaneously shoot them into the night air, right out of our hands or from precarious tubes in the ground. Everyone else in Reykjavík was doing the same and the sky was alight with a rainbow of colours and the kind of deafening bangs that make your insides shudder. Fireworks are sold in the run-up to NYE (as the kids seem to have it these days), with all profits going to the Icelandic search and rescue team (ICE-SAR), which is pretty neat, and also lucrative. Last year over a thousand tonnes of fireworks were imported and it is not uncommon for Icelandic families to spend hundreds of thousands of krónur on their rockets and bangers. It is fantastically impressive and a real spectacle.

While we were sending our rockets skywards, a neighbour came out into the car park area where we stood with our little party and other families from nearby apartments. Clearly a fan of Icelandic beer or something harder, he stumbled out carrying a huge cardboard box. This, it transpired, was an industrial-sized firework, the sort usually reserved for U2 concerts and deployed by men in goggles from behind a safety desk. Our new friend merely lit the fuse and then ran for cover. The firework exploded to life in a riot of colours and sound. Animals ran for cover, car alarms sounded, children cried and windows rattled. Perhaps this particular firework shouldn't have been enjoyed from such close proximity – but what a celebration, or as Jools would have it, a Hootenanny.

It was during one big night out in Reykjavík that I was told a secret by a beautiful young Icelandic woman with piercing blue eyes and butter-blonde hair. She had been drinking, yes, but I have no reason to doubt her. I'll keep her name secret to protect her identity. That's how shocking this information is.

She told me that once a year, the staff at Reykjavík Zoo sit down to a very special dinner. At this dinner they eat the residents of the zoo itself, all in the name of managing numbers. Before you recoil in disgust (is it too late?), let me tell you about the zoo, and that no exotic or endangered creatures are eaten, obviously. Just the domestic ones that are breeding too quickly and normally would be finished off by predators. That said, it's still shocking, isn't it? That reindeer little Inga just petted? It's being roasted in red wine tonight, and served with a light salad.

Reykjavík Zoo might just be the most disappointing

zoo I have ever seen. If you have seen the Roundabout Zoo from the TV comedy series *League of Gentlemen*, you'll have some sort of comparison, but honestly, don't bother visiting. If you think I'm being overly negative, this is from the zoo's own website: 'In the Zoo you will find: horses, cattle, pigs, sheep, goats, foxes, mink, reindeer, seals, hens, chickens, turkeys, pigeons, rabbits, guinea pigs, geese, ducks, dogs and cats.' Dogs and cats? Pigeons? Hens and chickens? I was expecting animals from the frozen Poles, penguins, polar bears, that sort of thing, all with a conservation slant – the rescue and rehabilitation of Arctic and Antarctic animals. Instead, we saw a frightened fox at the back of a cage and the kind of animals and birds that are usually encountered as roadkill in Britain. I never envisaged a zoo where the animals were harvested by the staff.

There is a place where numbers do need to be managed. The hill – Öskjuhlíð – on which the Perlan building stands is the location for this bunny yarn. 'The Pearl' is a strikingly modern structure. Opened in 1991, it is a glass dome sitting on top of several aluminium tanks, each of which can hold millions of litres of geothermally heated water – part of the city's heating infrastructure. The reason the Pearl has such an expansive glass dome is so that the Northern Lights can allegedly be seen from inside. As if. It also holds exhibitions and concerts, has a Christmas shop, a museum, and boasts an expensive rotating restaurant. People often come for the views over the city and the photo opportunities. It even has its very own fake geyser. Trees have been planted on the hillside around it, and the grassy knoll slopes towards the city in one direction and the geothermal beach at Nauthólsvík in the other. The geothermal beach isn't as exciting as it sounds, by the way – the sand is imported and the sea is artificially heated by warm water being pumped into it. It is somewhat lacklustre. The bunnies, though, make me smile. *Oryctolagus cuniculus*, aka bunny-kins, are not native to Iceland, but over the years countless escaped and abandoned pet rabbits have made their way to the grassy hillside beneath the Pearl, leading to an infestation. The little critters are everywhere. Kind of like those hedgehogs in Uist, Scotland, but without the environmental impact and ill-considered intention.

World Book Night is celebrated every April. Designed to promote the joys of reading a proper book – one with actual pages and everything – it centres around the giving away of one million books in one night by an army of volunteers. World Book Night also distributes an impressive 620,000 books to hospitals, shelters, care homes and prisons throughout the year, across the UK.

I really liked the idea from the outset. Firstly, I am a sucker for books and a visit to a bookshop, a really good one, can take hours out of my day. Staff at the Austurstræti branch of the Eymundsson bookstore in central Reykjavík can confirm this. I think that there is a simple pleasure to holding and reading a book, one that e-publishing may ultimately struggle to recreate.

I also think it is commendable to give books to people that wouldn't normally get the opportunity to read; the objective being to increase literacy rates. The 620,000 books given to institutions can only be a good thing, right? But it's the actual giving of the books from person to person that inspires me.

I was lucky enough to be given a copy of Swedish author John Ajvide Lindqvist's *Let the Right One In* by a complete stranger at my local library. 'Would you like one of these?' she said, pushing the thick copy into my hands. 'It's about a twelve-year-old vampire.' It's not the sort of book I would usually read, admittedly, but I was thrilled to receive a gift from this pleasant lady, who clearly was just as thrilled to be making people happy by giving out copies of her favourite book. I went home and gave the book a try. I loved it; it's fantastically dark.

I was sorry to see, then, that World Book Night does not currently operate in Iceland. It's a bit like the American baseball 'World Series', in that the use of the word 'world' has been somewhat overplayed.

But it got me thinking. Does Iceland really need World Book Night? First off, the literacy rate is already extremely high (99%). There is little room or necessity for manoeuvre here. Iceland is rightly proud of its high standard of education. Reykjavík is a UNESCO city of literature. What more could a single twenty-four hours provide?

Secondly, Icelanders already love their books. If the often-quoted fact that 'Iceland publishes more books per capita than any other country' doesn't prove this (it's reckoned that every year five books are published per every thousand Icelanders), then try standing in a bookshop in downtown Reykjavík in December. You will be lucky to stay on your feet in the stampede for books to give as Christmas gifts. This is known as Jólabókaflóð, the Christmas Book Flood. Icelanders are already well aware of the pleasure of giving and receiving books.

There is something to be said about Iceland's history of literature at this juncture. I'm not going to harp on about it, but you may have heard about something called the sagas? And a certain Mr. Laxness? Halldór Laxness was a Nobel Prize-winning Icelandic writer, who, despite passing away in 1998, still has a huge influence on Icelandic literature. He was prolific, and his work showed a side of Iceland and Icelanders that the world hadn't seen before. The point I'm trying to make here is that Iceland has literature running through it like a strand of DNA.

Icelanders are – generally speaking – a creative bunch and writers are welcomed and celebrated in Iceland. One in ten Icelanders will publish something in their lifetime. I feel much more comfortable discussing my own book with Icelandic friends than I do at home, where it's viewed as something geeky, almost abnormal, not necessarily something to be proud of.

Happily, Icelandic fiction is now bigger than ever. Authors such as Arnaldur Indriðason and Yrsa Sigurðardóttir have got their feet well and truly under the Nordic crime table and are reaping the benefits. Their books are selling out all over the world (as in the whole world, this time) and in many languages.

The simple fact is this: Icelanders love books. They love to read them, they love to write them and they love to give them as gifts. I think it's fair to say that every night is a book night in Iceland. And that's fine with me.

✳✳✳

Another Reykjavík landmark is Hallgrímskirkja ('the Church of Hallgrímur'), a Lutheran church. It is the largest church in Iceland and certainly dominates the Reykjavík skyline, not only because of its height and striking design, but because it is built on top of a hill. It was designed in 1937 by our old friend Guðjón Samúelsson, he of the Sundhöllin swimming pool, who was State Architect at the time – obviously a busy lad. He is said to have designed it to look like staggered Icelandic basalt columns, but I think it looks more like a rocket ship. It took nearly forty years to build the church, and the lofty grey tower was completed many years before the rest of the church in 1986. Insert your own builder's joke here. As you are walking towards the church, you pass a statue of Leif Ericson, son of the aforementioned Erik the Red, and the chap who may have discovered North America almost 500 years before Christopher Columbus – a gift to Iceland from the US.

Frakkastígur, one of the streets leading up to the church, is on a fair gradient and to my detriment I found that it could be slippery underfoot during winter. As I took an ungraceful tumble on the tarmac, I'm sure that curtains twitched, and an Icelandic mum on her weekly shop hid her face as she privately giggled at my inability to cope with such tame conditions. 'You should come back when it's half a metre deep,' she said, according to her eyes anyway. Some streets in Reykjavík are geothermally heated to prevent ice forming; clearly not this one. Red faced and bruised, I made my way to the church. As you go in through the door, there is a little gift shop on the left where you can purchase tickets for the elevator to the top of the tower. It's only about 500 krónur (a couple of British pounds), but the two English ladies in their seventies with whom I shared the lift were openly proud of having sneaked in for free. Cheeky, indeed. The top of the church affords views over the entire city, and is breathtaking in terms of both the vista and the bone-chilling wind. You can take photographs of the city below and attempt to capture the 360-degree panorama, then try to match the shots up, Rubik's cube-style, when you get home. Or maybe that's just me. Back on the ground, it's worth checking out the impressive interior and organ. I followed those old ladies on the way out, by the way, and they never did pay.

On one occasion, I was lucky enough to visit the top of Hallgrímskirkja's spire at sunset. The effect was truly magnificent. The wind still howled through the open windows but seemed to bring in fresh, clean air rather than just a case of the shivers. The traffic was too far below to disturb the peace, and even the small planes gliding into Reykjavík's domestic airport seemed to do so without sound. The views stretched out in every direction: to Perlan on top of its hill; and to Esja, rising up in the distant north-east, dusted with its icing-sugar snow, as if tempting you out of the city and into the Icelandic wilderness. The best, though, was yet to come. As the sun sank slowly into the sea, it cast a magnificent orange glow over the city that resonated through the coloured rooftops and quiet streets; then the light turned pink, catching the lining of the mackerel-sky clouds that had formed high above us.

Back on the ground, I did what I like doing best in

Reykjavík: nothing much. I could spend – no, wait, I *have* spent – days, weeks even, just mooching around the city. Everything is within walking distance, which I love; I often find that after arriving from Keflavík, the best thing to do is to walk around. Maybe a *kaffi* in here, or a *bjór* in there. Pop into a bookstore, or a music shop. Life here seems to be about quality, not speed. People enjoy talking to each other in bars, or eating an Icelandic twisted doughnut (*kleinur*) while reading in a bookshop. Pop into Dogma and have a look at their funky and strange T-shirts. Walk down to the harbour. Go for a swim at Laugardalslaug. Keep an eye out for Icelandic rock stars. Grab some bread and feed the ducks, swans and other birdlife at Tjörnin, the lake near the City Hall. Take a dog for a walk.

Take a dog for a walk. Sounds like a grand idea. Except in Reykjavík it hasn't always been an easy thing to do. Dogs have been banned from within the city limits since 1924, although they are now permitted if you have purchased an expensive licence. They were traditionally seen as working animals, capable of spreading disease, rather than cute little pooches kept as pets. These days, the licensing system allows the monitoring of vaccinations, worming and micro-chipping. There are also regulations about having your dog on a collar and leash, and so forth.

I learnt all this from a friend of a friend, Þorleifur. An 'older' chap, is Þorleifur, who works for something to do with promoting Iceland and regularly takes his Icelandic sheepdog, Mosi, for a walk. Here is the great thing, though: Þorleifur and Mosi frequently invite people to join them for their walks around Reykjavík. I was all too keen to go, despite the trace elements of the previous night's beer still hurtling around my system, and the snow having turned to thick ice underfoot.

I met Þorleifur and Mosi just off Sæbraut, on the narrow footpath that runs alongside Reykjavík's sea defences, on the outskirts of the city. Þorleifur handed me Mosi's leash and we set off. Or rather we would have, if Mosi hadn't been so keen to mark his territory at every available opportunity.

The wind was blowing in off the sea, making the clouds race quickly over the city. I adopted a slightly slower pace on account of the slippery ice, to ensure I didn't embarrass myself (again!) in front of either Þorleifur or Mosi. Mosi, though, was keen to see me fail and frequently gave a good sharp tug on the leash to see if he could pull me off balance.

Mosi was light brown, with – not unlike myself – some grey around his ears. He had blonde fur around his back and eyes, a white stripe over his nose and the typical Icelandic sheepdog tail, which curled upwards onto his back. He was short and squat, but powerful, and very clearly intelligent. I was told that the breed is not dissimilar to the Shetland sheepdog or the Welsh corgi. Either way, Mosi wasn't bothered, and became frustrated with Þorleifur and me waffling on about dogs. He preferred to look out across the sea to Mount Esja, which was partially covered in a scattering of snow. Þorleifur took the opportunity to show me some extra claws on Mosi's legs, which some people say are used for walking through snowdrifts. I'm not so sure though.

We continued to walk down Sæbraut: Harpa, the new concert hall, was visible in the distance and to our left I saw Hallgrímskirkja up on the hill. Further on, we reached the Viking ship statue 'Sólfar' (Sun Voyager), which sits on a plinth covered in snow, set against its own perfect maritime backdrop. We stopped for a few photos, and even Mosi posed for the camera with a toothy grin, before spotting another dog in the distance and running off at full pelt, leaving me to feel the true power of this hardy breed by nearly having my left shoulder dislocated.

Back in control, we continued our walk. Þorleifur was an intriguing chap, full of tales and information, and this, along with the cool sea breeze, was helping my hangover no end. Þorleifur pointed out some sea birds: kittiwakes and eider ducks bobbed around on the sea, which was deep blue, and mirror still. There can't be many capital cities than can boast this, surely?

We were not far from the venue for one of my favourite Reykjavík pastimes. Kolaportið is an experience that is quintessentially Icelandic, and a million miles away from the groomed, sophisticated image of Reykjavík peddled by the posh bars, swanky hotels and myriad tourist booths. Kolaportið is an indoor market, located near the harbour, and it sells pretty much everything. I hesitate to use the phrase 'flea market' as this doesn't really do it justice. Open only on weekend mornings, its cavernous space is crammed with Icelanders buying and selling, well, everything. You can buy second-hand records, sweets, children's clothes, fishing tackle, videos, even fermented shark. The chatter of Icelandic buying and selling seems to be everywhere. I've been to the new shopping malls in Reykjavík and they are not a patch on this, certainly not in terms of atmosphere. I love it.

Outside Kolaportið, I observed a number of babies

lying in their prams. No parents in sight. This is not unique to Kolaportið; it happens outside shops and restaurants all over Reykjavík. The babies are actually left there for their own good, because Icelanders believe that the fresh cold air is healthy for children, even in freezing conditions. I can't see this catching on any time soon in the paranoid streets of Britain, and it shows just how safe the streets of Iceland are. Crime exists here; just at a super low level. It was still an arresting sight, and I remarked on it to Þorleifur, who failed to see my point entirely.

We ended our walk at Harpa, the concert hall with bubble-like windows. I had enjoyed meeting Þorleifur, and Mosi even more so. Mosi was a cute little pooch and I was glad he could now live his life here in Reykjavík. As we parted ways, Þorleifur told me that Mosi had sired pups all over the world; they are exported. I took his number. It might come in useful.

Reykjavík is just one of the best places in the world to be. I feel safe in Reykjavík. I feel the stresses of home leach from me. It's never long before I find myself thinking: do you know what, I could really live here. I find myself looking at the price of accommodation in the newspaper, or searching for jobs on the internet. I walk past schools and nurseries and wonder if my children – I did this even before I had any – could go there. I think that I would probably work as part of the mountain rescue team; that way I could get my fix of adrenaline by rescuing people from craggy mountain tops, while spending the rest of my time lounging in hot pots and drinking coffee in the city, quite possibly surrounded by quietly charming Icelandic women. My dreams are routinely punctured as I am reminded that I probably couldn't afford to live here, the Icelandic language is impossibly hard to learn, and I have a crippling fear of heights. You can't blame a man for dreaming, though, can you?

In fact, I do find Reykjavík incredibly inspiring. Everywhere, everyone seems to be involved in something creative. People are in bands, or writing books. Even the graffiti in Reykjavík is creative. This seems to rub off on me (the creative spirit, not the graffiti). It's where I got the idea for this book, certainly. I like this feeling. The feeling that if you try, you could do anything. It's incredibly empowering and motivational. I haven't been anywhere else like it.

One man who can't bear to be away from Reykjavík for too long is Snorri Helgason. Formerly of the band Sprengjuhöllin, but now going it alone, this singer-songwriter of folksy Americana can never be too far from his home city, or a *pylsa*. Especially at Christmastime.

I met up with Snorri at an East London record store, where he told me all about it over – what else? – a strong black coffee. Snorri was sporting a Viking-esque beard that belied his youth, an Iceland-hipster standard-issue woolly hat, and a thick scarf against the cold. He had a warm handshake.

Snorri had moved from Reykjavík to London the previous year. For someone so strongly associated with the Reykjavík music scene, it seemed a strange choice. 'I wanted to get out of Iceland, and the music scene there,' he said. 'Yes, it's close and collaborative and that's brilliant, but at the same time it can feel claustrophobic. With my solo career, I wanted to break away from that.'

Snorri had been touring extensively in Europe and was now ready to go back home. No, scrap that: he was desperate to go back. He told me that he missed the food, his friends and the Reykjavík music scene. I could see why.

'The break worked. I love London, but it didn't inspire me like Reykjavík. It's that ultimate break-up thing – it's not you, it's me.' As if to prove this, Snorri had returned to Reykjavík for the annual Airwaves festival, playing a staggering eleven shows in four days. How's that for a statement of intent? 'It's easier to just turn up and play as a solo artist, so I thought I'd go for it.'

I told Snorri that I hadn't been able to make Airwaves the previous year.

'Oh,' he said, 'you should have come. It was really good. I played in coffee shops, house parties and at Harpa.' Harpa is the concert hall in Reykjavík that opened in 2011, the one I'd seen on my walk with Þorleifur and Mosi the Icelandic sheepdog. Snorri was clearly a fan. 'It's beautiful,' he said. 'My girlfriend doesn't like it, because she says it blocks the view of the mountains, but I think it's a small price to pay.' It had apparently worked well as a venue at the festival. 'You could just hang your coat up and spend the evening going from room to room listening to different artists.' Gallingly, Snorri told me that even the Northern Lights had turned up at the festival, putting on a spectacular show.

He talked about the making of his latest album, *Winter Sun*. He said that the close network of musicians in Reykjavík made it so much easier; Sindri from Seabear agreed to produce the album after a New Year's Eve phone call, and Sóley, another Reykjavík luminary, played on the record too. He made the whole recording process seem like a meeting of friends, and deceptively easy. It's a formula that clearly works.

I asked Snorri for the secret of a good night out in Reykjavík. 'House parties,' he said, without hesitation. 'Find a good house party, that's where it will be at. A couple of beers downtown maybe, and don't forget the *pylsur* – they are the best in the world.' I pointed out that Snorri might just be biased. He laughed.

We discussed Reykjavík's first big snowfall of the year – the biggest since 1921, by all accounts. A friend had sent Snorri a photo and he had felt a pang of homesickness. 'Reykjavík is a big part of me,' he said. 'It's a big part of my consciousness. The houses. The places. The people. It's all very important to me.' And with that he put on his hat and headed for the door. I had a feeling Snorri would be booking a flight back home to Reykjavík just as soon as he got to his laptop.

Reykjavík never seems to disappoint. One January, I found myself in Reykjavík on a dull, wet Thursday. Having made the trip across to Iceland in January purposely to indulge myself with picturesque snow scenes and frosty-haired pool-languishing – perfect for washing away those post-Christmas blues – I was perturbed to find myself in a week where the rain barely stopped, the wind rattled the windows and any chance of Northern Lights was chased away by temperatures of up to a balmy 8 degrees Celsius. Everyone had a look of despondency about them as they dashed from shop to shop, and the tourists were turned away in droves from pre-booked Northern Lights mystery tours.

It was on this soggy Thursday, in one of the city's tourist information centres, that I heard my favourite rebuff to a tourist. The attendant was asked whether there would be a Northern Lights tour that evening. For the umpteenth time, she smiled and in a polite voice said, 'Yes!', before adding, 'I think you will not go.' Brilliant. So I did what I have learnt from Icelanders. I went to a café and ordered coffee. It arrived in a flask – which I still find thrilling. I poured cup after cup and read a book in the comfort of my own booth. I might even have ordered a slice of warm chocolate cake with whipped cream, but that would be telling.

After an hour or so, my clothes had dried and I couldn't people-watch any more due to the steam on the window. Then I caught a snippet of a conversation that sent my body tingling with excitement. Either that or the sugar rush from the cake. I understood just enough to know that I should gather my stuff, pay the bill and hit the street. It worked. It was five o'clock in the afternoon, on a dreary Thursday, but Reykjavík had just spun her magic again. Amiina were playing a concert in a tiny record store.

Amiina – for those of you that don't know – are four classically trained young women who are best known for being the string section of Sigur Rós. If you don't know who Sigur Rós are, I can't help you. Amiina are a band in their own right and have added a drummer and an electronic artist to further enhance the rich sound they already made. The result is downright amazing; the girls play all manner of instruments, including the much under-used saw, while the two lads keep a tight percussive mix going to help things along. The sounds are layered, warped, wrapped around each other. The style is at once reminiscent of Sigur Rós but at the same time different.

I enjoyed the gig immensely. The room was small and crowded, and the music reverberated off the walls, but the feeling was that something special was happening. As I stepped outside, hands full of CDs and head full of tunes, I realised I'd found what I'd been looking for. Reykjavík had worked its magic, again.

Chapter 3

The Beautiful South

Höfn appeared in the distance. The distance was about 2 metres, due to a horrible, pervasive, thick fog that seemed to have settled overnight and did nothing for the town at all. I was scheduled to stop off here, not for the remnants of the 1950s fish-freezing factory or the glacier exhibition, but to pick up supplies. With haste, that's exactly what I did – and then moved on quickly. Maybe Höfn transforms itself once the sun is out, like a Victorian English seaside town, but I didn't stick around to find out. It felt like an abandoned town in the American Midwest, with its spread-out low buildings, petrol stations and grid system of streets. I couldn't even pronounce the town's name correctly; apparently it sounds something like 'Hup'.

I pushed on to the hostel at Vagnsstaðir, a 50-kilometre drive west along the coast from Höfn. The hostel turned out to be a rather quaint house standing on its own between the sea and the mountains. Sea birds swooped low and their calls were the only thing to be heard over the wind, which rushed in from the coast. Once settled in the hostel, I headed straight out to explore. The first thing I found was an elderly and arthritic piece of machinery designed for pulling crowds of tourists across glaciers. Best described as a cross between a small locomotive and a tank, it was painted a fetching blue and yellow. It looked like it hadn't been used in a while, which was a shame as I'm sure it would have been terrific fun on the glacier, pulling intrepid explorers to the start of their journey, or entertaining grannies and grandkids on their holidays.

The other thing I found was a traffic sign warning about reindeer. Or caribou, I couldn't be sure. It was more likely to be reindeer, the only difference being domesticity. I thought this was fantastic: a huge red triangle with the silhouette of a large bull reindeer in the centre. It reminded me that I was far from home, where reindeer are only found on Christmas cards and Advent calendars.

I jumped back into the car as, unusually for Iceland, I had an appointment and couldn't be late. It was only a few kilometres from the hostel, but I had to make it to the junction of the F985 and Route 1 by 2pm or else I'd miss my only chance to go snowmobiling. I was really excited at the prospect. It was my first time and I felt like a child on Christmas morning. I parked the car in a rough car park at the junction and waited. I needn't have worried about being late; the organisers were seemingly running on Icelandic time. And I don't mean that they don't recognise British Summer Time. I think the Icelandic term is *þetta reddast*, 'it will all work out'. In Iceland, it's less of a saying, more of a way of life. I must use it more.

The weather deteriorated yet again, the low-lying grey cloud and drizzle made all the worse by a heavy wind buffeting the car as I checked my watch. So much for *þetta reddast*.

I was soon picked up by my hosts, well within the hour, to make the somewhat treacherous trip up the

F985 towards Skaftafellsjökull, a subsidiary glacier of Vatnajökull. The F985 – where do they get such crazy names? – looked fairly straight on the map, and I would have considered attempting it myself had this not been against the vehicle's insurance policy (a warning in itself?). I was very glad I hadn't. My Icelandic guides drove a heavy, robust-looking 4x4 with monster-sized tyres. If you have ever seen the BBC *Top Gear* episode where Jeremy Clarkson drives to the North Pole, you'll know exactly what I mean. Interestingly, the support team for Jeremy and co on that trip were Icelandic. During the trip they were called on to show the skills and knowledge only found in the most experienced Arctic explorers: rescuing vehicles with bungee cords, re-inflating tyres with accelerants and cutting through shards of ice with chainsaws. The sort of thing that obliged Jeremy to accept that he wouldn't have been there without them. Something that quite a few people took pleasure in, I'm sure.

The track was twisty at best. At worst, it had eroded to nothing and had an alarmingly sharp gradient. The clearly seasoned driver handled the track expertly, knowing exactly where to place the tyres and where would send bits of rocky debris crashing to the depths below. The only comfort at this level was the thick cloud, which obscured the steep drop to the jagged rocks to our left. Approximately half way up the track, the driver brought the vehicle to a stop. The first reason was that they wanted to show me signs of a glacier at work. They pointed to a large flat rock that had very pronounced glacial striations; these had been gouged out by boulders set into the glacier's icy underbelly. The boulders act as sandpaper and erode the base rock as the glacier gains and retreats over centuries. It looked like the scratch marks cats put into the paintwork of your car if you don't shoo them off.

The second reason for our stop was the Lada Niva just ahead of us. By coincidence, I recognised the car as belonging to an Italian couple who were staying at my hostel. In direct contrast to their fashionista exterior – think over-large sunglasses and ponytails for him and her – they had hired an olive-green Lada Niva 4x4. Somewhere in Reykjavík an Icelander was simultaneously laughing and rubbing his hands together at having managed to hire out such a decrepit old banger on the strength of its 4x4 'capabilities'. Seeing the couple in their Lada Niva on this precarious terrain, I couldn't decide whether to describe them as brave or stupid, but it caused much hilarity with my guides, who merely pointed at the vehicle and shouted 'Russian Hummer' before collapsing into laughter. By the end of the day, I had decided. Despite the fact that our Italian friends did make it to the base station, I concluded that they were bloody stupid and that we could easily have been looking at two bodies on our return journey. Fashionably dressed bodies, at that. You'd probably find that the sunglasses were glued to their faces.

Base station turned out to be a very isolated but rather out-of-place-looking wooden building complete with veranda and curtains in the windows. It was surrounded by all sorts of snow machines, diggers and ploughs. I couldn't get *The Shining*'s Overlook Hotel out of my mind and, once inside, I checked over my shoulder for Danny on his tricycle. No sign of him.

I was asked to dress in an all-in-one suit and crash helmet

before heading out onto the glacier. Miraculously, the murk had lifted and the white of the glacier was met by a deep blue sky, and lit by an unobscured sun. The perfect white snow stretched on and on; I felt like a toy from a Christmas cracker that had been placed on a large, perfectly flat white cotton tablecloth. It was a study in perfection. I rushed to take photographs, but I needn't have hurried. I must have been above the cloud as the glorious conditions stayed with me the whole time I was on the glacier.

My first attempt at snowmobiling was disastrous. Snowmobiles are like land-based jet-skis, with a large seat to the rear and handlebars and a screen to the front. They come only in garish colours, and the one I tried was racing-car red. To allow the machine to scoot across the snow, you need to get up a certain amount of speed. Unfortunately, I wasn't confident enough to go fast, which led to the snowmobile either sinking into the soft snow or, even worse, tilting at a slow yet irreversible rate, causing me to topple off in the most embarrassing fashion. My embarrassment was compounded by the fact that every time I alighted – voluntarily or not – I sank bodily into the 5-metre drifts that lay on top of the glacier.

Eventually I got the hang of it – it's all about shifting weight – and began zipping across the glacier at speeds of up to sixty kilometres per hour. I emitted what I took to be shrieks of joy, although, in hindsight, this could have been abject terror. I scrabbled for superlatives in my mind. It was fantastic. The speed and exhilaration of guiding something so fast and quick, combined with the stunning glacial scenery rushing by was worth every króna. And it cost quite a few of them.

I stopped at a jagged peak of rock that was jutting out of the glacier for the obligatory photo call. I was glad of this as I was struggling to take it all in. You know when in films the camera focuses in on the main character and then starts to rotate slowly around them? Like Tom Cruise in *Vanilla Sky*? I kept imagining this happening to me, with the pristine white landscape and far-off mountain peaks and the sunlight glinting off my shades. If this is what is meant by 'being on top of the world' then I've been there. I am a lot taller than Tom, too, so I would have the edge there.

The trip was over all too quickly and I returned to the Overlook Hotel to get ready to leave. Before we set off, though, there was a moment of excitement as the guides received a radio message: we were requested to return to the glacier. Just a few hundred metres out on the snow and ice was a stationary 4x4 vehicle. As we approached, the single occupant got out of the vehicle and walked towards us. I initially thought he was drunk, due to his slow and deliberate movements, but he turned out to be elderly. Late seventies, I'd say. His face was red and gnarled and just as you'd expect an Arctic mountain man to look. He wore dungarees and a workmanlike thick woollen jumper. The lads helped him with a tyre problem – probably by setting light to it – and then we were all on our way. They told me that the old fellow was driving from one side of the glacier to the other in order to see his family, a journey of tens of kilometres, and that, incredibly, such a journey was not uncommon. I found this amazing, especially as most British pensioners struggle with a set of traffic lights, let alone an immense ice sheet.

On returning to the car park at the junction with Route 1, there was a sense of despondency in the air. Actually, it was probably more in my mind and the result of a chemical infusion – in the biological sense – but that's what I had felt. I had quite literally peaked and I was not sure that anything could compete. Like the comedown after an all-night party, or how people must feel after running a marathon. What was the answer? Ice cream of course.

Off Route 1, heading west, and demarked by bales of hay with huge letters on them, a single-track road led to a farmhouse. I travelled down this track, flanked by luscious green carpets of grass either side. At the farmhouse I was met by a twelve-year-old girl wearing a Mickey Mouse T-shirt. She quickly ushered me indoors and introduced me to a range of organic ice creams, served from a counter just in front of the family's living room. All of the ice creams had been made on the farm, with milk from cows that had spent the summer grazing on the soft new grass of the glacial plains. There were a myriad of tempting flavours, but I went for vanilla. It was sublime; a million miles away from the processed white sludge served in fast food restaurants that liquefies after thirty seconds. It was creamy and delicious. It would have been delicious wherever it was eaten, but it was certainly enhanced by the location. I believe the French call it *terroir*; like eating fish and chips in Llandudno, or bagels in New York City, or drinking champagne in, well, Champagne. The location adds to the experience. The farmhouse, the sea behind it, the dark green mountains rising from the grassy meadows and punctuated by the striking white and grey tongues of the glacier poking through. I could have stayed forever, with the Mickey Mouse girl handing me cone after cone of that frozen heaven. You would have had to crane me out like one of the poor half-tonne souls you see on television.

❊❊❊

The following morning I started early. I had one of those awful, dribbly showers normally found in the holiday resorts of northern England; the polar opposite of the consistently rip-roaring, hot and powerful ones you find across the Atlantic. Perhaps I was on the wrong side of the continental divide, I mused, as I tried to wake myself up with strong black coffee instead.

My first stop of the day was Jökulsárlón. This is a stretch of water between the glacial nose of Breiðamerkurjökull (an outlet glacier of Vatnajökull) and the cold sea. Icebergs of all shapes and sizes calve from the glacier and float around the lagoon, sometimes for up to six or seven years before they either float out to sea or else melt into the lagoon like an ice cube in your Diet Coke. I arrived early, well before the bus-loads from Reykjavík. It was spectacular and eerie at the same time. I had never seen an iceberg up close before, but they are really beautiful. More blue than white, they come in handsomely carved (and, yes, calved) shapes, all curves and abstract.

Icebergs have different names according to their different formations – 'dome', 'pinnacle', 'dry dock' – but I prefer the more childish-sounding 'blocky', 'wedge' and 'bergy-bit', as described by the super-hero sounding International Ice Patrol. My absolute favourite, though, are 'growlers'. Growlers are the smaller icebergs that show about 1 metre out of the water and earn their strange name from the noise made by escaping gases as the centuries-old ice starts to melt.

Inuit people believe that their ancestors live on in icebergs, which is a nice idea as they float around so gracefully. I don't believe it though. I spent time – I lost track of exactly how much – just standing by the edge of the lagoon, looking out into the turquoise ocean of 'bergs floating around each other. It was just breathtaking. Every few metres or so, there were chunks of ice washed up onto the black-sand shore. Some were clear, others were baby blue, complete with the black striations of ancient snowfalls. I really liked looking into the glass-clear cubes, seeing my face reflected back and contrasted against the black sand beneath it.

I took a trip on the 'duck' – an amphibious vehicle that carts boat-loads of tourists out amongst the floating icebergs. The Icelandic guide was informative and told us all about the lagoon and its features. She talked about the danger of 'bergs flipping over and even let us try some of the centuries-old ice. Mine tasted stale, if I'm honest, but I was told that was because nearly all the air had been compressed out of it.

I didn't really enjoy the duck, despite the guide's *joie de vivre*. I guess it was because I was part of a crowd again; like I was sharing the experience with too many people. This is incredibly daft, as the lagoon has already been shown to millions of viewers in films such as *Tomb Raider*, *Batman Begins*, and Bond films *Die Another Day* and *A View to a Kill*. I kept an eye out for Angelina Jolie, by the way. I didn't see her, but then the Gore-Tex jacket-and-scarf combo can disguise anyone.

I couldn't wait to get off, but while the guide was pointing out an iceberg the shape of a penguin, and everyone strained their necks and pointed their zoom lenses, I spotted a seal. He was playfully ducking and diving amongst the ice before poking his whiskery head out of the water to check the boat's progress. No one else had spotted him – he was on the other side of the boat to the iceberg that looked like a witch's nose – so on landing I darted around the shore to where I had last seen him. After a few minutes, he emerged and gave a show that SeaWorld would have been proud of. Or that would have prompted them to put him in a small glass tank; one or the other. He repeatedly dived down, very gracefully, and I would then track the bubbles he made before he remerged again. At one point, I wondered whether he'd given me a grin. Now, if my ancestors were seals, goofing around the glacial lagoon, rather than icebergs, I think I would be OK with that. This seal was one happy soul. It was a pleasure to see him at such close quarters in his natural habitat. He did grin at me. I'm sure of that now.

I eventually tore myself away from Jökulsárlón and headed west towards Vík í Mýrdal on R1, as I had started to call the highway that encircles the whole country. The views on this stretch were fantastic. At one point, I could see the tongues of four glaciers. There were sharp sea cliffs, from which birds wheeled, and then flat glacial vistas with the odd erratic. I learnt all about erratics at school and the facts have stuck with me ever since. It's when a glacier transports a huge rock and then leaves it behind as the glacier retreats. An erratic. A lad at school once called it an 'erotic', which still makes me chuckle now. That's probably why it's stuck after all these years.

The glaciers in this region of south-east Iceland feature in *Chasing Ice,* a documentary produced by James Balog, a scientist, photographer and former global-warming sceptic. He decided to document the retreat and disappearance of glaciers across the northern hemisphere, providing tangible photographic evidence of climate change taking place before our very eyes. To do this, James – and his crew (more of them later) – set up 'Extreme Ice Survey', essentially twenty-five time-lapse cameras that recorded the movement of glaciers in Alaska, Washington State, Greenland and Iceland. *Chasing Ice* is the story of EIS, the trials and tribulations of setting up such a far-reaching project and the breathtaking, awe-inspiring result.

There are a couple of highlights to watch out for; the first is Svavar Jónantansson, an Icelander who guides Balog in the Iceland part of the mission. The film starts and ends at Jökulsárlón, amidst the frozen chunks of translucent blue ice and black sand. The shots here are exactly as you would expect: the shining shoes of Iceland's best party outfit.

Balog placed five cameras on Sólheimajökull, an outlet glacier of the Mýrdalsjökull glacier (Number 4 on the Iceland glacier size chart), not that far from Vík. The glacier is a blur of light blue and dirty black/grey ice, but it is 'dying', as Balog puts it. It's at Sólheimajökull, while checking one of the cameras, that Svavar inserts a much-needed slice of humour. Picking up a camera unit smashed by falling rocks and ice from the glacier itself, he says, 'Looks like they didn't read our signs,' and points to a warning sign on the obliterated box.

The science pieces, the talking heads and the constant barrage of bad-news clips culled from around the world are occasionally annoying and occasionally unsettling but also a constant distraction from the main star of the show. The ice.

Balog is an extraordinary photographer; the ice is photographed from such delicious angles and perspectives that whenever I watch it, it makes me shudder and grasp my coffee even tighter. Shots of gaping moulins (vertical shafts within glaciers), striped glaciers from above, striated blue/black ice, trapped micro air bubbles and icebergs against the night sky backlit by aurora – these images fizzle and crack on the screen. The finale is a calving event in Greenland, when an entire glacier seems to buckle and explode in front of the cameras. The ice is the real star of the film, and in a way, exactly what Balog has set out to capture.

Whether a single film has the power to influence thinking and the politics behind global climate change remains to be seen, but this is powerful stuff. The star of the show is on the verge of bowing out forever.

As you approach the town of Kirkjubæjarklaustur, 'Klaustur' to the locals, the gravel plains deposited here by glaciers and their run-off stretch as far as the eye can see – sometimes as far as several kilometres. There are red and yellow warning signs along the road and the gigantic metalled bridges that span this stretch, alerting drivers to the possibility of apocalyptic sandstorms. I've never experienced one, but apparently a sandstorm in full flow is something to behold and not ideal driving conditions. I did, though, manage to catch sight of one of the greyish-white

Arctic foxes that the guidebooks speak of. It was tiptoeing silently across the gravel, preparing to gorge itself on some unlucky sea birds and their eggs.

After a while I reached the village of Skógar and its waterfall, Skógafoss. You might not know the village, but you will definitely know the waterfall by sight. It is used in almost every piece of promotional material about Iceland, and has adorned many a guidebook cover, postcard and TV advertisement. There was even a TV ad for a UK investment firm filmed here; odd, considering the financial crisis (*kreppa*, as the Icelanders call it) hit both Iceland and the UK, and given that it's not that cheap to get here. Not the best place for promoting life insurance and savings plans, surely? She is a widow though, so maybe she has a substantial inheritance to fritter away.

The village of Skógar isn't much to look at, but the 62-metre-high Skógafoss certainly is. The waterfall plunges right off the edge of a cliff in a pleasing free fall before thunderously entering a deep pool, creating a rainbow spray and then continuing seawards in an ill-behaved stream. It's a proper waterfall, and it makes your heart pound just to stand near it. It's just the sort that Disney might try to recreate; you really believe that if you could just get behind this one there would be another world or at least a pot of gold.

Speaking of waterfalls you can walk behind, it's always worth a visit to Seljalandsfoss, just a few kilometres from Skógar. It's not as chunky as Skógafoss, but its feisty plume of water is catapulted some 200 metres over a sheer rock face. It's as if the stream delivering the water has been caught by surprise, as the water seems to come over the cliff with some force, leaving a clear gap behind. It's possible to walk behind Seljalandsfoss, and stand there, slack jawed, in a cave cut into the cliff face, while you slowly but surely get drenched from the spray. So that is exactly what I did. It is a fantastic, refreshing experience, especially after a long drive. I was there on a summer's day, and the bright blue sky, combined with the glowing greens of the spray-fed bracken, ferns and grasses made me feel like I was almost somewhere tropical. Almost, I said. I stood there transfixed as the water surged over my head, and then came crashing down just in front of me. It sounded powerful, like a jet taking off, or a continuous roar of thunder. I loved it.

If there is one thing that put Iceland on the global map in recent times, other than financiers or Björk's new hairstyle, it's Eyjafjallajökull.

Eyjafjallajökull, also known simply – and helpfully? – as E15, erupted in March 2010. It was preceded by a smaller eruption at Fimmvörðuháls, which is situated between Eyjafjallajökull and its neighbour glacier, Mýrdalsjökull. If you are struggling to place where this is in Iceland, think of the country as a duck. Eyjafjallajökull would be at the start of the duck's legs. Geography is easy, isn't it?

There are thirty-one active volcanoes in Iceland, and the tourist board calculates that there is a major volcanic event every five years. The eruption at Fimmvörðuháls may not have got more than a passing mention and some spectacular pictures on the news, but Eyjafjallajökull certainly grabbed the world's attention, even if most of the world couldn't pronounce it. There is a very amusing clip on the internet of various newsreaders word-mangling their way through the Icelandic name. Perhaps they should have stuck to its literal English translation, the very pronounceable Islands-Mountain-Glacier. Kind of does what is says on the tin, doesn't it?

Earthquake activity in the area began on 20th March 2010. It started as only a fissure vent, but went on to become one of the most major global tectonic and volcanic events in decades. Eyjafjallajökull began to erupt in earnest on 14th April and melted part of the glacier sitting on top of it, sending melt water cascading down to the sea, and dust, ash and steam spraying up into the sky. Molten magma was shot out and the volcano caused its own weather system, including so-called 'dirty thunderstorms'. Eighty nearby farms had to be evacuated. Residents received three automated text messages: one for the initial eruption and a subsequent pair for glacial floods. This is a rural area of Iceland, so evacuations caused relatively little disturbance to the population. I'm sure that you would disagree with me, though, if you lived at its base and were one of the families displaced by the eruption; receiving a phone call in the middle of the night and having to dash for safety must be simply frightful.

Reykjavík residents, however, found that their urban lives were largely unaffected. Sure, you could turn on the news and laugh at the attempts at pronouncing 'Eyjafjallajökull'. But apart from the odd sprinkling of ash over the city, everything remained pretty much the same. Even Keflavík Airport remained open for most of the time.

The reason for this? The wind was blowing the ash plume towards the east, away from the city.

Eyjafjallajökull, after reaching an impressive four on the Volcanic Explosivity Index (out of a maximum, but unheard of, 8), then started to belch its ash many kilometres into the air (somewhere between 6 kilometres and 10 kilometres), causing disruption in the airspace over much of Europe and as far away as Canada, because of the jet stream. Airlines were concerned about the effects of the ash on airplane engine turbines, and newsreaders called in scientists to explain the potentially catastrophic effects of this, using computer-generated models. The airspace over much of Europe was closed for a record six days, leading to the loss of millions of pounds and the stranding of passengers around the world. It is estimated that globally, airlines lost about £1.1 billion due to the restrictions, which lasted for six days, and affected 1.2 million passengers each day. Nissan suspended car production for a day, when it could not import the required components, and even the Japan Moto Grand Prix was postponed, after several teams were left stranded. Fruit and vegetables, usually air-freighted, were left to rot in airports across the world. The British Royal Navy was deployed to Spain and France to repatriate stranded members of the British public. This was reported to be the highest level of transport disruption since the Second World War. While this is not to be laughed at – and I saw the pictures of passengers sleeping at airports who certainly weren't laughing – it did lead to some amusing anomalies. Such as John Cleese spending £3,300 on a taxi ride from Oslo to Brussels, and Jens Stoltenberg, the Prime Minister of Norway, running his country from the United States using only an Apple iPad.

Near the base of Eyjafjallajökull, at the family-run farm of Þorvaldseyri, an enterprising and intriguing exhibition has been set up. The exhibition appeared to have been placed in a converted garage, but is really rather excellent. It opened exactly one year after the eruption and tells the story from one family's perspective of the eruption and the direct affect it had on them. That the volcano looms large over the family farm is startling enough already; the film that shows their ordeal once the eruption starts is nothing short of jaw dropping. The hurried moving of cattle indoors, the lightning storms and booming sound waves, the dense ash falling over everything like snow in negative, and the emotional drain it had on every member of the family is shown in close, intimate detail. This isn't a Hollywood movie, it's a family film.

One image shows a twenty-something blonde Icelandic woman shovelling ash from the back garden, as if it's the most normal thing in the world. She waves to the camera. Slowly, the movie shows the farm's return to normal, save for the hordes of tourists turning up to collect souvenirs of the ash from the roadside. At one point in the movie, a farmer is seen sweeping ash from the back of a trailer. He then places it into a bag and hands it to a gathering crowd of Japanese tourists. He can't help but smile at the bizarreness of the situation either.

Afterwards, I ambled around the photo exhibits and the shop. To my surprise, the same young woman from the film was serving in the shop. I went over to say hello, and asked her how she felt about being a film star now. 'Oh,' she said, 'I don't think so, not yet,' then blushed intensely.

I shut my pie shoot, stopped embarrassing the poor girl, and bought a pot of finest Eyjafjallajökull ash. I was still a tourist, I suppose.

✳✳✳

Vík í Mýrdal was my next stop. Situated 165 kilometres from Reykjavík and still on R1, Vík is a small town that has the unusual distinction of being linked with Hull in England. An unlikely pairing, I know, but one that has grown out of the friendship between sailors from both towns. This is not just a notional link; both locations have sculptures by Steinunn Þórarinsdóttir of male forms on tall basalt columns facing out to sea. The sculptures supposedly represent the harsh environment in which seafarers from both ports work, and the friendship that has developed over the years.

There was a touching expression of this friendship in January 2009, when the UK was embraced by a severe cold snap. Temperatures plummeted, snow fell, and even the iconic London buses were halted for the first time since the Second World War. Local charities in Vík were mobilised; they sent a shipment of *lopapeysa*, good old-fashioned Icelandic jumpers, to the elderly people of Hull, to keep them warm in the bone-chilling cold. Cue photographs of Hull's pensioners wearing Icelandic knitwear, and looking, I have to say, very snug indeed. I think that's brilliant. I already have a *lopapeysa* so I know how warm they are, and I love the idea of Icelanders helping out Hull's pensioners.

The *lopapeysa* is quintessentially Icelandic, but it is

not as old as you might think; the earliest examples of the unique pattern are from the 1950s, though there is no doubt that they are here to stay. These thick, extra-warm jumpers are made out of the finest Icelandic wool and often have a concentric pattern around the collar, technically called a yoke. There is a rumour that the original pattern was brought back by Halldór Laxness and his wife after a trip to Greenland, but this is unconfirmed and was probably just made up to ensnare yet more tourists. The majority of *lopapeysur* are sold to tourists, but only because Icelanders still like to make their own. It used to be that every Icelandic girl had to knit one; I'm sure that is no longer the case, but if an Icelandic girl feels the need to knit one for me, that would be fine. No protest from me. I love them.

Vík hasn't got much in the way of culture or shopping, though it does have a serviceable garage, a church and a bank. What it lacks in urban chic, though, it makes up for in the most dramatic vistas. The town rolls away from the sea up a gentle slope. This affords glorious views of the sharply pointed 'troll' rocks – black volcanic stacks out at sea. Called Reynisdrangar, they are supposedly petrified trolls caught out by the sun as they attempted to pull a boat ashore. I'm not sure about this, but I agree that it's a nice tale to tell the kids. The kids will probably swallow this, with the postscript that if they are naughty, the trolls will come for them too. Still, the rocks are an arresting sight, and form a striking pose against the blue horizon.

Having been to Vík, I decided, once I was back in the UK, that I had better go and have a look at Hull too.

It took me longer to travel to Hull from my home than it does for me to travel by air to Reykjavík, but eventually my 'Trans-Pennine Express' train pulled into Hull station. It was an overcast, windy day, which would be about right for August in a northern UK town that just happens to be twinned with Reykjavík.

Just off the High Street, in the rather pompously named Museum Quarter, is the *Arctic Corsair*. This deep-sea trawler is now permanently moored there and since 1999 has been seeing out its days as a museum and testimony to Hull's past as a sea-faring community. The *Arctic Corsair*, though, is no ordinary boat and has a colourful past, to say the least. Built in nearby Beverley, it was Hull's last side-winding trawler and was designed specifically for fishing in the perishing cold and treacherous Arctic seas around Iceland.

Like I say, the *Arctic Corsair* had quite a time of it. In 1967, when heading home from fishing near Greenland, she was in a collision with an Irish boat just off the Scottish coast. Her starboard side was heavily damaged, and both boats were taken to Wick for repair. She bounced back though and in 1973 took the world record catch for cod and haddock, which is no mean feat.

Her moment of fame, however, came in 1967, when she was directly involved in the Cod Wars. On 30th April of that year, she was in a collision with the Icelandic gunboat ICGV Óðinn. The *Arctic Corsair* was badly damaged and had to be patched up by the Royal Navy, but full repairs back in Hull took several months. These days, she has to contend with only the 20,000 visitors that come to see her every year; an easy task compared to what she was used to. I was sad to find that the boat was closed for the day I visited, and that there were no tours operating. I cursed myself for not having checked ahead, and made do with walking along the quay next to her considerable bulk, occasionally pressing myself against the railing to peep inside.

Victoria Pier is the site of the sculpture 'Voyage'. Commissioned by Hull Council and the Icelandic Government, Steinunn Þórarinsdóttir has crafted two pieces. Both are male figures, stood atop tall basalt columns. They are, it has to be said, close in style to Anthony Gormley's work, although not as creepy as his figures that stare out to sea from three kilometres of beach in Crosby, near Liverpool. 'Voyage' looks out across the Humber, in the direction in which the fishing fleet would have left, heading to the cold Icelandic fishing grounds to ply their trades.

The second of the two sculptures, named 'For', is in Vík, some hundreds of miles away. Both were commissioned to mark the relationship between the two communities, to celebrate the hardy fishermen that set sail from both ports into inhospitable seas, and to cause 'good will to ripple through Vík and Hull alike'. I know this because it says so on the nice plaque on Victoria Pier, and the distance – 1534 kilometres – is actually on a brass plaque at the base of the sculpture.

The Hull sculpture is made of brass and has turned a light, coppery green, which makes it stand out against the cold steel grey of the sky and the muddy brown of the Humber that stretches out in front of it. On the day

I went, the Humber was the colour of the tea my nan used to make, the sort you could stand a spoon upright in, and it swelled angrily at the pier. Its setting couldn't be more different than its brother's in Vík. 'For' has its back to the green Icelandic cliffs and is framed by jet-black beaches, purple lupins and the blue sea. It is a study of colour and nature. 'Voyage' is framed against a monstrous building across the harbour called 'the Deep', and a road bridge behind it hums with cars and lorries. Power stations and pylons line the horizon and litter blows around its feet.

I like the idea of the twin sculptures, though, and I was pleased that I'd come. There wasn't a single soul in sight, and I took my time. I thought about how hard life must be for fishermen in the cold northern seas, and though my only frame of reference is TV shows such as *Trawlermen* and *Deadliest Catch*, I do feel for them. Steinunn has said that the sculptures were inspired not only by the people out at sea, but also by the loved ones left on the shore. I thought about which would be harder: being out at sea or being left behind, not knowing if your husband, father or son would ever return.

The wind blasted my thoughts away, and I noticed a forlorn-looking hot dog stand nearby. In a tribute to Iceland, I decided to perform my own little ceremony. I ordered a hot dog. With everything. It wasn't a patch on its Icelandic cousin, although admittedly I was stone-cold sober rather than fully inebriated on Icelandic beer. In a funny sort of way, though, it felt right. As if I'd come full circle. A pleasant, warm, fuzzy feeling of completeness. And I'm sure that the statue blinked his left eye, just once, just for me and my imitation *pylsa*.

A few months later, I was left agog by the news that the statue in Hull had been stolen. Yes, that's right, a statue weighing 300 kilograms and measuring a huge 1.8 metres high was stolen. CCTV apparently showed several men dragging it from its plinth and into a waiting, and presumably reinforced, van. What staggers me though isn't the physical logistics of the incident; it's the barefaced, disgusting cheek of the thieves. It really angers me, that sort of thing. The mayor of Hull swiftly placed an order for a new one, I was told, but that's not the point, is it? I hope it falls on one of them. I need to think of happier things. I need my faith restored in humanity. Back to Iceland it is then.

After many hours of driving along Iceland's extraordinary south coast it was with some relief that I pulled into the sleepy coastal village of Stokkseyri, my last stop. Not only was I ravenous, but it had been an extremely hot day by Icelandic standards; the skies had stayed clear and blue, allowing for the sun to beat down non-stop. In other words, I was gagging for an ice-cold bottle of Einstök Icelandic White Ale.

Stokkseyri is a small village of 445 inhabitants. It's a forty-five-minute drive from Reykjavík. It seemed perfectly nice, and has even attracted the attention of Jónsi from Sigur Rós, who once named a song after the place. That's not why I was there though. I was there for Fjöruborðið.

The menu at Fjöruborðið made some bold claims, such as 'golden lobsters hook their claws together and dance a belly dance while mermaids serve tables amongst shrimp wrapped in seaweed, clapping shellfish and inquisitive haddock'. Hmmm. They said of the soup: 'People have struggled against storm after storm to get here and enjoy this soup. The desire for it can be so strong that rational thinking simply blows away with the wind.' But do you know what? They might just have been right about the soup. The soup was ridiculously good; creamy, thick, full of tomatoes and a good portion of succulent white lobster tails. It was divine. If I'm ever in the position of having to choose my last meal, soup from Fjöruborðið would be the starter.

Next up, perhaps not surprisingly, was lobster. Other dishes were available, but it seemed churlish to have anything else. The lobsters were actually langoustines, but, really, who cared? They were freshly caught every day, not far from there. They arrived at my table in an iron skillet, having been sautéed in wine, butter and garlic. There were 'trimmings' on offer, but with the exception of a chunk of rustic bread, I gorged myself solely on lobster after lobster, getting my fingers greasy and my stomach to bursting point. Accompanied by a well-deserved ice-cold beer – the Einstök that I had dreamt about – it was superb. Seldom have I enjoyed a meal quite so much. This is proof that exceptional ingredients need little messing with; other restaurants, particularly some in the UK, need to sit up and listen.

The desserts looked particularly fine: massive delicious wedges of sticky-toffee this, chocolate that and a messy but cream-filled pavlova. I was too stuffed with lobster, sorry, langoustine, to even consider one.

Instead, I took a walk on the seashore that lies only a few metres from Fjöruborðið's back door, and from which it takes its name. It was a glorious evening and the sun was still high in the sky despite the late hour. The sea was silvery and shimmering.

Chapter 4

Hopelandic

I used to work in a record store. I have always enjoyed music, so it was a pleasure to work there. I can't play a note, on any instrument you care to name. But when it comes to listening to music, I don't think that I can be beaten. I'm really, really good at it. I'm also quite a contender when it comes to carrying large stacks of CDs.

I also became really good at identifying tunes hummed at me by the Great British public. They would come in: grannies humming the Police; love-struck teenage boys looking for the Goo Goo Dolls; and shy kids with mum and dad, forced to sing the song that was slowly driving all three of them mad. I would be good, no, really good at getting the tune, finding the CD and making the sale. But first I would cheer up my day by calling a colleague over and getting my poor victim to sing the whole thing again. Nine times out of ten, that colleague would be Andy.

Andy delighted in my game and would often call other staff members across and make the customer repeat the ditty for a fourth or fifth time. He was thirty-ish in age but had the mindset of an overgrown student. I hate to admit it, but Andy was cool. He ached 'cool'. He seemed to survive on fast food – especially after an alcoholic binge the night before – and always had some madcap idea on the go. I once found Andy asleep at a music festival. In the afternoon. Once roused, and supplied with red wine (it was cool to drink red wine at this point in time), he began to remove various articles of clothing to reveal a series of tattoos in the shape of arrows inside circles. They adorned his feet, shoulders and abdomen, as I recall. Andy pointed out that each had a meaning – arrows pointing down kept his 'feet on the ground', those pointing upwards 'kept dreams alive', and those on his abdomen… I can't possibly remember, sorry.

Working in the record store had many perks, but one of the best – nearly as good as the slices of pizza sold next door – was getting to play obscure music really loud. Andy and I both relished this, taking it in turns to choose the next album and 'out-weird' each other. I would often go for Americana or alternative dance. Andy loved to play anything leftfield. Including, well, Leftfield, but also everything from world music (Manu Chao's 'King of Bongo' featured a lot, I remember) to hard rap.

One of our favourites was a band called Sigur Rós. I don't recall whether it was Andy or I that played them first, and I'm definitely not conceding this one. You may have heard of Sigur Rós now, but back in 2000 they were unheard-ofs from Iceland. Not only that, but you could – cliché alert! – almost hear the sound of wind sweeping across volcanic rock while Jónsi warbled and wailed in a language dubbed 'Hopelandic'. *NME* journalists wept in praise and I was hooked. I'd never heard anything like it before, and cranked up loud, it would result in a 50/50 split in the customer base. Half would quickly make for the door; others would linger longer amongst the racks, seemingly frozen to the floor. Not that I minded: 'Starálfur' or 'Ný batterí' would often be the highlight of my day. The manager didn't seem so keen, obviously thinking of his sales targets rather than aural pleasure.

Sigur Rós translates as 'Victory Rose', but because it's Icelandic (number one hardest language in the world to learn ever), this is not a literal translation. Sigur Rós is also the name of lead singer Jónsi Birgisson's sister. Still with me? Good, because Sigur Rós' second album was entitled () – yep, two brackets. None of the tracks was titled either, and how the bloody hell do you say () anyway?

This interest, fuelled further by unpronounceable Icelandic titles (where they existed), soon turned into an addiction. The addiction peaked with the band's third album, *Takk* ('Thanks' in Icelandic), which I could have worn out, were it possible to wear out a CD. The obsession then became all-consuming. Not only for Sigur Rós, but for anything Icelandic.

I wasn't the only one developing this obsession, incidentally. Around this time, Damon Albarn, the lead singer of Blur, the man behind Gorillaz, and the person responsible for superlative songs such as 'Sing', as well as the jarring 'Country House', also developed an interest in Iceland. In the 90s he spent a good deal of time in Reykjavík and for a time he became something of a permanent fixture in the Kaffibarinn, a famous café/bar (bloody hell, even I could translate that!) in Reykjavík. The rumour goes that he was offered shares in the place then and there if Blur were to use the bar as their headquarters while in town (recording their eponymously titled album, if you're interested). He agreed of course, and hence the London Tube sign outside. Kaffibarinn also features heavily in

101 Reykjavík, a film our friend Damon composed the soundtrack to. He is believed to currently own a house in Grafarvogur, a suburb of Reykjavík, the lucky fellow. The local rumour would also have you believe that the 'woo-hoo' refrain from *Song 2* was stolen from a little-known Icelandic band. I don't know if this is true or not, but it's quite a nice thought that this song, famous world over, is actually Icelandic in origin. Woo-hoo.

Talking of record stores, next time you're in Reykjavík, try to get yourself to 12 Tónar on Skólavörðustígur. It's tiny, but it's painted bright yellow, so you won't miss it. It's a great little place, and they run a record label too. It has become a meeting place for Icelandic musicians and music lovers. The complete opposite of chain-run record stores, and a survivor of the encroaching preference for digital music, it is a record store that is run exactly how record stores should be run world over. You are encouraged to take your time and browse. You can listen to anything that tickles your fancy on CD players that are scattered around, and the owners even provide you with free coffee. How lovely is that? I have spent far too many hours in the basement of that little shop, lounging on leather sofas, sipping coffee and playing new Icelandic music one CD after another.

✳✳✳

The one time you might want to avoid 12 Tónar is, perversely, during the Airwaves weekend, purely because it will be jam-packed in there and hard to find anything. Airwaves is an Icelandic music festival that takes place in the downtown district of 101 Reykjavík every October.

There is a whiff of suspicion hanging over it that, like Valentine's Day and Mother's Day, it was invented by businesses that would otherwise struggle to attract custom at this quiet time of the year. Nevertheless, Airwaves has picked up a reputation for its Icelandic debauchery, soundtracked by up and coming Icelandic bands. It has become world-renowned.

The festival has been running since 1999 and has a reputation of nearly mythic proportions; you know the sort of thing – unscheduled secret performances, watching bands while standing next to Björk, stepping out into the frozen night while the Northern Lights allegedly arc overhead. These experiences are nearly always described only in glossy coffee-table magazines or by a friend of a friend – they never really happen, right? Like the mouse in a fast food restaurant's burger, it's an urban myth, surely?

I thought that it was about time that I found out for myself and promptly booked flights, reserved a hotel room, and sought forgiveness from my family in double-quick time. Festival tickets, however, had sold out quickly and were proving difficult to source. My Icelandic contacts were nonetheless confident that they could get me in and were not nearly as fearful as me that I would cross the North Sea only to find myself unable to access any of the musical delights on offer. In fact, Icelanders often taken this laid-back approach to life; it really is quite Mediterranean in style. Maybe they are just getting ready for EU membership, or perhaps they are simply confident that everything will work out just fine. In this case it was the latter, although I'm sure that the introduction of siestas wouldn't be wholly unwelcome.

It turned out that my friends were right and a ticket – actually one of those scratchy plastic wristbands that makes you feel like a tagged cow on a Texas ranch – was sourced from the ginger-haired curator of the festival. He would later be pointed out to me in a full club of people while a Swedish DJ tried to simultaneously pierce my eardrums and smash my beer glass with reverberating beats.

I saw Björk once, by the way. It was on Sjómannadagur (Sailor's Day) – the day when Iceland's seamen and fishermen are celebrated – in Reykjavík. The rain was pouring down, and while the adults hurried to keep out of it, the kids enjoyed looking at the ships and poking the various strange and wonderful deep-sea fish – in various stages of decay, I should add – on the dockside. Through this melee Björk sashayed, wearing her usual hair-bobbles and a blue dress. No one took any notice. I went back to poking the fish.

I have always admired Björk. That's never been the problem. Björk has constantly caught my attention, but somehow adoration, even enjoyment, has been beyond my grasp. It was with some trepidation, then, that in 2011 I found myself at a world premiere of her new Biophilia show, performed as part of the Manchester International Festival.

As grand entrances go, it was astonishing. Accompanied by a twenty-four piece all-female Icelandic choir, Björk entered wearing a preposterous outsized orange wig, reminiscent of a cartoon dog, and a heavily ruffled blue dress. A caged Tesla coil was lowered from the ceiling. Purple-white forks of lightning fizzled and crackled. Björk let rip with *that* voice. The audience could not help but take notice.

Björk patrolled the stage, ensuring that everyone felt included and involved. It's a strategy that worked: Björk in a fearsome wig, standing all of 2 metres away from you and looking straight into your eyeballs really does get the heart beating. But it's her choir that I really enjoyed; sometimes choreographed in bizarre square-dance formations, and dressed in sparkly blue and gold outfits, they added a touch of humanity that counterbalanced Björk's often esoteric concepts. I later heard that afterwards they performed in central Manchester and I was genuinely sorry to have missed them – even more so because they were apparently excellent, singing in the late-evening sunlight. Björk doesn't wear the wig when shopping in Reykjavík, in case you were wondering.

Back to Airwaves. Arrival at Reykjavík (well, Keflavík, really) was as per usual. An architect's dream of clean lines, polished metal and imported wood, followed by an unannounced and always surprising emergence into the most inclement weather. I honestly, there ought to be warning signs by each door. Keflavík was voted Europe's best airport in 2011. No one told the voters about the weather, clearly. You exit from a centrally heated aircraft cabin (and your superfluous yet comforting fleece blanket) and a balmy airport arrivals lounge into whatever sub-Arctic weather system has been chosen for you on this occasion. I had been selected for torrential rain that was flying sideways like in the scene from *Forrest Gump*.

I was collected by Einar, who presented me with my wristband – he knows that I worry, what with being English and all – and then filled me in with what was new in Iceland since my last visit. This opening gambit never changes, but it is always informative and essential listening. It will invariably include the weather, the financial situation and the number of murders that year so far (usually one, two at the most).

The radio was alternating Icelandic Indie with international Beyoncé-Britney-Shakira pop, and even through the rapid-fire Icelandic I could tell that excitement was building for Airwaves. That, plus Ikea had a sale on that weekend. I had already made my choice, although an image of that crunchy chocolate cake you find only in Ikea crossed my mind momentarily.

Einar drove quickly, seeming to have forgotten that the last time I had been a passenger in his car he had nearly killed us both. I might be exaggerating here slightly, but he did hit a snow bank at such speed that I nearly lost control of my bodily functions. This time we arrived safely in Reykjavík after about forty minutes, both in one piece. The city was buzzing. The bohemian and ultra-cool were yet to emerge pupa-like into the night-time scene, but ordinary folk were filling the pavements and coffee shops, reading reviews, studying venue maps and planning out the night ahead.

Einar and I adjourned to a café to join them. We began to make arrangements for the weekend and the conversation was peppered with Einar making calls to friends and contacts to see what was going on and when. All of the calls were conducted in Icelandic, but I was beginning to grasp a few words here and there.

A few hours later I found myself at Reykjavík Art Museum. For the course of the Airwaves weekend the museum is transformed into one of the festival's prime venues. We were pretty early, in the scheme of things, and I assumed that most of the people there – filling approximately a quarter of the floor space – were not Icelandic, it being the wrong side of midnight and all. This super-late night revelry can be disconcerting if you don't understand the protocol. I distinctly remember being at a dinner party with Einar and friends and having already drunk too much and eaten twice my body weight. The drinks themselves had been substantial – cocktails, beer, wine, dessert wine, the ubiquitous Icelandic spirit *brennivín* (for my enjoyment of course), and after-dinner brandy. I was not in such great condition then, when at 1am it was made clear that the evening had only just started and we would now be going downtown. I don't know how I managed it, but I am assured that my dancing skills improved significantly as a result.

The Art Museum started to fill. The opening bands were somewhat eclectic, but things improved as the evening progressed. One of the first bands was a group of Icelandic teenagers. All fifteen of them were wearing pointed conical hats and they concentrated not on the music but on asking the audience to move from one side of the room to the other. I wasn't convinced that this would catch on – I couldn't see Damon Albarn or even Björk adopting the practice – and I was relieved when the lead cone-head announced that it was their last song and, better yet, their last gig ever.

Music goes hand in hand with Icelandic culture. I could bore you with tales of ancient instruments discovered by archaeologists, and the *rímur* – a traditional form of Icelandic poetry – that lives on with musicians such as Steindór Andersen, but I won't. What I will say, though, is that the long dark winters of Iceland seem to have contributed to a thriving music scene. Not just pop, but heavy metal, dance, opera, folk and classical are all thriving here. It seems that every young Icelander is learning an instrument, in a band, or making squelchy beats behind a computer. They don't seem to have that same nervousness or embarrassment factor that English teenagers have; they just want to play music, and they deserve credit for that. There also seems to be less of that mass-produced generic pop here. Less Simon Cowell and those fellows, and more organic, home-grown talents from garages and front rooms. Maybe that's to do with getting out of the Icelandic winter storms and doing something pleasurable and constructive; maybe it's not. I enjoy the results anyway.

Daníel, a friend of Einar's, and I continued to down beers (Icelandic beer really is excellent, did I mention that?) at the Art Museum and I started to feel relaxed and at home. This didn't last though. The next band were English but bloody awful. Ear-splittingly bad. They were talentless and tuneless at the same time. I noticed that the young woman next to me was making notes in her notepad and I asked her if she was from a magazine or newspaper. She was from the *NME*, the British music paper. She told me that the band were from London and were hotly tipped to be the next big thing. I didn't comment, but if they are to be the next big thing, I'll eat my hat, or some of that rotten Greenlandic shark Einar keeps threatening to feed me. I'll stick with the hat, actually.

To retain my eardrums in un-perforated condition, I slipped away to the bar. Icelandic beer is really excellent, but goes down far too quickly. I returned to find that in my absence things had gone all Icelandic on me. Daníel tried to point out the current Miss Iceland. To be honest, I couldn't quite hear his directions and all the Icelandic girls in the vicinity looked like possible contenders. Icelandic girls are something else: not conventionally beautiful, something more than that. I decided to drink more beer and try to figure out what makes them so special. Even Tony Soprano agrees; he frequently has a 'Miss Reykjavík' round to entertain him. But then you wouldn't ever disagree with Tony Soprano, would you?

I was brought back from thoughts of fictional gangsters and nubile Icelanders to the real world when I caught movement out of the corner of my eye. It was a human-sized cartoon monkey swimming towards me atop the densely packed crowd. The crowd were loving it. The combination of Norwegian power pop and a crowd-surfing monkey is a heady combination at the best of times; in Reykjavík at midnight, drunk on Icelandic beer while a storm raged outside, it was a contender for my personal highlight of the year.

✻✻✻

The next day I was suffering from the effects of too much alcohol, too much loud music and too few *pylsur* too late. My stomach was churning, my head was throbbing and my ears were ringing. But I needn't have worried. After a breakfast that I feared might have been all too temporary, Daníel picked me up.

Daníel is a good man all round. He is into his Icelandic music and enjoys poking fun at me for two reasons: my obsession with Iceland and my inability to see the Northern Lights. In fact, we had ended the previous night by walking to a huge display-board depicting the Northern Lights, to prove that they really do exist. I was starting to doubt it, to be honest. We had then taken turns at photographing each other in front of the display in a frankly rubbish attempt at fooling friends and family back home that I had seen them at last.

Iceland is the best place to wake up with a hangover. The water from the tap is so pure, so crystal clear that it makes great drinking for your dehydrated brain, while a pounding, geothermally hot shower – just ignore the slight smell of sulphur, you get used to it – works on the rest of your body. Once you are well enough, head for a hot pot to complete your therapy. That reminds me, Icelanders never buy bottled water – they believe their tap water is the best in the world. They are right. Singer Hafdís Huld once told me off for buying a bottle, so it must be right.

Daníel was a man with a plan. He drove us out to the Blue Lagoon, for a hangover party. This was a fantastic idea. The Blue Lagoon, not far from Keflavík Airport, is actually a by-product of the geothermal power plant next door that provides power to thousands of Icelanders, and hot water and heating to even more homes, by pumping super-heated water from the earth's depths. Don't let that worry you, it's perfectly safe. In fact, the waters are said to be good for skin complaints such as eczema and psoriasis, although in some areas the water is a little too hot for my liking and every time I visit I can't help thinking of those lobsters being tossed into boiling pans at Fjöruborðið, that fabulous restaurant in the village of Stokkseyri. Apparently they make a little squeal as they meet their death. I know how they feel. The lagoon contains an astonishing six million litres of water, which is renewed every forty hours. The temperature is super-warm, like bath water, and the luxurious and eponymous blue colour comes from the minerals, silica and algae that form the soup.

A visit to the Blue Lagoon is Iceland's number one tourist activity, so you might think that I would rail against it in the same way the Spanish complain about the saturation of Ibiza, but I really like it. Basically, the 'hangover party' was the same relaxing experience I'd had there before – the whole poster-endorsing light blue lukewarm waters and apparently skin-enriching white silica mud – but with a DJ at the side of the lagoon playing what I think are termed 'fresh beats'. People were selling Viking beer next to the lagoon, but we agreed that was a step too far. Floating around while being serenaded with chilled-out music had the desired effect and I was quickly beginning to recover from the excesses of the night before. Daníel was feeling the same, and the colour began to return to his face, although that might have been down to his new face pack. Our ability to make conversation also began to return. Admittedly, this conversation was about what makes Icelandic girls so special. From where we were standing, of course, it was getting increasingly obvious.

The beats quickened as if to remind us that the evening was coming and Airwaves was set to start again. By the time we arrived back in Reykjavík, we had time for a quick burger before examining the schedule and meeting with some of Daníel's friends.

We started off with a trip to Iðnó, a converted theatre

next to the Tjörnin lake. We were there to see For a Minor Reflection, a post-rock band, pigeon-holed into the same genre as Sigur Rós, Explosions in the Sky and the improbably named God Speed You Black Emperor! (exclamation mark copyrighted and necessary). The Reflection boys were in a buoyant mood and tried out a combination of new tracks and ghostly minimal lighting. The effect was mesmeric, before crashing crescendos brought us back to reality. But when reality is watching new Icelandic bands in Iceland, with a cool beer in your hand, it's no bad place to be.

✳✳✳

Another Airwaves highlight was my meet-up with Sóley at Café Haiti near the harbour in Reykjavík. Sóley Stefánsdóttir is a twenty-something musician from Hafnarfjörður near Reykjavík. She has all the correct musical credentials – she learnt classical piano from an early age, then moved on to big band, brass and composition, but she really cut her musical teeth while in the band Seabear. She has also played with Snorri Helgason. She provides sweet, enchanting vocals over layered, blurred piano and guitar. It's as elegant as it is unique.

On arrival at the café, Sóley immediately ordered a double espresso, saying it would warm her up; I was worried about the effect it might have on her already bubbly personality. I started by asking about her music, and if she connected it to Iceland.

'I try not to,' she said, 'because it can be a cliché, but in a way, of course I do. I don't know if I would compose different music if I lived in a small apartment in New York, but it does affect me. Like this weather. It's really windy outside now. It makes me angry. You are walking against the wind, and it's like *Rarrrr!* There is a power, an energy here. I try not to write about Iceland and all the clichés.'

'Are you tempted to move away from Iceland to see if it affects your music?'

'I love it here. I tour a lot. I travel a lot, but when I come home to Iceland, I love it. I don't want to move. Not yet. I just bought an apartment here with my boyfriend. I feel really grown-up!'

'Do you miss Seabear?'

'They are lovely people, and good friends. It's different working in a group to working solo. When I'm alone, I can be my own boss and do what I want to do. No one is bringing any weird ideas to the table. In a group, you bring in an idea, someone else brings something, and we just jam it together. When you work alone, it can be really selfish, but I really like it. If I could, I would play everything. I'm actually really shy though.'

'You don't seem shy,' I said.

'I'm not really. I could talk forever!' Sóley laughed.

As I sat with her and slurped coffee, while the wind whipped at the sea behind the steamed café windows, I felt pleased to have met Sóley. She is so enthusiastic about her music, I've no doubt she is going to become highly successful. I think she deserves every bit of success she gets. I'll raise a coffee to that.

A different sort of Airwaves 'high light' is the one emitted by the Imagine Peace Tower on the small island of Viðey, just a few minutes by boat from Reykjavík. Installed at the request of Yoko Ono Lennon (to use her full name) in memory of John Lennon, the tower is made up of fifteen extra-powerful lights that send a thick column of light into the Icelandic night sky. The tower was installed to mark John Lennon's sixty-seventh birthday and is re-lit on 9th October every year; it remains illuminated until 8th December, which is the date that Lennon was assassinated. The tower's strong beams can often be seen penetrating the cloud, of which there is usually plenty, but on a clear night they reach up seemingly infinitely. Rumours of the Northern Lights being sighted at the same time abound. The monument was named after Lennon's anthem 'Imagine' – which isn't very, well, imaginative. The base has the words 'Imagine Peace' inscribed twenty-four different languages. You can't see those from Reykjavík, obviously.

I wouldn't call myself a Beatles fan, because I know that this is a serious title, borne by some seriously obsessional people. I do enjoy the Beatles' music though, and I appreciate that 'popular' music wouldn't be the same today without them. I've been to the Hard Days Night Hotel and the Cavern Club in Liverpool. I've even been to Strawberry Fields and the Dakota building in New York. What I can't get my head around, though, is this tower – or, more specifically, why it was built in Iceland. As far as I know, Lennon never stepped foot in the country. And, yes, I have heard that Ono and Lennon were planning to visit, and, yes, he would have agreed with Iceland's geothermal credentials and would have loved the place, but it's a bit odd, isn't it? Surely it should be in Liverpool's Albert Docks? Or on Gibraltar, where they were married?

The tower was completed on 9th October 2007. Yoko Ono is believed to have said on the day of unveiling that the tower was 'the best thing' that she and John had 'ever done'. I don't think John had much say in the matter. In my opinion, she has always been a bit strange, that Yoko.

I have a confession to make. Actually, I have a few, but I'm only going to share one with you. If you thought my obsession with Iceland was at the extreme end of things, you should probably stop reading now. My obsession with Sigur Rós is bigger. Not in a fawning, fan-girl sort of way. I don't make hand-made posters or flags, or wear a Jónsi mask, for example. Neither do I write stories about the band and me 'having adventures' like the Famous Five and Timmy the dog. I don't wear feathers in my hair, or one of those tweed caps with ears. However, I do really enjoy their music and seeing them live. I think that they are unique and what they do is powerful; it certainly has the power to transport me back to Iceland. I have followed the band to the detriment of my wallet – at festivals in Spain, acoustic gigs in London, exclusive screenings of *Heima*. And don't forget Wolverhampton. But Icelandic gigs are a preference of course.

In 2006, Sigur Rós returned to Iceland after a well-received world tour. Wanting to repay the kindness and support of their fellow Icelanders, they set about touring Iceland, playing special venues such as abandoned fish factories (in Djúpavík), scenic craters and controversial hydropower sites. The tour was filmed and produced as

Heima, which you should definitely check out if you are an Icelandophile: the direction and photography are utterly inspiring, and you'll be booking your plane tickets before the film ends.

They also played in Reykjavík, which was attended by 30,000 people and me. This was the biggest ever outdoor concert in Iceland – 10% of the country's population was there, which is pretty amazing. I travelled across to Iceland especially for the concert, and I wasn't at all disappointed. The concert was free entry, which meant people of all ages were able to come: families with kids on their shoulders and older people with picnic baskets. It also meant that the usual branding and corporate messages were missing, leading to a more relaxed atmosphere. More of a welcome home party than a money-making event. It was actually where I first met Daníel and his long-term fiancée, Inga. I remember specifically complimenting Inga on a spectacular pair of *lopapeysa*-style gloves she was wearing. I really must get a pair of those.

The concert was staged in Miklatún, which is a green and appealing open space on the edge of the city, surrounded by dark green conifers. Sigur Rós played a storming set that night, and ended with 'Popplagið' (Pop Song). This was anything but pop, and descended into a pulsating marcato of feedback, with Jónsi wailing over the top. One of the funniest things in *Heima* is when Jónsi explains that his grandmother, who was watching the concert on national TV, was forced to turn the TV set off during 'Popplagið', mistakenly thinking her set was broken. I think that is kind of sweet.

Another of their memorable gigs was the closing

concert of their world tour in November 2008, which took place at Laugardalshöllin in Reykjavík, in the arena there. Part of the concert was performed from behind an indoor waterfall that cascaded across the entire stage front.

I also went to see Jónsi on the first UK date of his solo world tour in 2010. The concert was amazing. Jónsi played his Icelandic woollen socks off, which isn't unusual. What was unusual, though, and made it unforgettable, was the quality of the visuals. Jónsi had teamed up with a production company that was used to staging operas and classical music and together they created something special. The set was based on a French taxidermy shop that had burnt down a few years back, and the special effects included fire, storms and animals being set free, all soundtracked by our boy Jónsi. The image of the deer being chased through woodland has been indelibly printed on my brain, probably forever.

After the gig, I noticed that a small number of people were wearing 'After-Show Party' passes. I asked a young woman how to get one of those exclusive little numbers. She pointed me in the direction of a chap clearly in the know. Despite never having met him before, I shook his hand like a long-lost friend. I gave him eye contact, and my best spiel. He responded by giving me two passes. We made our way upstairs to the party. There was an excited hubbub of English and Icelandic being spoken in equal measure. Jónsi soon made an appearance and began to mingle with the crowd. As he came closer and closer to where I was standing, I started to wonder what I should say to him. Should I ask which Icelandic bands to look out for? Who Damon Albarn had stolen that song off? Why

Icelanders love music so much? What were his thoughts on the Peace Tower? Why I couldn't get Icelandic music out of my head? Why was music so important to him? Why was music so important to Iceland?

He moved towards me.

'Can I have your photo?' I heard myself say.

What a berk. Maybe I am just an obsessional fan after all. I could hear Daníel's laughter in my ears.

Chapter 5

Urban Puffin Patrol

I was sitting on top of a volcano. Just read that again. I was sitting on top of a volcano. It was a gorgeous summer evening, and I'd climbed 200 metres of its red lava slopes to get to the summit. Beneath me lay the town of Heimaey, in the Westman Islands (Vestmannaeyjar), which are off Iceland's south coast. The town's white buildings contrasted sharply with the deep green of the rest of the island, the evocative blue of the sea, the orangey pink sky and the purple fields of lupins. Out to sea, uninhabited islands dotted the skyline. To the west was a harsh-looking octagonal skerry, Elliðaey, with a single white building perched on it.

I had got there just in time. It was a few days after the summer solstice, but I wanted to be there for midnight. It was now 23.58, but it could easily have been 3pm. It was perfectly light, albeit a very soft, glowing light. The sun barely dipped below the horizon, but lent some delightful soft pastel colours to the sky. I've seen Iceland in deep mid-winter, when the sun barely rises above the horizon – actually, up in the north, it doesn't rise at all – but I love the light Arctic summer nights too. (Even though there's absolutely no chance of seeing the fabled Aurora Borealis.) It makes me want to stay awake all night and do stuff. Like climb a volcano.

My volcano of choice was Eldfell. It's still active, but hasn't erupted since 1973. When she goes, though, she really goes. The 1973 eruption caught the attention of the world – and the inhabitants of Heimaey, obviously. They were all evacuated to the mainland – or to Iceland, as they say here, like it's somewhere abroad. The evacuation, by boat and air, was successful. Only essential workers stayed behind and, amazingly, only one person perished. This comes as a surprise when you see pictures of the 'wall of fire' the fissure produced and learn that 400 houses were either damaged or swallowed by the lava and tephra. The lava flowed through the streets at a speedy 40 metres per hour and the tephra was up to 4 metres deep in places. The 200-odd essential workers did their job though, and by pumping seawater onto the approaching lava, managed to eventually halt it, thereby saving the island's harbour. Not only that, but submarine eruptions actually improved the harbour, making it more protected and yet still accessible. The island grew by two square kilometres. The abundant volcanic deposits were used to create new land for 200 houses, and were also used to improve and extend the Heimaey's airstrip. The heat from lava flows was used for heating. Icelanders always turn things to their advantage, don't they?

The crater of the volcano is accessible by foot and, for that matter, by vehicle. I was told that, in places, you can still feel the heat of the volcano, that the ground is still hot some fifty centimetres below the surface, but I didn't have a shovel with me, so I was reduced to digging with my hands in random spots. I didn't find anywhere remotely warm. There's a story, though, that brings a smile to my face. The locals here used to use the warmth of the ground to cook bread. Some time in the 80s the Swedish prime minister visited Heimaey, and locals promised he could taste some of their specially baked bread. However, the chef had forgotten to bring flour – a rather crucial ingredient in bread, I find. Time was short, so a shop-bought loaf was shoved into the ground instead. This was produced for the prime minister, who was somewhat bemused to find the loaf was already sliced.

Eldfell, then, is a fairly recent addition to Heimaey, whereas its neighbour, Helgafell, is 5000 years old. I was thinking about this when I realised that midnight had come and gone. It was still light, and there was still a stream of Icelanders climbing up to the summit to join me. I don't quite know why. I mean, the view is spectacular, and for me as an outsider a complete one-off, but if you lived here, would you still bother? At midnight? Some were dressed head to toe in lycra, and carried walking poles; others were groups of teenagers, looking for a place to pair off and smooch.

I made my way down the slopes. I've always struggled heading down slopes at speed, not because I'm scared of tumbling arse over tit, as my grandmother used to so eloquently put it, but because my over-large feet and toes seem to bunch up at the end of my shoes, causing intense pain. I didn't moan, though, as there was no one to hear me, and I might have seemed a little wimpish considering what the residents there had suffered. As if to highlight the point, I passed wooden signs emerging from the bluey-purple lupin fields. They were street signs, demarking the streets that had been swallowed whole under metres of lava. I struggled to comprehend that under my feet, under the twisted and sharp volcanic rocks, lay streets and houses from 1973. It was a sobering thought. As I continued to descend, I saw a white concrete building, half crushed under the lava flow. It was waiting either to be completely swallowed or to be rescued. It was an arresting sight. I kept my foot complaint to myself.

I was staying in Heimaey that night and I had booked into my hotel already. Unusually for Iceland, the place was filthy, with hairs in every corner and the light switch actually hanging from the wall by its wires. I would have complained, if it hadn't been a gorgeous twenty-year-old Icelandic girl on reception. She just had to look at me and I melted inside. Instead, I asked her where was the best place to eat in town. She told me about a restaurant across the road. I tore myself away from her presence, just as she seductively twirled hair around her fingers. She didn't actually, I made that up. I went to the restaurant; it was excellent. I had monkfish with a salsa, and the obligatory cold Icelandic beer. I then saw that the girl from reception had transformed herself into a waitress. No wonder she had recommended the place. I hope she got commission. In fact all the waitresses there were super good-looking nineteen and twenty-year-olds. The town seemed to be run by them.

Outside, the girls were taking time off from running the town – everyone needs a break – and were being pursued by an army of greasy-looking male teenagers who had adopted skateboards (the younger ones) or souped-up vehicles (the slightly older ones) in an effort to attract the opposite sex. It didn't appear to be working, despite them cranking up the music really loud and screeching off from junctions at speed. I guess that Friday nights are the same everywhere, even on a volcanic Icelandic island. That's when I decided to climb Eldfell. I was glad I did. Later, I tried to sneak into my bed without being electrocuted or getting twisted in other people's hairs.

❄❄❄

I awoke to a morning full of sunshine, and still without a cloud in the sky. Feeling lucky, I headed straight out into Heimaey in search of breakfast. The boys and girls of last night were presumably still sound asleep in bed, and it felt like I had the place to myself. Every August, they have a huge music festival there. I couldn't imagine what it would be like with thousands of drunken Icelanders in various states of revelry about the place. It's quite the party, I'm told, although I couldn't help noticing that Ronan Keating had been booked that year.

In 2012, Tim Burgess, lead singer of UK band the Charlatans, inadvertently created a new breakfast cereal – the improbably named 'Totes Amazeballs'. Posh London slang for 'Totally Amazing', this breakfast cereal contained shortbread, raisins and soft marshmallow. Personally, I prefer something a little more refined for my breakfast. And always accompanied by some decent music, usually of the Icelandic variety.

On this trip, one of my breakfast bands of choice was Rökkurró, a folk/rock five piece from Reykjavík. Rökkurró have produced an EP and two albums, my favourite of which is *Í Annan Heim* (In Another World). This record is all opulent strings and haunting vocals that are gently insistent at getting into your head. The name 'Rökkurró', I was reliably informed, comes from the Icelandic words for twilight, *rökkur*, and quiet or calm, *ró*. Makes sense to me.

My alternative – related – breakfast soundtrack was by Lily and Fox, a side project of Rökkurró's lead singer, Hildur Kristín Stefánsdóttir. The band were having a break, as Hildur had temporarily relocated to Japan, but her cover versions of 'Interpol' and 'Kavinsky' were more than enough to keep me enthralled. Sweet, breathy vocals accompanying a quietly plucked koto harp. She also has her own material, which is well worth a listen. It goes nicely with a croissant and a strong coffee, I found.

A month earlier I had decided to contact Hildur in Japan, to see if she could tell me more. I started off by asking where the name Lily and Fox came from.

'It is so confusing to explain, but I'll try! Basically I'm a huge animal lover so I wanted it to have animals in the name but I also wanted it somehow to be connected to Japan because my connection to Japan is such a big part of me. Foxes, or *kitsune*, are thought of as mythical creatures in Japan; they have magical abilities and appear in many folklore stories, which made my love of them even stronger. And from that I started forming a story in my head of these characters, Lily and Fox. Lily is a human in my mind, but the name was based on my favourite flower – well, and my mother's name! See how confusing this is? Ha ha!'

I asked if it had been difficult to leave Iceland, and Rökkurró.

'Yes, it was extremely hard. I had always had this dream of going, but I couldn't bear the idea of leaving the band for such a long time. But then I changed my mind as I felt afraid that if I didn't go now I would never go! But saying bye to friends, family and the band at the same time was really tough. Rökkurró is taking a break while I'm away, so I know it's hard for the others in the band as well.'

Hildur had recently done something truly special. In February 2012, Japan played Iceland at football at Nagai Stadium in Osaka. Hildur, surely after skipping breakfast due to nerves, stood and sang the Icelandic national anthem before a crowd of 50,000 people. Oh, and it was broadcast live in Iceland and Japan, just to add to the pressure.

'The Icelandic national anthem is also one of the hardest songs to sing that I know and with its very broad range, it is even more nerve racking. But of course it was a once in a lifetime experience and also a great lesson for me in seeing how stress affects your body. Because for those ninety seconds it took to sing the song, I stood so ridiculously tense and stiff that actually when I woke up the day after, my whole body was sore!'

From singing with a band as high calibre as Rökkurró, to producing intimate cover versions of her favourite songs, to performing in front of 50,000 football fans – that takes some doing. Totes Amazeballs, as they say in London. Time for some breakfast, say I.

After breakfast, I went looking for another sort of gathering. A gathering of puffins. The Westman Islands are renowned for puffins, not just for the catching and returning of pufflings that lose their way in August, but for the millions of puffins that call Heimaey home. At one point, Heimaey had the world's biggest puffin colony. These days, puffins are in decline. Some blame the lack of sand eels, the puffin's natural food source.

The Latin name for puffin isn't *Puffinus puffinus* as you may have thought. That moniker belongs to the madcap Manx shearwaters, who are a different 'kettle of fish' altogether, and who were apparently puffins, before the puffins were. The puffins here are *Fratercula arctica*, or Atlantic Puffin. You can get them in three others models – tufted, urban and horned – although those are not found in Iceland. And I made one of them up.

Over half of the world population of Atlantic Puffins breed in Iceland, although numbers are thought to be in decline. To put a figure on it, there are around 3 million pairs that breed in Iceland each year and an estimated total population of between 8 and 10 million.

I think they are great little birds and I am intrigued by them. I am fascinated by their appearance and habits, and by that handsome, show-stopping face. Members of the auk family, they are often nicknamed the 'penguins of the north', which I can understand. Their other nickname, 'clown of the sea', I find a little demeaning. I can see how the name came about, with their colourful beaks, white faces and distinctive marking around the eyes (all of which are temporary, by the way; they shed this after the summer season), but there is so much more to them. I could spend hours watching these little critters: the way they pop up unexpectedly from holes in the ground, fly past your head making a swishing noise as their wings flap 400 times per minute, and land feet first on the water like a sea plane. I love that classic image of puffins carrying sand eels in their mouths. They hold the eels between their tongue and the top half of the beak, allowing further fish to be caught.

The record is sixty-three fish, although that will be hotly contested at the next Puffin Olympics, I'm sure.

Puffins can live to the ripe old age of twenty-nine. How crazy is that? And that's just the age of the oldest known ringed puffin; it is thought that some might live a lot longer. It is especially crazy considering the hard life the little birds have. Puffins nest in often precarious burrows in grassy banks on cliff tops. Females lay only one egg per year, and the chicks, known as pufflings, have to hide from many predators, including gulls and Arctic foxes. Grey powder-puffs of fluff, they are prey to anything bigger than them. Most things then. If they survive, all the pufflings leave their burrows for the open sea on the same date in August, under the cover of darkness. This is the end of any parental care – they are now on their own. This strategy, designed to avoid most of the daytime predators, has been undermined by the invention of the electric light. Pufflings are drawn to lights: they become confused and head towards them, get increasingly baffled and invariably become prey. In Heimaey, children are encouraged to patrol the town and collect up the pufflings in boxes before releasing them, presumably with directions and a map.

Puffins spend April to August on land to breed and rear their young. The rest of the time they are at sea. That is eight or nine months bobbing around at sea, which sounds like an awful thing. They aren't daft though: puffins have been found in exotic places such as Morocco, the Mediterranean, and even Newfoundland. Perhaps it's just like an eight-month holiday. If they do survive long enough – it's not all-inclusive – to return to their breeding grounds, it's still not straightforward. Sand eels have disappeared in places, and there are other dangers.

Only a few years ago, approximately 250,000 puffins were caught and eaten in Iceland every year. They were caught in huge triangular nets that hunters waved in the air from the top of cliffs, a practice known as 'sky-fishing'. This sounds like a lot of puffins, but the catchers were heavily licensed and only non-breeding birds were taken. No licences at all have been issued in recent years. It shouldn't have made a huge impact on the population if you consider the numbers – at that point there were an estimated 4 to 5 million puffins in the Westman Islands alone. I used to think that this was a shocking number of puffins to be eaten, but that would be deeply hypocritical of me and there is no indication that the practice has impacted on numbers. I wouldn't want to turn into one of those people that become vegetarian because animals have 'cute faces'. I wouldn't refuse a burger because cows have big eyes and flutter their eyelashes, so what's different with this? So long as it's ecologically sound, which I am told it is. The dark smoky meat of a puffin, eaten together with blueberry jam, is to die for, apparently.

I once saw a documentary in which world-renowned chef Gordon Ramsay travelled to Iceland to catch and sample an Icelandic delicacy – the heart of a puffin. Gordon was taken to the cliffs of the Westman Islands, for a spot of sky-fishing. On catching a feisty puffin, he untangled it from the net and held it up for the camera to see. Quick as a flash, seizing his opportunity to make a stand for puffins across the world, the puffin turned and nipped Gordon's nose, causing a shriek and a bloody injury. The puffin made good his escape. I don't think there were many people watching that didn't silently cheer for that little puffin and his televised protest.

An ever decreasing number of puffin catching licenses are still granted. The Westman islanders' traditional approach was to scale the cliff faces with a rope in order to capture the puffins and their eggs – an activity known as *spranga*. Down by the harbour in Heimaey I came across a *spranga* rope hanging from a cliff and had a go, but merely ended up swinging aimlessly, not a puffin in sight.

I headed out to Stórhöfði, the southern tip of the island. This place is allegedly the windiest place in Iceland, with only four days per year when the wind doesn't blow. I must have visited on one of them, as it was completely calm when I arrived. The sea was a stunning blue, and I could see all the way across to the mainland, and even the glaciers on the horizon. It was truly glorious. All I needed was a puffin. The puffins didn't agree. I saw three sitting around, but as soon as I approached they buggered off. I decided that a more daring approach was necessary and, finding a suitably dangerous-looking overhanging crag, I crawled on all fours out above the sea. I felt very brave; maybe it was the sun. The grass was slightly damp and slippery, and beneath me was a drop of, say, 40 metres directly down to where the ocean bashed against the sharp vertical cliffs. It would be worth it, I told myself. To my left was a puffin crouching among some vegetation, gathering grass from between some perky tufts of pink flowers. I observed the cheeky little bird for a while, before he noticed a six-foot-tall, gangly chap trying to manoeuvre himself in a somewhat ungainly fashion nearby. He let out a little puffin laugh and took flight down to the sea and safety. I extricated myself; my puffin obsession had been tickled but not nearly fulfilled.

I may not have seen more than five puffins at Stórhöfði, but I did see something else. On the horizon, I spotted a line of smaller islands and skerries. Some had been battered and beaten by the Icelandic seas. The same seas that were perfectly calm that day, but were undoubtedly extremely rough throughout the winter months, eroding the islands with the raw power of their waves. Following the line of islands, my eyes rested on the newest addition to Iceland. Surtsey is a freshly formed island. Freshly baked, or whatever. The new southern outpost of Iceland. On 10th November 1963, fishermen noticed that the sea had warmed in the area, and then, and this would definitely catch your attention, plumes of smoke began rising from the sea. Within five days, this would form into a small island, accompanied by an ash cloud some nine kilometres high. This was Surtsey, the newest island in Iceland – and the world. The eruption continued for another three and a half years, eventually creating an island of 2.64 square kilometres. Colonisation started in 1965, not just by flora and fauna, but seemingly by scientists in white coats who designated the place a reserve and prohibited anyone else from entering. The very same scientists, incidentally, who wouldn't even reply to my correspondence. There seemed little to no chance that they'd let me land on Surtsey, I realised this, but to not even reply? Shocking. I'm not bitter though. They are probably too busy searching for new species of moss on Surtsey to reply to me. Or watching the puffins that have only recently moved in.

Anyway, Surtsey is the second largest island in the

archipelago, after Heimaey itself. That said, Surtsey is being eroded by those naughty waves I spoke of earlier. In 2006, it had already reduced to 1.38 square kilometres, and the nice lady in the Surtsey exhibition in Heimaey pointed me in the direction of models of the island that predict its shape and size up to the year 2050. It was a pretty good exhibition, to be honest, and I learnt all I needed to about this new island, apart from how to actually see more of it or set foot on its newly formed soil. It was so good, in fact, that I felt obliged to buy a Surtsey T-shirt from the very same lady. Is it cool? Is it geeky? I don't care. I wear it with pride. I have seen Surtsey from a distance.

The distance, it seems, is destined to remain. Not only did the obtuse scientists choose to ignore my pleas, I couldn't even get a boat to take me anywhere near it. I appreciated that I couldn't set foot on its scientifically important soil, but I wouldn't have minded casting my beady eye over it from a boat, with binoculars.

The only boat making waves that day was stuffed with tourists, but not being proud, I hopped on too. I secured myself an excellent position at the rear, and used my elbows to keep any intruders at bay. I was thoroughly disappointed with the tour. The captain/tour guide pulled on a dirty, ex-navy-type jumper, otherwise I wouldn't have known he was the captain. I couldn't hear a word he was saying over the noise of the other forty-odd passengers and the chugging diesel engine. So I settled for admiring the view, and scaring myself silly when I realised just how precarious my perch had been when puffin spotting; one slip would have caused a 40-metre tumble onto sharp volcanic rocks. I wouldn't have been able to finish this book, and my family would have had to claim on my extensive life insurance cover. Pros and cons, then.

The captain did have a surprise up his filthy sleeve though. At one point he turned the boat into a cavernous sea cave. The acoustics inside were marvellous, even the dripping from the roof sounded melodic. To make his point, the captain produced a saxophone and played a mournful tune, which sounded crystal clear and was certainly both loud and beautiful. In fairness, though, he should have told the fellow in front of him what he was planning, as the first note clearly startled the chap, whose 'Ooh' was also sent echoing around the cave.

I did see Surtsey again in the distance. It was a hulking shape of hazy blue-grey, the furthest island in a direct line of skerries and outcrops leading from Heimaey. It was the closest I'm likely to get.

Chapter 6

Great Find, Huh?

At first I couldn't find it. I had driven a series of rough tracks that either led nowhere, or worse still, led back to each other. The landscape was black volcanic rock that had created plateau-like formations and had folded and warped around itself. There was little plant life and the dark rock seemed to be turning darker under the sun and the deep blue sky. I kept searching, checking different maps and asking others, but only getting more and more lost. Tracks petered out. Tracks had gates across them.

And then I saw a flash of another windscreen glinting in the sunlight. I headed towards it, thoughts of breakfast and giving up now pushed away. The car was parked at an odd angle against a ridge of volcanic rock that seemed to go on forever in both directions. I couldn't see the end of it, and neither could I see over it; it was the height of a double-decker bus. Or two normal buses. Or if you don't measure things in buses, it was the height of three cars.

As I approached the parked car, sending up a plume of dust behind me, I saw a panic-stricken couple dash to cover themselves up; skin was seen but nothing indecent. A flash of thigh here, an errant belly button there. Nothing more. But it was enough. I had found it.

I pulled alongside the car, confident and proud that

I had cracked the code and found this exclusive little place. The couple, now dressed, seemed to have pre-empted my next move. I opened the car door and got out, sending the usual cascade of crumbs tumbling to the ground. 'It's through there,' the female said, pointing to a vertical crack in the rock wall. 'Or there is another one, just there, but it's hotter.' She pointed a few metres away. Her face broke into a smile. 'It's brilliant,' she said.

I would have stuck around to chat, but I was already whipping off my shirt and jeans. Any English shyness or prudishness was forgotten in the excitement. I dashed towards the gap, as quick as I dared without cutting my soft feet on the rocks. In an uncoordinated and ungainly approach, I made it up a few rocks and to the crack. I peered inside, my skin pricking with anticipation. I saw a perfectly hewn cave, which had a roof and smooth sides. From where I stood, the sunlight illuminated a set of natural rock steps that led to a perfectly clear pool of water. The sunlight refracted off the water, sending fragments of light bouncing around the cave. A light steam came off the surface of the water.

I stepped slowly and carefully down to it, and placed a toe carefully beneath the surface. It was the most perfect temperature; warm like a bath run by your mother. I eased myself in, until I was completely submerged. It was fantastic, exhilarating, all of those things. It was life-affirmingly good, being able to float around in this hidden pool of naturally heated water. I had never done anything like that before; I'm not sure I ever will again. I should imagine that it is even more special in the winter as the snow falls softly outside and you are cocooned in your warm pool sheltered by your own personal cave. Some lucky sod has even probably done so while the Northern Lights ricochet in the sky.

It was the perfect start to the day, and as soon as I was as wrinkled as a plum, I decided it was time to go. As I drove away, I saw another couple approaching. Clearly searching for something, they were checking maps and in the middle of a heated discussion with much hand waving and gesturing. I didn't want to get involved, so I drove on smugly.

Speaking of exclusive hideaways, I had spent the night in a really special little place. So special in fact, I'm worried about mentioning it here. If you have ever read any of the late Pete McCarthy, you'll know that he had a 'convent' in east Ireland. I would say where, but he never let on where it was located, just that he went there to recharge his batteries, eat fresh food and sleep the sleep of kings.

I don't have a 'convent', but I have found something pretty close. Maybe even better. The farm. Situated just off R1 in the Mývatn region of north Iceland; I'll say no more than that. It looks just like a normal farm, with bales of hay and tractors standing by in the farmyard. There is a large plywood cow, keeping lookout, otherwise you'd probably drive straight past it. Once there, though, you'll be directed back over the road to the accommodation, which consists of wooden chalet-style buildings, each with a neat patio area outside and gingham curtains tied back in the windows. Inside there is a luxurious bed with crisp white sheets and everything you need. After a hard day, this place is heaven. But the best is yet to come.

Back at the farm, you are directed to the cowshed.

Although this doesn't sound promising, it turns out to be a somewhat unique building. Half of it still belongs to Daisy and friends, but they are separated from the other half by a wall and large Perspex windows. Here comes the twist: the other half is an ultra-modern dining area – pristine white walls, wooden tables and chairs, and large windows that look out over the countryside, should you get bored of watching cows while you eat. The food is simple and yet fantastic. Chefs the world over pine for this standard of food, and yet here it is, tucked away on a farm in northern Iceland, on the far edge of Europe.

I had a mozzarella salad, fresh Icelandic rye bread and a crisp white wine. It was fantastic. Did I already say that? The mozzarella had been made on the farm, from the cows who were watching me eat it. The rye bread had been made in a pot lowered into the geothermally heated ground and left to bake slowly overnight. As if that wasn't enough, I finished with a divinely sticky chocolate cake. I ate until I was achingly stuffed, and a bit merry, then waddled back to my cabin, crawled between crisp, clean linen and slept the sleep of kings.

I didn't wake until the sunlight hit the windows of my little cabin. I rubbed my eyes and stumbled over to the cowshed café: it was milking time for the cows and breakfast for us humans. Despite vows that I'd never eat again after last night's feast, I tucked into a local lake trout, fresh breads, cheese and fruit. *Nammi namm*, indeed. The weather, unbelievably, had remained dry and sunny. I couldn't believe my luck. There is a saying in Iceland that goes, 'If you don't like the weather, just wait five minutes.' I just hoped that it didn't apply to good weather too.

On my way out of the cowshed café, a driver in a rental car pulled alongside me. It was an American guy, and I recognised him from the meal the previous night and breakfast that morning. I ducked down so that I was at eye level with him. He shouted, 'Hey, man! Great find, huh?' I just shrugged and waved noncommittally. He was right, of course. It was brilliant. Excellent. Every superlative you could think of. But we didn't want everyone going and spoiling it for you, did we? I vowed to catch up with the American guy and give him a stern talking to. He needed to keep the place our secret.

✻✻✻

I've never really got on with Akureyri. We just don't seem to see eye to eye. Calling herself the 'Capital of the North' doesn't help, in my opinion. With a population of only 17,700, she might be the biggest urban centre outside of Reykjavík, but there isn't really a great deal of competition, is there? I generally feel uneasy whenever I'm in Akureyri, but maybe that's because my first visit was so unsuccessful that it tarnished my view forever.

I had boarded an Air Iceland flight from Reykjavík. Immediately I was put at ease by the cabin crew. 'Can you please move to this seat?' The stewardess indicated a seat across from where I was sitting. 'It will balance the plane.' Bloody hell. Balancing the plane? We hadn't even left the tarmac yet. The plane was tiny, with about twenty seats. You could hear the luggage being thrown on in the compartment behind us. I couldn't even see a toilet on board, but then remembered that this had probably been removed to prevent passengers wandering around and unbalancing the plane.

I'm not a nervous flyer; don't get me wrong. I've done quite a bit of flying in my time. This flight wouldn't be that bad, I told myself sternly. I couldn't see anything out of the window. We flew through thick grey cloud right across the country, before arriving at one of the world's most impressive runways. Built on a spit of land out in the fjord, it is surrounded on three sides by water and runs parallel to the fjord's steep sides. It's pretty stunning apparently, but my view was obscured by the thick cloud base that had lowered itself over the town like a tea cosy.

I alighted and waited for five minutes for the weather to change. It didn't. No time to waste: I was only there for the day. I suppose the joke about Icelandic forests isn't true either (see below). Disheartened, I looked for a taxi or bus to take me the five kilometres into town. There wasn't one. There wasn't anything. I appeared to be the only one who hadn't already realised this, the only one who hadn't called ahead and made arrangements. The car park, previously full of 4x4 super-trucks, started to empty and I was the only one standing outside. The cloud had started to drop its load – I probably should have brought a hat. Instead, I pulled my collar closer to my neck and started walking towards the town.

It seemed to take an awfully long time. Cars sped past and sprayed me with the fresh cold water that Iceland is so famous for. I began to fantasise about a hot pot of tea and a slice of cake, and some dry clothes, rather than having to schlep all the way into town with my jeans becoming heavier with every step.

Once there, I managed to find the swimming pool. I tried to take some perverse pleasure in the fact that I had taken off my soaking-wet clothes to go for a swim in an outdoor pool in a storm. I jumped straight in and floated around for a bit, avoiding elderly swimmers and young children trying to drown each other by seeing what happened if you put inflatable armbands on your feet. I experimented with the pool's hot pots. A sign said they were 45 degrees Celsius, and had a symbol depicting a fifteen-minute maximum. I had already been in twenty-five minutes, and felt a bit light-headed, as well as having a fierce red glow to my skin, from the nipples down. I could only take so much and made a hasty exit before I cooked myself like an egg. Even the torrential rain landing on my head and shoulders didn't cool me.

On spotting a café, I headed towards it for shelter. I was ushered to a seat that was clearly kept for the town's unsavoury characters or soaking-wet foreigners. It was on its own in a corner, away from everyone else. I was given a menu that was entirely in Icelandic – or rather it was thrown on the table in front of me. The waitress was a stern Icelandic lady, wearing black clothing which I'm sure she thought was slimming. She gave me a look that said 'Don't drip on my floor.' I took off my jacket, and promptly dripped all over the floor. My jacket had decided not to be waterproof on my left shoulder, so my clothing was soaked through, but on the left side only, which felt peculiar to say the least.

I gave up on the menu and ordered the somewhat strange combination of coffee and soup, both of which I can manage in broken Icelandic. The coffee, in fairness, was excellent. Scalding hot, strong and full of flavour. The soup, however, was scalding hot, and full of scraggy meat. I assumed it was lamb, but it tasted awful and I ended up eating the vegetables and leaving the stringy, chewy mutton in the bowl. This didn't much endear me to the waitress, who clearly wasn't keen on me in the first place, and slighting the food put me right out of favour. I tried to read my guidebook, and some soggy leaflets from the airport, but I couldn't. She was standing staring at me. She whispered something to a colleague, and they both laughed. I might have been paranoid, but I definitely felt uncomfortable. I decided to leave, so I paid the bill and stepped back out into the pouring rain.

I took a walk around the town. I found the town square – Ráðhústorg – and two rows of shops, one of which was a cavernous bookshop that I took some time to explore, what with having plenty of time on my hands. There was another eight hours to go before the plane left to return to Reykjavík. I then walked the same streets again, and felt simultaneously wet and sorry for myself.

I had never seen a 1-metre-tall model of a Viking look depressed before, but the one in Akureyri did look unhappy. Even the horns on his headgear were drooping slightly. I knew how he felt; it's not often that I feel down and depressed in Iceland, but Akureyri had sucked all the life out of me. I couldn't find a bar, or a coffee shop, or anything to keep me entertained. I had read most of the books in the bookstore, and dripped snot in some of them. There was only one place last to go: the cinema.

I have always loved cinemas. My granddad was the manager of a chain of cinemas across the Midlands, and it seems to be in my blood. I love the rituals involved: getting your ticket, a bucket of popcorn, trying to find a seat in the dark, telling people to 'Shhh!' I love all that stuff. Akureyri has only a small cinema, but it didn't matter. It's probably one of the northernmost cinemas in Europe, and to get in there, out of the wet and the rain, felt pretty good. It was warm and dry and had those fat velveteen seats you used to get in cinemas in England before all those chains took over. I ended up watching a cute Disney-esque film about animated furry critters living in a hedge. It wasn't Oscar-winning stuff, certainly, but it cheered me up no end.

Akureyri might have shown me its worst, but a cinema had saved me. Until I had to walk back to the airport, that was. At least the thought of racoons and bears running around and having a whale of a time kept me busy, and took my mind off the horizontal rain that had simultaneously soaked my clothes for a second time and stung my face.

It was with some trepidation, then, that I made my second visit to Akureyri. But this trip turned out to be a different kettle of fish entirely. Transformed by the bright sunlight and seemingly Mediterranean temperatures, Akureyri seemed to be trying to make things up to me.

I arrived by road this time, and my eye was immediately caught by Akureyrarkirkja, the large twin-towered church that dominates the town, keeping a watchful eye from the hill on which it stands. I walked up to it through beautifully tended gardens, which feature gentle waterfalls and genuincly huge blooms that seem to belie their near-Arctic location. It's the same warm micro-climate that allows Akureyri its botanical gardens and the northernmost 18-hole golf course, apparently. Two rows of blue and yellow flowers led up to the door of the church.

Akureyrarkirkja's resemblance to Hallgrímskirkja in Reykjavík was easily explained by the fact that it was the same chap that designed them both. My favourite thing about the church, though, notwithstanding the views of the town and fjord from its steps, was that it contained a stained glass window from Coventry, not far from my hometown in England. Coventry was heavily bombed during the Second World War. Large areas of the city centre suffered severe damage and Coventry's cathedral was shattered by the bombing, leaving only a partial shell and a forlorn spire. The stained glass windows, though, had been removed to keep them safe, and one of them ended up in Akureyri, which I think is fantastic. Apparently it was bought by an entrepreneurial Icelander who found it in a London antique shop – a lovely story, even if the excess baggage charges would have been extortionate. I'm surprised that Coventry hasn't asked for it back though.

After admiring the church and exhausting myself on its steep steps, I wandered back into the town. The bookshop and cinema were still there, my saviours on my last trip, but I didn't require them today. Instead, I plonked myself down outside a rather wonderful café, where a smiling waitress supplied me with coffee and cake while I sunned myself. It felt like I was in Rome rather than Akureyri, and slowly it dawned on me that I might have got the place a little bit wrong. Akureyri, it seems, has a cosmopolitan spirit at heart and a thriving music and arts scene. I'm not saying it's Camden or TriBeCa, but I like the idea that the small community here, up on the edge of the Arctic Circle, tries hard to keep culture going and enjoyable. Akureyri has also become something of a transport hub for northern Iceland, with domestic flights to locations across the country, as well as to Grímsey, an island that partly falls within the Arctic Circle itself. Airlines have started routing international flights there, too. Akureyri has museums, galleries and even a university – surely not many towns of that size can boast the same?

Another reason I've changed my mind about Akureyri is because of Kjarnaskógur (the Kjarni Forest), a woodland reserve just south of town. Iceland has very few trees, and those it does have tend to be short and stunted, so Kjarnaskógur is very unusual. The wood was planted entirely by residents of the town, who began work on it in 1952 and now use it for picnics and bike rides in the summer, and skiing in the winter. The forest is mainly birch and larch, but other species flourish there as well with one species lending shade and shelter to another. This allows plants from warmer climes such as primroses and bluebells to make an appearance. Akureyri has an ambitious plan to completely encircle itself with forest in the future, and I think it definitely should. It's a great idea.

The Iceland forest joke? Go on, then if you haven't already heard it.

Q. What do you do if you are lost in an Icelandic forest?
A. Stand up.

Kolbeinsey is the northernmost outpost of Iceland, but that's just a dot of rock in an ice-cold sea. Grímsey is the most northerly inhabited point of Iceland, and the only place where Iceland is intersected by the Arctic Circle.

It's not easy to get to Grímsey. You either have to fly or take one of the infrequent boat trips from the mainland. Days on Grímsey are not named as the rest of the world names them, but rather as 'ferry days' and 'non-ferry days'. The arrival of the ferry is often the only thing that distinguishes one day from another up there. I chose the flight.

The flight, in true Icelandic style, left slightly late. I was travelling from Reykjavík to Akureyri and then on to Grímsey and my fellow passengers were a female handball team and businessmen returning home for the weekend. The plane was only partly filled. I took the opportunity to kick back and listen to some music. It was Sóley.

We took off, and I started to relax. I was quite looking forward to seeing Grímsey; I'd read a fair bit about it and I was intrigued. I wanted to find out why people would want to live there. I wanted to find out what it felt like to cross the Arctic Circle for the first time. I wanted to find out about their obsession with chess. For now, I sat back and relaxed, occasionally trying to work out which glacier we were flying over, which glacier was so brightly, brightly white that it caused me to scrunch my eyes and furrow my brow. It reminded me of being a child and going snow-blind during winter days. You could close your eyes and see a ghostly green silhouette of the snowman you'd just built. It was a happy memory, and my mum was calling me back in for tea (sausages and mash) as I drifted off to sleep in my seat.

After a tedious couple of hours twiddling thumbs in Akureyri, I boarded the twin-otter plane to Grímsey. The passenger list was getting gradually smaller. There were no air hostesses on this flight, and I could see into the flight deck from my seat. Announcements were made by the pilots simply turning around to face us.

The only other two passengers were two massively obese Canadians. They were huge; he was slightly smaller than her, but there wasn't much in it. His trousers were under extreme pressure. I'm not sizeist or anything, but when you have to have extension pieces added to your seatbelts, that's being too big, isn't it? To add to their already sizeable bulk, each of them was carrying three cameras. Two huge long-range lens things around the place where their neck used to be, and another in their hands. Throughout the flight, they did not talk to each other but just shot photographs. Whirr, click, click, click. Maybe it was Morse code? Either way, it prevented me from relaxing, and towards the end of the flight I began to feel murderous.

We flew through a dark narrow fjord and out into the open sea. The mountains, still topped with snow, disappeared behind us. I kept checking the ocean below my window, convinced I could see whales breaching and pods of dolphins.

Four minutes away, the co-pilot put a call in to Grímsey. The reason? To clear the extensive birdlife from the runway. I'm told that a Land Rover is driven up and down to clear the way for the plane. I think that is brilliant.

Grímsey has to be the smallest airport in the world. It's just one tiny green building, but one which proudly bears

113

the island's name. The vastness of my fellow passengers seemed to make the petite airport look even smaller. Some enterprising soul has built a hotel next to the airport, and just behind this lay the close-to-mythical Arctic Circle.

Grímsey is roughly diamond shaped, but with an extended point at the north end. The island is encircled by cliffs, and to warn ships there is a squat orange lighthouse that looked as if it had been placed there by an avid Lego fan. There was a wind blowing, which I suspect never stops, and an incredible soft blue haze to the light, which I believe is from being so far north. The island was surprisingly green, with dashes of yellow summer flowers.

My guide for this part of the trip was Halla Ingólfsdóttir. Halla is a summer visitor to Grímsey, but her family live there year round, along with the other eighty-odd residents. I mean 'odd' in the sense of an estimate, not that they are odd, I should add. Halla certainly wasn't odd. She was in her early forties with a face full of freckles and a huge smile. She greeted me like a long-lost relative, and as I climbed aboard her rusting fifteen-year-old van, she was talking non-stop. Her phone rang and she barked something Icelandic into it, then apologised profusely to me and sat on the phone to prevent any further interruptions to her magical mystery tour of Grímsey. Even this northern outpost has a mobile phone signal.

Grímsey is 5.3 square kilometres in size and Halla had something interesting to say about every centimetre of the place. She pointed out where her young niece lived, in a row of white houses that formed most of the town. It was her birthday soon, she told me. 'Children here ask for chickens and ducks for pets,' she said, before going on to point out the brightly painted chicken house her niece had already carefully prepared in anticipation. I thought this was great, a far cry from the nine-year-old kids in my town, who want the next games console, and probably have no idea that those nuggets they are eating used to cluck.

The houses were all carefully kept, and looked cosy and inviting. There were problems with gardening, Halla told me, due to the wind and salt from the sea. Nothing really grew there, but some of the houses had compensated for this by painting stones in bright colours and putting them in the garden instead. It brightened the place up, in a landscape that was otherwise predominantly greens and greys.

The same salt and damp air played hell with vehicles, Halla told me, which might have explained the ailing condition of her van. That, or just the way she drove it across the unpaved and rough tracks that passed for roads around there.

The day was overcast, and I suspect that a lot of days up there are the same. It was not raining, though, so I was pleased about that. Halla continued to talk as she drove me to the southern point of the island. I got out of the van with my mouth gaping. Halla was still talking in the background, but I was not listening. In front of me was what I'd been searching for. In front of me was a puffin colony. A proper one. The puffins were everywhere. I was on top of a sheer cliff, but all along its length, for as far as I could see, and directly downwards, were puffins. Puffins on top of puffins. Puffins next to puffins. Puffins squeaking, puffins cawing. Puffins with perfectly white fronts and super multi-coloured beaks. Puffins with orange feet.

I was able to walk up to about a metre from them before the suspicious staring began and they took flight to the sea below. There are no natural predators on the island for puffins, unless you count the islanders. I grabbed my camera and took some of my best ever puffin photographs. No, they were better than that, they were world class. Puffins, on that northern outpost, are alive, well and extremely photogenic. Halla stood by, arms smugly folded across her chest. 'I told you this place was special,' she said, her smile nearly as wide as mine.

Back in the truck she continued to show me around: the oil-heated swimming pool, the church built from washed-up timber, the school (children up to fourteen go to school there, after which they have to go the mainland to continue their education), the busy little harbour, and the shallow pond where local young children get their sea-legs by building and sailing their own boats. The island is surprisingly self-sufficient, if you count the exchange of fish for vegetables on ferry days. The weather isn't too bad either, with the Gulf Stream and the sea preventing the temperatures from dropping below minus 10 in the winter, but also keeping it cool in the summer. Even the snow finds it too windy to stick around. I bet it can be a cold and desolate place on a mid-winter's day though. I imagine the thing that keeps people going is each other's company, and community spirit was much in evidence – children were out playing in the street, one neighbour was helping another with their fence, and elderly residents were sitting around talking about nothing in particular.

One pastime that has taken hold on Grímsey is chess, undoubtedly encouraged by the philanthropic actions of a certain Willard Fiske, a nineteenth-century scholar from New York. Despite never having set foot in the place – the closest he got was passing by on a ship – Fiske became besotted with Grímsey. He sent the island eleven marble chess sets – one per household and one extra. One of these boards still lives in the community hall on the island. Chess (*skák* in Icelandic) has at times been taken so seriously on Grímsey, apparently, that a local story talks of how one match ended with the loser facing the ultimate forfeit: throwing himself off one of the island's many cliffs. Fiske also sent wood and finances to build and maintain a school and library. He passed away in 1904, bequeathing $12,000 to the island. Not surprisingly, there's a monument to Fiske down by the harbour. It's the one that looks like the ship that presumably sailed past with Fiske on board.

I asked Halla about crime on this island. She pulled over to a meadow covered in dandelions, a rare shock of yellow against the green grass and dark grey skies. She told me that there was no crime on Grímsey. Consequently, there were no police either. People left their doors open at night, but one day, about ten years ago, there was a summer festival. A foreigner arrived with a shotgun and in a state of inebriation. His behaviour deteriorated until the islanders decided that everyone should retreat indoors; the police were called but took several hours to arrive.

The big problem around there, Halla told me, was not crime but Arctic terns. Arctic terns are slight birds, with white plumage, a forked tail and a black cap. They have an alarming call, something akin to an 80s car alarm, and have a habit of swooping down, no, sorry, dive-bombing intruders. This is done at speed, and can be quite frightening, particularly if you have ever seen Alfred Hitchcock's *The Birds*. These slim birds have sharp beaks and a protective bent, which means that they will attempt to injure anyone or anything that comes too close to their nests. Halla had warned a recent visitor about this, she said, advising him to wear a hat and carry a stick when out walking. The stick was for holding in the air – they only attack the highest point – and the hat was in case the stick didn't work. The visitor had clearly ignored the advice: he returned from his walk a couple of hours later with blood streaming from his face. As she was telling me this, I heard a sharp thud on the roof of the van. 'That,' said Halla, 'was a tern.' And she turned to look at me, as if to say, 'I told you so.' I decided to stay inside for a bit.

Our next stop was the Article Circle, just behind the airport. It was actually a small metal platform with handrails, and a signpost attached: '325 kilometres to Reykjavík, 1949 kilometres to London, 4445 kilometres to New York'. I set foot across the Arctic Circle. I didn't feel any different. Nothing changed. There were no fireworks, no trumpets. It felt somehow hollow. I crossed back and forth, but it was no good. I still didn't feel any different. I don't know what exactly I was expecting. I had the obligatory photo taken, and on the flight back, I was 'awarded' a certificate from the pilot as I had now crossed the Arctic Circle. It all felt so incongruous. Halla noticed I was not smiling. 'It affects people in different ways,' she said. 'And besides, you had already crossed the line when I was showing you the terns earlier.' She was a cheeky one, that Halla.

Halla took me to another puffin colony on the other side of the island. There was already a crowd of birdwatchers there, with all the kit, long-range lenses and camouflage clothing. Halla parked the van in such a position that it would ruin every single shot they were trying to take. I don't think she did this intentionally, but it made me laugh, and I quickly had the colony and the bay all to myself.

I sat in the long grass and pretty pink flowers on top of the cliff. I gazed out to sea. I didn't need any more photos. It was all there. I enjoyed the present. The sound of the sea against the stones below, and the noisy puffins appearing from their burrows. The sea breeze blew the grass in one direction, liked combed hair. The smell of good, fresh air. The next stop from there was the ice sheets of eastern Greenland, but it felt like I was sitting on the edge of the world. I loved the feeling. Halla was right. The place was special.

Chapter 7

Lord of the Arctic

Not all visitors to northern Iceland are welcomed with open arms.

On 17th June 2008, twelve-year-old Karen Helga Steinsdóttir raised the alarm that one of the world's most dangerous predators had invaded her mum and dad's sheep farm in Thverárfjall in the middle of the Skaga peninsula, between the towns of Sauðárkrókur and Blönduós. She had spotted a polar bear. Polar bears are not native to Iceland, but it's believed they catch lifts with the ice floes that break off the Greenlandic ice and slowly float to Iceland. Having enough sense not to give the polar bear a hug, the girl ran back home and let everyone know what she'd seen. She initially thought it was a plastic bag, apparently. Unfortunately, despite offers from Copenhagen Zoo, and despite eyewitnesses stating that the bear did not appear hungry, having already gorged itself on birds' eggs, the bear was shot and killed by the Icelandic police. It had allegedly run towards a group of journalists, although the details seem a little sketchy. Given that a polar bear can cover 200 metres faster than the fastest sprinter, the police obviously didn't want to take any chances.

What made matters worse was that this was the second sighting, and subsequent shooting of a polar bear in Iceland within two weeks. There had been no sightings in Iceland for twenty years, and then two in a fortnight. This bear had come ashore not far away from Hraun, at the tip of the Skaga peninsula. The animal was seen – I love this description – 'nonchalantly strolling along a road' in early June 2008, and quickly caused a crowd to form. The police were called and made the decision to shoot and kill the bear rather than detain it or use tranquiliser darts. The reason given for this was that the bear was moving quickly and they were concerned it might wander off into the fog.

Polar bears have the Latin name *Ursus maritimus* ('maritime bear'), coined by a British naval officer, but they are also known by different names to different peoples around the world – white bears, ice bears, sea bears and even Lords of the Arctic. The Sami people of Scandinavia fear offending a polar bear by using its real name, so they use other expressions instead, such as 'God's Dog' or 'Old Man in a Fur Coat', although these days 'Old Man in a Fur Coat' could be just as offensive, if you ask me.

They spend most of their lives on sea ice, hunting seals in a way that belies their cute and cartoonish image. In fact, the word 'Arctic' comes from the Greek for 'bear'. This makes sense, as polar bears only inhabit the Arctic, rather than the Antarctic, which means 'penguin'. No, it doesn't. It means 'without bear', obviously. I never knew this, and now take great pleasure in regurgitating it at every opportunity, but especially when I see a Christmas card with both penguins and polar bears having a magnificent time together.

There are approximately 20,000 to 25,000 polar bears

in the Arctic, and they are believed to be vulnerable to extinction, although they are notoriously hard to count – nothing to do with their natural camouflage, you understand. One of my favourite polar bear 'facts' has to do with whether they camouflage themselves or not. Apparently it's been proved that there is no evidence whatsoever that polar bears cover their black noses with one paw while hunting, to conceal themselves fully from prey. I love the image of a polar bear doing this while a couple of seals chat away next to their ice hole, but I also love the fact that a research team spent considerable time, effort and funds just disproving this fact. Sometimes, I think I'm in the wrong job. They live for fifteen to eighteen years, typically, although I was startled to hear that the oldest known was a bear called 'Debby' who lived to an astonishing forty-two years in a Canadian zoo.

Polar bears are twice the size of Siberian tigers and just as nasty. You wouldn't want to pull a polar bear's tail, for example. They are the world's largest land carnivores, although in recent years the Kodiak bear has fiercely contested this. Not in any official way, you understand. There is no Bear Olympics or anything of the sort. They have the strength to decapitate you with a single strike – and will do so instinctively if hungry. Most polar bear attacks on humans are predatory; in other words, they attack for food – they actually want to eat you. Polar bear attacks are significantly more likely to be fatal than attacks by other bears, who tend to maul and maim humans rather than, well, finish the job. I'm not sure which I'd prefer, but the thought of being consumed or mauled by one of these massive carnivores just leaves me full of fear, whether they are called 'Debby' or not.

Another bear arrived in Iceland in May 2011. This was the fourth in only three years. It appeared in an uninhabited area of the West Fjords and wasn't near anyone or anything. The Icelandic authorities shot it dead. Again, I'm not going to judge whether this was right or wrong. What has clearly emerged, though, is that the Icelandic government has no set policy in place for dealing with polar bears. There is policy and legislation in place to authorise shooting of bears that are posing a danger to humans, which is understandable. I realise that rescue and detention attempts can be expensive and dangerous, but considering the country's proximity to polar bear habitats, the alleged vulnerability of the polar bear species and the seeming frequency of the bears' arrival on Iceland, I don't just call this daft. I call it negligent. I fully support the campaigners that are urging the government to reconsider this; surely they need a plan of action? Polar bears cannot keep getting shot because the Icelandic authorities have little or no idea what else to do.

❋❋❋

The sun was shining as I headed out of Akureyri and back on to R1. I drove past an inexplicably large statue of a man wearing a cap, and hit the open road. Like millions of ducks, I was heading to Mývatn.

'Mývatn' translates literally as 'Midge Lake' and it's easy to see why, with bloody millions of the little sods driving you mad. It's worse as the summer goes on, apparently, so I have vowed not to come back then, or only if wearing a full beekeeper's suit. Mývatn is a large expanse of still water created by a lava flow some centuries ago. Today, it is quite rightly a protected nature reserve. The lake makes a delightful scene, never mind from which angle you approach; its still, calm waters contrast pleasingly with the sharp towers of volcanic rock that jut out around it.

The lake itself is fed by nutritious spring water that sustains large numbers of water-bugs and other creepy-crawlies for the ducks to feed on, and also keeps some areas of the lake free from ice in winter, allowing the ducks to paddle. The ducks like nothing more. Barrow's Goldeneye – a duck, not a Bond villain – nests nowhere else outside of North America, so it must be good. Not that I'm turning all twitcher on you, but I was quite disappointed not to catch a glimpse of the peculiar *húsönd,* or house duck, as Icelanders call the Goldeneye. I didn't spot any eider ducks either, which was a shame as I've always wanted to see where those feathers come from – the ones you find when you shake your duvet too hard at home – but they are sea ducks and nest near the coast. There is apparently quite a large colony of them where the Laxá river empties Mývatn's contents into the sea. As they float on the sea, Eiders even form giant, presumably cosy, rafts of ducks, all in the name of warmth. Perhaps they could explain to me about the tog system for measuring duvets, which I've never really understood, and you don't seem to find measuring anything else. If I can find one of the buggers, I'll ask him whether I should go for the 13 or 13.5 tog duvet. Or he might just quack and fly away, fearing I'll pluck him like the rest of his relatives. Just watch how you say that last sentence, mind.

On the east shore of Mývatn is Dimmuborgir. Not the Norwegian heavy metal band, but a maze-like structure of weird volcanic formations that you can walk around. They were created when a river of lava flowed across a marsh. The water in the marsh began to boil and frothed up through the lava, creating vaporous bubbles that cooled, leaving empty chambers and pillars up to 10 metres high. A tourist centre is being built, and there are designated trails. 'Dimmuborgir' means 'dark castles': it's apparently connected to hell, and a favourite place for Satan to visit. I couldn't see it myself, and found the whole thing a bit disappointing, and dull. Maybe it's all that ash-grey and black rock. Maybe I'm just not enough of a Goth to enjoy all that darkness. I vowed to return wearing more black eye shadow, and moved on with no sign of the fork-tailed beast.

Only moving on wasn't quite so easy. The road heading east was initially as smooth as a runway, but then degenerated into something worse than driving on corrugated iron. Instead of leaving it as a rough stony track, the Icelandic authorities had decided to use some sort of powerful machine to literally cut a track into the rock base. The result was not one to be proud of, and should, by rights, have cost someone their job, or at least have had them making the tea for a month. The track was pitted with contiguous channels running perpendicular to the edge, making it feel like the car had square wheels. I was bounced around inside like I was in a tractor ploughing a field. I feared that my hands would cease to work from the constant vibration, and that the car would shake some crucial component loose and I would be stranded there forever. The sun was beating down and my thoughts turned darkly to newspaper stories I'd read about tourists in the Australian outback – the ones where one half of a couple waits by the broken-down car while the other person sets off for help but never arrives. I placated myself with the thought that it would all have been worth it, while at the same time feeling in my door pocket to check my bottle of water was still there. They've built a new road now. About time too.

This was the infamous R864 in the Jökulsárgljúfur National Park. It led to Dettifoss, a waterfall that waterfall fans make pilgrimages to from across the world. If there is such a thing as a waterfall fan, then I'm sure that they would. Dettifoss is the biggest waterfall in Europe, if you measure waterfalls by water volume discharge, which waterfall fans usually do. Its discharge – lovely word, isn't it – can be over 500 cubic metres per second during the massive spring run-off. The road was hellish, and I considered that I was being punished for being so dismissive of Dimmuborgir and Mr. Satan. It's a mere twenty-six kilometres north from Route 1, but feels a lot longer. You can't see anything either, just a flat grey-green landscape of thick lichen and moss over the volcanic rock. The moss there is ecologically important; it's slow growing and highly delicate. One footprint in this sensitive stuff could be there for years before it grows out.

Occasionally, a 4x4 vehicle rocketed past, shaking my car and spraying a thick fog of dust. When this happened, I just used the sun to navigate until the dust settled. The dust was so bad that I had all the windows closed, and yet it still seemed to percolate through and the air felt thick with it. I could see particles of dust floating around in the sunlight.

After a dusty forty-five minutes, I arrived at Dettifoss,

or rather the car park nearby. I parked up and then ambled over to the waterfall. What a sight. And sound. White water flowed at speed before dramatically cascading 44 metres down to the canyon floor. It was 100 metres to the other side. The water looked really angry and powerful; there was nothing calm about it at all. It was a huge torrent and it sent a fine spray up into the air that refracted with rainbows before it was blown away.

Dettifoss is on the Jökulsá á Fjöllum river, which gushes melt water from Vatnajökull and gathers further water from a large drainage area. Downstream of the falls, the river has carved an impressive canyon, which looked like something out of a film. It was not hard to imagine a rugged cowboy riding up the riverbank and coming to a sideways stop to admire the mighty cascade. In fact, it has been in a film – Ridley Scott's *Prometheus*. I sat as close as I dared to the falls and it was so loud, I couldn't hear myself speak. The words were drowned out by the sheer noise of the water plummeting downwards. It was really beautiful. I stayed for a while, but then I remembered the road and, not wanting to be stuck there at night, I drove back.

On returning to civilisation, or at least the village of Reykjahlíð, on Mývatn's eastern shore, I opened the door of the car and about a tonne of dust fell out. It had been worth it.

Hverarönd is a couple of kilometres south of Reykjahlíð, just east of Mývatn, and is absolutely outstanding. It is entirely otherworldly. It's like the set of a sci-fi movie, and probably has been at some point. It's a collection of geological geothermal features; a freak show of nature. It's set on the most gorgeous plain, with snow-streaked mountains at each perspective, and a unique pastel-peach-orange-coloured soil that looks like it's been smudged together by an over-enthusiastic art student.

There are wooden footpaths to save you from getting boiled to death in the natural hot pots, but there is no escape from the billowing plumes of sulphur. Signs advise visitors not to stray from pathways, or to stand in the caustic sulphur plumes, but the smell of sulphur is intense. It smells like eggs, and not in a good way. A good lungful would make the strongest person gag, for sure. Whereas near Geysir in the south-west there are hot pots of water, at Hverarönd there are mud pots. They look like a mistake in the Dulux paint factory; thick, gloopy emulsion bubbles and spits in the most alarming manner. Some are several metres across, complete with caked mud sides that have cracked like porcelain in their own heat. Then there are fumaroles, which look like pyramid stacks of rocks that have pushed up from the earth and are continuing to push and heave. They are the source of the sulphur; they hiss and scream angry shoots of white sulphuric steam. Between the mud pots and fumaroles are streams and vents, all red hot, all belching and bubbling. The colours are exquisite. The white-out of the steam clears to show the orange scenery: there are yellows and whites on the ground, the fumaroles are streaked with red and greens, and the mud points range from grey to blue. They are familiar colours, but in the wrong places, like the printer had malfunctioned. It's weirdly, weirdly beautiful. It's exactly the sort of strange yet compelling landscape that drives me to visit Iceland. Scenery like that can't be found anywhere else, except my dreams.

If there is one place to wash the sulphur out of your hair and the dust out of your ears and other orifices, it's at the nearby Jarðböðin nature baths, close to Bjarnarflag. Similar to its southerly counterpart the Blue Lagoon, Jarðböðin is a large lake of geothermally heated water designed for bathing. It is a great way to relax, and I think that the UK should consider revitalising spa towns such as Bath into something similar. Unlike at the Blue Lagoon, beer is on tap at Jarðböðin, should you find it hard to relax in the gentle blue warm waters without the aid of alcohol.

It wasn't particularly busy when I visited, and save for a group of teenagers flirting near the hot pots, the nature baths had a hushed tone, not unlike a library. Opened in 2004, the baths have built on a centuries old tradition of harnessing subterranean power in the area. Steam baths and saunas have been on the site for hundreds of years, and there are also underground bakeries. I kept looking under rocks and bin lids, hoping to find a loaf baking, but no such luck. I had to settle for floating right up to the edge of the lake and looking out over the steaming landscape as dusk came. And that's not settling at all.

Just north of Mývatn is the small fishing town of Húsavík. Previously only famous for whale watching, it went on to gain notoriety as the home of the Iceland Phallological Museum. The museum's founder and curator is Sigurður

Hjartarson. Sigurður first set up the museum in Reykjavík, but when he retired and moved to Húsavík in 2004, he simply took his collection of formaldehyde members and dried tally-whackers with him. Since then, there has been no looking back. The museum catches the eye of every journalist and TV researcher looking for kooky, strange Iceland, second only, perhaps, to elves and trolls. Articles on the museum have been published in twenty-six different countries, and it still ranks as one of the twenty-five things to do in *The Rough Guide to Iceland*. Let me give you the facts, and then maybe you'll understand why.

Sigurður has amassed 272 specimens from ninety-two different animals, ranging from a dormouse to a walrus. He concentrates on Icelandic animals – both from the land and from the sea – and this is why he has fifty-five specimens of whale penis (including the impressive 170-centimetre sperm whale penis) and one polar bear penis, from another unfortunate that floated to Iceland on a floe a few years back. It doesn't explain, however, the inclusion of twenty-three 'folklore' penises, which I assume are those supposedly from trolls and elves. Not only am I sceptical about the very existence of such creatures, I am even more sure that you'd struggle to catch one and then remove its penis. You are, at the very least, going to end up with a nasty curse, surely.

Sigurður has collected forty foreign specimens; his star turn, however, arrived on 12th April 2011. A human penis. I'm not kidding. Ninety-five-year-old Páll Arason donated his penis to the museum a good few years back, but I don't think that anybody, anybody at all, thought that he'd go through with it. We were told that it was removed by a doctor, but nothing more. I wasn't sure whether to congratulate Sigurður on his achievement, or not, but either way, it has certainly put Húsavík on the map.

Sadly, the Penis Museum has now moved back to Reykjavík. Part of me thinks it is over-hyped, but I still popped in to have a look at its new home. Nothing much had changed; flaccid members still resided in their test-tube homes. One new addition, though, was a contract from one Tom Mitchell of the United States, pledging his penis to the museum on his death. His penis, and I'm not making this up, is named 'Elmo'. There was a picture of Tom and Elmo hanging in the museum, right next to the signed contract. Perhaps Elmo was feeling shy that day.

Húsavík is also a great place for whale-watching trips, although I've never had much luck with them. I usually end up with a handful of sightings of black, shiny humps surfacing in the distance. On one trip, on which I have never been so cold, I managed to spot a harbour porpoise, and on another, on which I have never been so seasick, I managed to spot a pod of dolphins racing alongside the bow of the boat. As pleasant as this was, I wanted to see something more spectacular. Do I sound ungrateful? Well, the whale-watching companies of Iceland – of which there are many – are not shy of showing photographs of whale tails against snow-capped mountains, or whales leaping clear of the sea in front of boats of mouth-wide-open tourists. I'm sure this does happen, but it never happens to me. I thought the Northern Lights were elusive; you should try a blue whale.

Mark Carwardine, zoologist extraordinaire and Stephen Fry's mate, is on record as saying that Húsavík is one of the best places in the world to see blue whales. Blue whales are the big ones – 30 metres in length, and up to 180 tonnes, and yet they still manage to evade me. That said, so do the fin, sei, orca, humpback, sperm, northern bottlenose, and long-finned pilot whales. Twenty-three species of whale circulate in Icelandic waters, either in passing or because they live around Iceland. Even the funky-nosed narwhale passes through.

I'm going to talk about Keiko, the orca (killer) whale best known for the 1993 film *Free Willy*, then I'm going have to address the elephant in the room, as they say. Keiko, it seems, was Icelandic. He was caught by Icelandic fishermen in 1979, and spent some time in an aquarium in south Iceland before being moved to an aquarium in Ontario. He was then moved again to a park in Mexico City. That place wasn't so good for Keiko, who was placed in a tank too small for a whale, designed for dolphins. The water was also too warm, and chlorinated. As a result, Keiko began to suffer badly and had to be rescued and then rehabilitated in Oregon. This was after Keiko allegedly saved the life of an eighteen-month-old child who fell into his enclosure, by using his nose to punt the child back onto dry land before his father even realised what had happened. He repeated this feat during filming. He was eventually flown home to Iceland in 1998, where an expensive training program went ahead off the coast of Heimaey to teach him to catch fish and consequently survive in the wild. On release, Keiko swam for Norway, in all likelihood looking for a mate. He died in Norway in 2003. Keiko means 'Lucky One' in Japanese.

That elephant? I'm going to dodge it. Iceland does

still hunt whales. Sometimes this is for scientific reasons; sometimes, and historically, this has been for food. This is a near-Arctic country after all. You call still buy whale meat in Iceland, in supermarkets and even as kebabs in Reykjavík. Commercial whaling recommenced in Iceland in 2006, with quotas set for minke and fin whales. Minke whales are consumed locally, and the hunting quota is seldom met, whereas fin whales are usually for export to the Japanese markets, although this has not happened in recent years.

Whaling in Iceland has, perhaps not surprisingly, caused a fair amount of controversy. Some of this controversy and objection has come from well-meaning US citizens, who probably ought to look at the whaling policies of Alaska before looking so far from home. Whaling is an emotional and political subject in Iceland. I'm not going to state an opinion either way; if that means I get splinters in my buttocks from sitting on the fence, so be it. I do think about it, though, mainly when I see those big black whaling ships docked in Reykjavík harbour, demarked with a huge 'H' for *hvalur* (whale).

There is a love story in Húsavík too. Mike Lindsay, best known as a founder member of English folk-tronica band Tunng, first went to Iceland for the New Year's Eve celebrations in 2006. He describes this as a 'war-zone, where everyone is more drunk than you, and yet still setting off fireworks out of their hands'. It was during these mad celebrations that he met an Icelandic girl named Harpa.

Mike returned to London and tried to forget about Harpa and Iceland and, presumably, attempted to clear the ringing from his ears.

Until 2010, when Tunng played the Airwaves festival in Reykjavík. Mike met Harpa again and they were reunited. Harpa took Mike to Húsavík, a small fishing village in north-east Iceland. Mike came up with a plan. Not much of a plan, but a plan. He decided to spend two months in a small cabin in Húsavík, making music, spending time with Harpa and drinking up his new-found obsession with Iceland. To sort the first part of the plan, he borrowed instruments and a name from the local landscape. His cabin overlooked Kinnafjöll, which translates as 'Cheek Mountain'. Cheek Mountain Thief was born.

Cheek Mountain Thief, the album, was released in 2012. It is an aural pleasure; a mixture of layered vocals, soft strings, folky guitar, parping brass and surprising percussion. If hipster band Bon Iver were the last musicians to employ the 'disappear into a remote cabin' method of making music, it's proof that it works, but in very different ways. Bon Iver's album deals with melancholy and lost love; *Cheek Mountain Thief* is more positive, probably due to love found. Supplemented by top-quality Icelandic musicians at every turn (Sin Fang from Seabear; singer/songwriter Mugison) and given a final mix by a member of Múm, it certainly feels Icelandic. I would call it a triumph. Mike was also pleased with its reception. 'I didn't know if the media would get it; it's a very personal record, but they did, and they were very complimentary.'

Mike was similarly complimentary about the Icelandic music scene. 'It's amazing,' he told me. 'It's difficult to define, it twists and turns and overlaps. Our drummer is in ten different bands, I'm sure.' He has clearly embraced this different sort of scene. You can feel this influence throughout *Cheek Mountain Thief,* and especially on tracks such as 'Showdown', which features a shouty Icelandic backing vocal, or twinkling strings Sin Fang-style on 'Spirit Fight'.

Mike and I clearly share a passion for Iceland. We spent some time chatting this through. He started off by saying that the main attraction of Iceland was that 'it's not London', but he was joking. He described his appreciation of the landscape – 'alien, different and prehistoric' – but it's the Icelanders that have captured his heart. 'They are just so welcoming and warm. They have a general personality trait that is so positive; anything is possible. It's magical.' I would agree.

Mike told me that he was moving to Iceland on a permanent basis, and that he and Harpa were planning to get married. This is a love story. No wonder Mike can make such joyful, addictive music. I recommend you get your ears around *Cheek Mountain Thief.* It's the sound of an Englishman falling in love with a girl and with Iceland.

Chapter 8

A Feast with the Huldufólk

Sitting in Manchester Airport, north-east England, in one of those restaurants that have themes, organic credentials and prices to match, I spotted an Icelandic businessman. He was clearly waiting for the 2310 flight to Keflavík, as was I. Dressed in a power suit, and speaking grammatically perfect English with a pronounced Icelandic accent, he called the waitress over. He pointed a beautifully manicured finger at the menu.

'Fish, chips and what are they... these... mushy peas?'

The waitress thought. You could actually see her thinking. She replied in a thick Manchester accent. 'Like petit pois,' she said, 'but mushy.'

He looked somewhat mystified as I simultaneously spat out my drink and tried not to laugh. Genius.

Perhaps I laughed too soon, though, at this clash of cultures underscored by a misguided waitress. I didn't realise that what was to come would be worse, much worse than the emerald-coloured, chemically enhanced pulped seedpod of the pea. Nichola and I had been invited to Iceland for a wedding. Einar and Klara were getting married and I couldn't wait. What I was worried about, though, was the food. My forays into Icelandic cuisine had come up with successes, such as the gorgeous and addictive yoghurt-like *skyr*, and some failures. Einar had yet to feed me rotten shark, but he had fed me the dried fish – *harðfiskur* – that you see everywhere in Iceland. I hadn't been expecting such pronounced, well, fishiness, and I struggled to keep it down. So it was with some trepidation that we boarded the plane, not because of the wedding or the hospitality – we were looking forward to both – but because of the horror stories you hear about Icelandic food. My head was filled with thoughts of rotten shark, sheep's testicles, lambs' heads and puffin hearts.

The flight, uncharacteristically for Iceland's flag carrier, was running late. This was to be the first of a set of problems. It was running late by nearly two hours, pushing our take-off time into the early hours of the next day, and leaving us to observe – from afar – the rather different type of person awaiting flights to 18–30s destinations such as Ayia Napa and Tenerife. The time didn't matter to them, it was beer o'clock and they were drinking until the hands fell from the clock. It reminded me of a night out in Liverpool a few months earlier, with a close friend. We witnessed first hand a male off his head on mephedrone – designer drug *du jour*; a domestic dispute that required several security staff to resolve it; and another couple – newly acquainted – who were swapping trousers, leaving her in oversized jeans and him in hot pants, both showing far too much flesh. The time, I should add, was 8pm. We were in a different time zone, and several drinks behind everyone else.

If being an unwilling participant in this debauchery wasn't enough, I had also received a phone call from our hotel in Kópavogur telling us that they had unintentionally overbooked and that we had been rehoused in the Viking Hotel in Hafnarfjörður, some kilometres away. *Takk fyrir*, indeed.

After finally boarding the flight, taxiing away and having a lovely snooze until touch-down in Keflavík, we awoke to a sunny night. It was June, the season of twenty-four-hour daylight. It was about 3am, and the sun was fully out. Hat on and everything. It confused my body clock no end, and made me feel more than a little disorientated. We collected our hire car, and headed for the seaside town of Hafnarfjörður.

The hire car also confused the hell out of me in my befuddled and overtired state, and I found myself reaching for the gear stick and finding only the window lever, much to my annoyance. The roads were quiet though, and the night-time sun cast an orange glow and long shadows over the lunar-like landscape. Lava fields stretched away from the road, covered in thick green moss.

As we arrived at Hafnarfjörður, my mouth fell open. I rubbed my eyes, momentarily disbelieving them. It made no difference though; they were still there. Directly outside of the hotel, on the quayside, were about fifteen Vikings. All of them were in full Viking garb: horned hats, swords, animal skins and ginger beards. They were scattered among canvas tents that had been set up for the occasion and were still in full flow, or should I say, the alcohol was still in full flow. They were clearly in a celebratory mood, despite the hour. We later discovered that this was an annual six-day festival during which people dress up as Vikings and have a bloody good time. Despite the danger of rape and pillage, we slipped unnoticed through the Viking hordes to our awaiting room. Shattered but happy to be back on Icelandic turf, we flopped on to the bed and slept.

Hafnarfjörður is well known for its Viking festivals, and also for its 'hidden folk' – more of whom later – but arguably it's even better known for its townspeople. Hafnarfjörður residents are quite often the butt of Icelandic jokes. Not that they mind, apparently; they even tell the same jokes amongst themselves. The jokes might get lost slightly in translation, so please bear with me, but they go something like this: they walk quietly past the chemist so as not to awake the sleeping tablets; they take stepladders to the supermarket when the prices go up – that sort of quality joke. Like I say, maybe they get lost in translation, but I'm not sure I agree with the antilocution.

Hafnarfjörður is a small town about ten kilometres south of Reykjavík. I don't know whether you'd want to classify it as a suburb, but it's close enough for me not to care. I'm told that the town has so many roundabouts that the mayor is colloquially known as the 'Lord of the Rings'. I've also been told about a local that had to move from Hafnarfjörður on account of her dog becoming violently car sick on every trip to and from town. It's the very same roundabouts that always cause me problems.

Last time I came to Hafnarfjörður, I had some trouble too. I had trouble trying to find the tourist information centre, where I had arranged to meet Sigurbjörg Karlsdóttir, also known as Sibba. I kept getting sent off in different directions. I counted my blessings; at least I wasn't covered in canine vomit.

Sibba had agreed to give me a tour of Hafnarfjörður, with a difference. She had promised to show me the best places to find elves and hidden people in the town. I needed to get this out of the way; it's one of the things that is constantly peddled to visitors to Iceland. Was it all a big joke on tourists? Hafnarfjörður is famous for having one of Iceland's largest settlements of elves, dwarves and other mystical beings, which are collectively called *huldufólk* – hidden people. I've read somewhere that only a quarter of Icelanders believe in hidden people, but a much larger percentage of Icelanders wouldn't destroy an elf house knowingly.

Sibba, whether intentionally or not, had dressed herself as an elf. She had a red woollen pointed hat, and a red jacket. She even had elfin features: green eyes and a quick smile. She introduced herself and explained that while she herself was not a 'seer' – in other words, she didn't see hidden people first hand – she did get visits from them in her dreams. She had gained her knowledge from a local seer named Erla Stefánsdóttir, from other people that had had experiences with hidden people and, perhaps more obviously, from working in the local tourist office for a decade.

There is a big part of me that is hugely sceptical about this. I am, by nature, a believer in the scientific, in hard evidence, in the tangible. But almost immediately, I felt at ease with Sibba. She wasn't asking me to believe; she was asking for me to have a walk around the town with her on a Sunday morning, and have a listen to some stories. I'm was more than happy to oblige, especially as she was so damn good at telling stories. In fact, she was so good that she had started to travel internationally to demonstrate her craft.

Sibba started off her tour by showing me a rock with a large iron bar sticking out of it. She told me that work had commenced on the rock to have it broken down to make way for a new house. Older residents of the town stated that the rock was inhabited by elves and, sure enough, the rock could not be broken, the workers became ill, and machinery mysteriously broke down. The reason? The elves, of course.

Whether you believe this or not, many Icelanders certainly do. In 2011 mining work on a new tunnel in Bolungarvík in the West Fjords ceased after construction machinery stopped functioning and one controlled explosion went wrong, causing stones to crash down on to the town below. The local residents held a meeting to explain to the elves exactly what was going on, in the hope that work would be allowed to continue.

Elves aren't always bad or naughty though – generally only if they have been wronged in some way. Sibba was full of tales of fruitful negotiations with elf communities that had allowed successful alterations to the landscape. There were even stories of elves helping humans, such as the young lad who fell from a cliff in Hafnarfjörður. He landed without a scratch. When taken to see the doctor, he explained that he had seen a succession of small hands appear from the rock face and break his fall, lowering him to the ground safe and sound. The doctor was unable to provide any other explanation for the child's lack of injury. Apparently elves had been seen around that particular rock on a number of occasions. In fact, Sibba had been told on two separate occasions in the same week, by two different individuals, that the elf living there had a sore throat.

We continued our tour. Hidden people or not, I started to appreciate Hafnarfjörður a little bit more. We walked to a green, leafy park in the town centre, where Sibba told me a story that made me grin from ear to ear. On one of her tours, Sibba pointed out a small cave in the park to the group. A Spanish tourist, somewhat carried away by it all, or just desperate to see an elf, decided to crawl inside. She was gone for a few minutes, then returned looking shaken. She stammered out to Sibba and the group that amazingly she had seen an elf in the gloomy cave. She had seen his eyes glinting right at the back of the cave; they were large and round and reflected in the little light available. At which point, a scared-looking cat scooted from the cave, to the obvious embarrassment of the girl and the amusement of the group.

I should probably point out that there are many different 'elven' beings. Some believe there are up to thirteen different types. There are elves, gnomes, dwarfs, light fairies, angels, love-lings and mountain spirits. That's only seven. I get confused between the different types and sorts; some have big ears, others are the size of children, others are naughty and some – light fairies – are believed to be luminous. But one thing that I was told has stuck. If you are ever unsure whether you are speaking with a human or a hidden person, check their nose. Hidden people have no septum and just one nostril. So you can tell them apart straight away. If the need ever arises.

Sibba also talked about 'changelings'. Changelings are elf children that have been surreptitiously swapped for human children without the parents' knowledge. They may look the same, but will be naughty and mischievous.

Apparently the best way to deal with this is to strike the child with a branch from the garden and make it cry. At which point the elves will duly appear and reverse the swap, obviously unable to stand the cries of their own child. It sounded like a scare story to tell naughty kids to me; and smacking kids with sticks to see whether they are changelings or not is far from an ideal method of parenting. It's likely to get you arrested.

We wandered on. Sibba pointed out an elven palace (where music had supposedly been heard), house gnomes (they occasionally borrow things from owners; I have one that seems to borrow money from me), settlements of older hidden people, and communities of elves and dwarves together.

Eventually we ended up at a large traditional-style wooden Icelandic house. Sibba told me that the family that had moved there had had to agree with the previous owners not to do anything to one particular rock in the basement of the house, where an elf family supposedly lived. The family had agreed to this and moved in, taking care not to do anything to the elf house. The family had a young boy, and he too was told of the elves living in the basement. One day, the boy was on a trip with the local school, not dissimilar to the tour that I was on. An elf church was pointed out to him, which was some kilometres from his own home, at which he exclaimed, 'What? They have to come this far to go to church?'

I thought it was a cute story; one of wonder and joy. If believing in elves and hidden people can bring such wonder and joy, then I'm all for it. I didn't see any hidden people and I don't know if I'll ever believe in their existence, but I enjoyed the walk around Hafnarfjörður, and I especially enjoyed Sibba's storytelling. It was a great way to start a Sunday morning, and it felt a million miles away from Reykjavík's carefully cultured smooth and sophisticated image.

On waking on Einar and Klara's wedding day, we had breakfast – not Viking-style, I noted – before noticing a slight problem. Our luggage, which contained all of our wedding gear, was safely under lock and key. The locks were on the suitcases. The keys were in the kitchen, in our house, in England. Despite much tugging, amateur locksmithery and old-fashioned kicking, the locks would not budge. I had invested in tamper-proof locks and they were living up to their name, that's for sure. My only options were to cut through the material, or saw through the hasps. As I didn't want to ruin the cases forever, I decided to try and find a saw. After a cursory search of the hotel, and a blank look from the receptionist, I found myself back in the Viking village. One canvas tent, blowing open in the cool sea breeze, appeared to be full of tools; probably used for making weapons, longships and funky hats. I approached with caution; like the advice given in bear country, never surprise a sleeping Viking. Certainly not a hung-over one. I shouted a tentative 'Hello', but to no avail, only the slobbery snores of sleeping marauders. I tiptoed into the tent and located a hacksaw. Returning quickly to the room, I made neat work of the hasps, using all of my DIY skills. I ran back to the tent and deftly replaced the hacksaw. Job done. I had sorted the problem, and evaded the Vikings, and it wasn't even 10am.

Einar, still having no faith in my driving skills or sense of direction, and despite almost certainly having better things to be doing on the morning of his wedding day, insisted on meeting us at the hotel so that we could follow him to the church in Kópavogur. Kópavogur translates as 'Seal-Pup Bay' and is actually a town in its own right, although it now adjoins Reykjavík's sprawl. It's also home to Emilíana Torrini, the Icelandic pop princess. The weather, obviously at great cost to the bride and groom, had turned out fabulously, with vivid blue sky and sparkling sunshine. It looked like Hawaii rather than Kópavogur, and like most places, it looked better in the sun.

The church was a fantastically modern structure of the type they do so well in Iceland. All perfect lines, large glass plates, white walls and gracious curves. It's not that far from where the happy couple live, and where Nichola and I have shared mad barbeques, dinner parties and the best New Year's Eve of my life. So far, of course. Inside, the church lived up to its exterior, with a clean, pine-inspired feel and, best of all, theatre-style seating. No uncomfortable wooden pews there. Just kick back and enjoy. All that was missing was a bucket of popcorn.

The church started to fill with friends and family, and I started to feel self-consciously non-Icelandic. Everyone was making us very welcome, but I was pleased to see the friendly faces of Daníel and Inga. The service commenced in traditional style, but was conducted – perhaps not surprisingly – in Icelandic. I could just about follow what was going on, but the language barrier didn't really matter.

It was clear that this was a very special day for Einar, Klara and their families, and we were chuffed to be part of that. Any self-conscious thoughts were purely selfish and I pushed them to the furthest reaches of my mind. Klara looked stunning in her pure-white dress and fur shrug, Einar looked nervous and excited in equal measure.

The service was fairly brief, and everyone was in good spirits. There didn't seem to be any attempt to inject dour religious sentiments into what was essentially a celebration, as so often occurs in England's marriage ceremonies, which is probably due to them having a captive audience for a change. Another bonus, and one that I'm all for importing to the UK, was the absence of hymns. I'd been to a great many weddings in the lead-up to this one. So many, in fact, that I'd remarked upon the fact to my barber, whose services had clearly been required a lot more as a result. I reckoned on twelve weddings in a twenty-four-month period. We agreed that it was probably due to my age and that of my friends. An elderly customer piped up behind us. 'You are lucky; at my age, it's funerals.' I stopped my moaning and the rest of my haircut was completed in silence.

At all of the weddings we were asked to sing hymns. This has always generated a feeling of dread in me, as I am blessed with all the singing qualities of an Emperor penguin. The whole congregation usually struggles though, with tone and volume being key variables. Attempts to remedy this have included expensive choirs and even the passing out of instruments to the congregation, but generally it's been to no avail. No one comes away from weddings saying 'Such gorgeous hymns, and so well sung', do they? Icelanders have solved the problem. Einar and Klara, for example, had hired an Icelandic singer. She had previously represented Iceland at the Eurovision Song Contest, but that's not what made my day. She did all the singing, therefore relieving me of all the effort and stress involved. And she was bloody good at it too.

One of the big differences from weddings I had previously attended wouldn't occur until after the service. Actually, it wouldn't occur at all. Klara would retain her surname. Einar would retain his. In Iceland, neither partner takes on the name of the other.

Names and naming in Iceland are a curious business. Following the old Norse system of patronymics, Icelandic children take the first name (or occasionally middle name) of their father, coupled with the suffix *–son* for a boy and *-dóttir* for a girl. So, Sindri Jónsson would be the son of Jón, and his sister could be – and I'm making all of this up – Vigdís Jónsdóttir. Easy, isn't it?

No, apparently not. There are some exceptions to the rule. Children can take on their mother's name if they wish; for example, if the father is not known, or, more likely, if the father does not want to be known. This would be matronymics, and happens occasionally.

There are some family names in Icelandic society, but these are inherited, as it has been against the law to compose or take a family name in Iceland since 1925. In fact the Icelandic government takes a pretty hard line on names; for example, if an Icelander takes on a foreign name or that of their spouse while living abroad, they must discontinue it on their return. I can see why this is – to preserve the identity and naming culture in Iceland;

but I can also see the other side of it. It must get pretty tiring trying to explain why your daughter and wife have a completely different surname. It must really hurt some immigration officers' heads.

Seeing as I have started on names, I'll go on. First names are equally complex. They often have some meaning attached to them, for example Björk means Birch Tree, Örn means Eagle, Björn means Bear and Hrafn means Raven. Gods are popular too, as are names from history. Furthermore – and this is where the fun starts – Icelandic couples can combine names for their newborns. So, Þorbjörn becomes Daring Bear, and Hrafnhildur, well, that's Battle of Ravens. Awesome. Names can often occur to mothers during pregnancy. Pregnancy brain was clearly underway when a poor baby was allegedly named Freðsvunta – Frozen Apron.

Help, or hindrance, however you wish to look at it, is at hand. The Icelandic Naming Committee has to approve every first name of every newborn Icelander. This is to ensure that names comply with Icelandic spelling and grammar, that boys have boys' names and girls have girls' names, and, rather sweetly I think, that the name can't be harmful to the person carrying it. Hence Satanía didn't get though. I think we could do with something similar in the UK, to stop all those muppets naming their children Aston Villa or Ikea or something. There has been controversy, though, as names that have been approved by the Naming Committee have included the very un-Icelandic Dennis and Jane. Even Carla has been approved, despite there being no letter 'C' in the Icelandic alphabet. An Icelandic girl even took the Committee to court in 2013 after her name – Blær (Light Breeze) – was not approved. She won the case.

Icelanders are addressed by their first names, including celebrities and even the prime minister. Please try and remember this next time you meet Björk or an Icelandic dignitary. Or for that matter, when using an Icelandic phone book, which lists everyone by first name, and occupation. Not that anybody uses phone books these days, of course. Just remember not to call Björk, Mrs Björk. That wouldn't be good. She'd probably punch you for it.

Icelanders place huge importance on family life. They appreciate spending time together as a family, and the blessing of having children. This emphasis on family life was very obvious at the wedding: it felt like a celebration, and everyone was genuinely pleased to be there and be involved. I'm not sure I've seen the same genuine enthusiasm and delight at weddings back in the UK. Maybe it's just me.

As is tradition in Iceland, the newly married couple sloped off for a photo session. We grabbed a cup of coffee with a group of friends who lived nearby and had clearly been briefed by Einar not to let us out of their sight. The coffee was served with *kleinur* – small twisted doughnuts that are absolutely delicious. And then came the reception. I had been dreading this part of the day. Not because of the language barrier but because of the food. Or the threat of the food. What would it be? All stringy cuts of lamb. Fish with everything. Eyeballs and singed heads of miscellaneous creatures. My stomach was twisting and turning with just the thought of it.

There is one Icelandic food that I love, though. I adore

it. I crave it. It's *skyr*. I even found it in New York. Let me explain.

New York was baking hot, seeming to shimmer in the blazing sunlight. The skyscrapers turned from grey to silver as they reflected back the sun's rays. The sun beat down, sending commuters and hipsters running for shade and air-conditioned shops, and turning the subway system into an underground oven. Typically, the English tennis players had already been knocked out of the early stages of the US Open, citing the heat as the reason why. I was in New York for other reasons, but I couldn't let the opportunity slip by. I had to take the chance to find Siggi Hilmarsson and his Icelandic *skyr*. I had read about the guy, and was utterly enthralled by his story. Moreover, I couldn't resist a tub of cool Icelandic *skyr* in that sultry heat.

Skyr is an Icelandic dairy product. Although you wouldn't be wrong to think of it as part of the yoghurt family, it is actually a form of soft cheese and is slightly acidic. It is virtually fat free, which is a bonus. Like most things, it was brought to Iceland by the Vikings, although I'm not sure that they were particularly health conscious. I certainly can't imagine them counting the calories. *Skyr* is part of my staple diet when I'm in Iceland – I probably eat more than is strictly good for you, but it is delicious and there is nothing like it in the UK.

Siggi moved to New York from Iceland in 2002 for grad school. In 2004 he found himself all alone in the big city at Christmas, and, for the first time, not going home for the Christmas holidays. Feeling homesick for his friends and family, and for *laufabrauð* (the thin Icelandic 'leaf bread' served at Christmas) and *skyr*, Siggi asked his mother to send over some recipes so that he could attempt to make his own Icelandic food, especially as *skyr* was nowhere to be found in New York. Siggi told me that he was missing Iceland and the ability to drive only an hour to find that 'instant feeling of aloneness'. So, in his adopted city of 8.4 million souls, a lone Siggi made his first batch of *skyr*.

He didn't say whether it cured his homesickness or not, but it must have gone well, as Siggi went on to produce further batches from an agricultural college in upstate New York during the spring of 2005. It was rapturously received by New York foodies. So rapturously, in fact, that Siggi was able to start his own company – Icelandic Milk and Skyr Company. He moved production to Norwich, Chenango County, New York, where doe-eyed brown cows eating pristine green grass produced organic milk for Siggi to turn into yummy *skyr*. By 2008, Siggi had doubled his company's size (OK, from two to four employees), and was producing *skyr* for stores up and down the eastern seaboard. Not bad for something started in his own diminutive kitchen. He planned to focus on the North American market, with the next stop being Canada. I remarked that the Icelandic–Canadian connection should make that an easy transition, a ready-made market even. Siggi just chuckled to himself. I asked whether – fingers crossed – he was planning to start producing *skyr* in the UK, but despite a lot of requests, he wasn't. I almost shed a tear. He did have some tips for me though. 'Try the grapefruit one,' he said. It was his favourite as he didn't like anything too sweet. His biggest seller was blueberry *skyr*. My stomach is rumbling now, just thinking of it.

Later, I did try the grapefruit one, bought from one of

the best food shops I've ever been into. It was in Brooklyn, and although Siggi's *skyr* is available across all five New York boroughs, I recommend this store. Outside on the street, it was marked by huge boxes of green and red oversized apples, landslides of heart-shaped strawberries and juicy watermelons. Inside was a tribute to any food you could possibly desire; pastries and aromatic coffee, hot and cold buffets, cold sliced meats and hot spinning chicken, English Ale and exotic fish, olive oils and fresh bread. I found the *skyr* and sat in the shadow of the Borough Hall to eat it. The grapefruit *skyr* – Siggi wasn't kidding around – wasn't sweet at all, rather tart, if anything. It had a slightly stiffer consistency than its Icelandic relative, allowing the spoon to cut though, and it held its form in a pleasing manner. It was pleasant, but I was not bowled over, if I'm honest. The next day, though, I was back for more. I chose the blueberry one, and it was divine. No disappointment there. It had a purplish tinge from the blueberries, and I was pleased to find that they also lent an extra sweetness to proceedings. I scraped every last bit from the pot. I could see why it was Siggi's top seller – it was really delicious.

Siggi said that he was continually surprised by the success of his *skyr*, as he thought it was going to be a niche market, the preserve of speciality food shops and alternative restaurants. Ever modest, he put some of the success down to the media spotlight on obesity and heart-attack risks, and the subsequent craze for health food. But I think that it is more than that. It's not just the taste either, or that lovely thick creamy consistency. I think Siggi has managed to find a way of putting a little bit of Iceland into pots.

***

If you want something truly Icelandic, perhaps you should try *svið*, a sheep's head that is first singed to remove the hair, sawn in half while frozen and then boiled. They sell these delicacies at the BSÍ bus terminal in Reykjavík, and it is quite an experience to see them there, all cellophaned up like the most bizarre fast food ever. To see one eaten in the most graphic manner, on film, you should try *Jar City*, in which the main character, Erlendur, dissects one with a penknife for his supper. The film should have been rated eighteen as a result, if you ask me.

Svið is often served at Þorrablót, a traditional mid-winter feast that is celebrated at homes and public festivities all over Iceland between mid-January and mid-February. In addition to *svið*, the following suspects are all likely to be present: *blóðmör* (lamb's blood pudding), the aforementioned *harðfiskur* (dried fish – cod or haddock, usually), *hrútspungar* (boiled and pickled ram's testicles – yum!), *hákarl* (rotten shark meat; see Chapter 11 for more on this), *selshreifar* (cured seal's flippers – no, really!), *lifrapylsa* (a liver and suet sausage) and *sviðasulta* (sheep's-head jam, similar to brawn). The only dish that I really truly enjoy is the *hangikjöt* – smoked Icelandic lamb that is absolutely divine, especially at Christmastime when it's served with wafer-thin *laufabrauð*.

The polar opposite to potentially world-beating, kid-friendly, super healthy *skyr*? It has to be *brennivín*. This evil spirit is made from fermented potato mash and flavoured with caraway seeds and other flavourings. It is frequently brought to the table at Icelandic festivals, particularly those with strong, rich meats, and whenever a weak-hearted tourist is encountered. It is a clear liquid that is best served as close to 0 degrees Celsius as possible. Its name translates as 'burning wine', which isn't a bad description, but is more often called 'black death'. Which is about right. No, not really. It's not all that bad, but I don't think it's going to catch on anywhere else soon. But then, what would I know, right? *Brennivín* has seen a rise in popular culture references that may just elevate it from tramp juice and for washing down rotten shark. Quentin Tarantino is apparently a fan, and one of the characters in *Kill Bill* is seen drinking it. Foo Fighters' Dave Grohl is also a fan; he is often seen wearing a *brennivín* T-shirt in Foo Fighters promotional posters and even sings about it in one of the band's songs. So take that, *skyr*; *brennivín* might just rock.

The makers of *brennivín* would certainly have us believe that it is not just another drink that you will bring home and let go dusty in the back of the cupboard. They will have you believe that *brennivín* is the essential Icelandic experience. They have even started selling bottles that come smartly dressed in neat Icelandic jumpers. Now if that isn't rock and roll, then I don't know what is.

'*Brennivín* is essential with any Icelandic food,' Agnar Sverrisson told me. I can vouch for that. The more you drink, the less scary the food becomes. I went to see him at his restaurant to get some guidance on what to eat in Iceland.

From the look of the place, I could have been in any Scandinavian-styled restaurant in the world. The almost austere décor, the clean architectural lines, white leather upholstery and shiny mahogany tables – it could have been Stockholm, Helsinki, Oslo or even Reykjavík. It wasn't. It was Texture, a restaurant in London, a Frisbee's throw from Hyde Park.

I was seated by a waiter who was oh-so-well heeled and smartly dressed that I regretted not having put on my best tuxedo. Not that I had one. I placed my order and sat back, trying to relax in such formal surroundings, but struggling. The informalities of Einar and Klara's wedding seemed far, far away.

Texture is part owned by chef-patron Agnar Sverrisson. Aggi – as he prefers to be known – was the first Icelandic chef to be awarded the prestigious Michelin star. He started his chef's career in the now-defunct Grill Room in Reykjavík, where he became head chef, then moved to the UK in 2001 to work in the Gordon Ramsay-owned, Marcus Wareing-led Petrus Restaurant. A duo of chef appointments in London and Luxembourg followed, with a healthy cutting of teeth, I'm sure.

Aggi opened his Texture restaurant with Xavier Rousset, a world-class sommelier (where do you get these jobs?), in 2007 to much critical acclaim. The Michelin star was not far behind.

As I waited for my food, I was somewhat perplexed by the English tap water and the Czech beers on offer, as I was by the Greek waiter. So far, so un-Icelandic. And if the waiter had poured my water again, I would have screamed. I'm more than capable of pouring water, thanks. Slowly, subtle hints of Aggi's heritage started to creep in. Directly behind me – hence not noticed immediately by my ever observant self – was artwork by Tolli. It was an abstract piece but captured all the raw power and white heat of an exploding volcano. I spotted an Icelandic waitress exuding an understated glamour that did not go unmissed by the businessmen-dominated luncheon tables. My butter came served on a piece of black Icelandic granite, and I breathed a sigh of relief. The Icelandic touches were subtle, but they were all present and correct. Perhaps Aggi could help me after all.

The first courses passed in a whirl of fresh fish, pickled vegetables, Icelandic prawns, salty seaweed and purple cauliflower. The waiting staff continued to annoy me by brushing crumbs from my table in the manner of nursing-home carers – Oh, look! You missed your mouth! – and yet, improbably, they could not direct me to the bathroom. Maybe there wasn't one. Maybe they swept that up too.

The dessert arrived, and it was a bowl of fireworks on a Reykjavík New Year's Eve. It comprised a divine *skyr* ice cream, *skyr* (the real, genuine article, imported especially), rhubarb granita, rhubarb cubes, homemade muesli and a hint of mint. As desserts go, it was a real cracker – a delicious confection of textures and flavours. The *skyr* – a rare treat in the UK – was fantastic and partnered superbly with the tangy rhubarb. The muesli provided some crunch and the mint tasted like a summer garden. It was exquisite. I felt spoilt and licked the bowl and spoon clean to the obvious displeasure of my snooty waiter.

Afterwards, I got to speak to Aggi. I levelled with him: I was in need of his help. Icelandic food was confusing the hell out of me. It seemed to me that it was either terrifying – think sheep's head or rotten shark; or anything from Þorrablót – or absolutely divine: think *skyr, kleinur* or anything that Klara cooks. Aggi, clearly an expert in his field, would hopefully be able to shed some light on this dichotomy.

He started by telling me about food from his childhood. Old-school, traditional Icelandic food. 'It's going out of fashion,' he said. 'I used to eat it in front of the TV with my parents. It wasn't a case of getting to like it – there wasn't anything else.' I asked him about modern foods in Iceland; he told me that the influx of fast food had changed young people's diets and had led to obesity. When he was a child it wasn't uncommon to have dried seaweed as a snack; now it's unheard of.

There are some traditional foods that have lasted the course, though, and not just the *hákarl* (fermented shark). Aggi confided in me that this was often used to make tourists go 'Urghh' – Einar, if you are reading this, I'm on to you. Every 23rd December, the last day before Christmas in Iceland and known as Þorláksmessa (the Mass of St Þorlákur, Iceland's patron saint), it is traditional to sit down to a meal of *skata* (putrefied skate), often in the form of stew. This is usually accompanied by turnips, potatoes and – yum! – lamb fat. Aggi is a big fan of this, and told me that it is often the highlight of his culinary year. It is sold in every restaurant in Reykjavík and the West Fjords (where the dish originated), probably because many Icelanders now choose not to cook it at home because of the intense, putrid smell. Surprisingly, it comes in mild, medium and very strong varieties. Aggi recommended the medium; I think I'll just have the spuds.

Icelanders do have some good feasts though, such as Bolludagur (Bun Day) and Sprengidagur (Bursting Day), celebrated on the last two days before Lent. On Bun Day they are encouraged to eat all the sweet buns – similar to profiteroles – they can; and on Bursting Day it's tasty *saltkjöt* (salted lamb) stew until they explode. My sort of celebrations.

We went on to discuss the sheep's head (very good; not pretty), puffin meat (Chef Marcus Wareing wouldn't try it), lamb (he agreed that it's divine), and whale meat (controversial, but well liked by the chefs at Texture). As we talked, I saw that Aggi has a genuine passion for Icelandic food. His eyes twinkled as we spoke, and I saw his mind conjuring up recipes. At Texture, he uses Icelandic langoustines, lamb, dairy produce and fish. I asked him if he was concerned about flying in such beautiful ingredients from Iceland, and whether this could affect their freshness. 'No,' he laughed. 'I can have a freshly caught piece of Icelandic cod here within thirty hours. When I first started cooking in the UK, I had to prepare fish for other chefs – "This is shit," I would say, as it wasn't fresh at all.' I guess when you are used to such good-quality ingredients, it must be hard to compromise. 'The fish from Iceland is so good because they waters are cold, clean and of a high quality. You are always going to get a better fish.'

Next I asked him about the *skyr*. He told me that he gets a lot of phone calls about it from people all over the UK, mainly because he is the only place in the UK to sell it. There was a shop in Kensington, London he told me, but they couldn't get hold of it any more. Aggi also told me that a large supermarket had been looking to stock it, but that it had fallen through due to the banking collapse in Iceland. We both thought that was a real shame.

We chatted briefly about Siggi's success with *skyr* in New York, and agreed that he was doing a cracking job.

I couldn't resist asking Aggi about the Icelandic penchant for barbeques, and as soon as I mentioned the word, he started to smile. 'As soon as the temperature hits 10 degrees Celsius and we see the sun, Icelanders get naked and start to barbeque.' I thought this sounded like a bad combination of activities, but I saw his point; it's about making the summer last for as long as possible. What wasn't said was that Icelanders are using such fresh, local produce that all it needs is to be simply cooked on a barbeque. No burnt sausages and ash-ridden burgers there.

I asked Aggi if he missed Iceland. Not surprisingly, he said he did. He intends to retire there, probably with a summerhouse and hot pot nearby. I can't say I blame him; he is clearly working his socks off at Texture and deserves all he gets. His promotion of Icelandic food is something unique in the UK, and something he should be justifiably proud of. He said that being a celebrity chef made him feel 'tired and old'; I think it makes him an ambassador for Icelandic food.

As I stood up to leave, Aggi had one more piece of advice for me. 'Try lamb's testicles,' he said. 'They are delicious pickled.' I don't think I will, Aggi. 'Just don't go for fresh ones,' he went on, 'they have an awful texture, a gross consistency, kind of oozing everywhere.' Don't worry, Aggi, I definitely won't be having them anytime soon. I shuddered at the thought.

Back at the wedding, Einar's best man was delivering what was clearly a hilarious and entertaining speech, in the densest, most impenetrable Icelandic I have heard.

I only knew this because the tables of guests were clutching at their sides and laughing with gusto. Suddenly there was a break in the Icelandic patter. All eyes turned to us. 'Welcome to our English guests,' he said. 'And on our menu today, traditional Icelandic food, such as lamb's testicles, sheep's head...' He trailed off, each mention of Icelandic delicacies causing consternation on my face, and further amusement for the other guests. Perhaps I could relax though. As long as I didn't eat the raw lamb's testicles, looked forward to a *skyr*-based dessert and swilled it all down with *brennivín*, it would surely be fine.

And it was. The wedding feast turned out to be delicious, and we danced the night through.

Chapter 9

A Plump of Hook-Nosed Sea Pigs

The 'Golden Circle', a summertime tourist favourite, is a loop designed by tour companies that runs from Reykjavík through south-western Iceland via some of the most stunning locations in the region – and arguably the country. Despite the danger that bussing coachloads of tourists to some of these natural phenomena might have a detrimental effect on the very phenomena they are there to see, coaches leave Reykjavík all year long, twice a day in the summer. The big three sights are Gullfoss – a stunning waterfall; Geysir an area of geothermal activity and the chance to see the dependable Strokkur blast water into the sky; and finally Þingvellir – the site of Iceland's first parliament.

Although this isn't a guidebook, I think it would be remiss of me not to mention these attractions in a book on Iceland. OK, maybe I'm being a bit harsh on the Golden Circle. Yes, the coachloads can take some of the edge off a place, but we've all got to start somewhere, haven't we? And the locations themselves are pretty remarkable.

Gullfoss is approximately 120 kilometres north-east of Reykjavík. It translates as 'Golden Falls' and is a pretty impressive set of waterfalls, making it one of the most popular tourist attractions in the country. The Hvítá river is wide and lively. It appears on the horizon as a slate-grey colour with a light blue tinge but foams where the water is torn up by the jagged rocks. It cascades several times, in a blur of white noise, like a TV full of static, before sharply plunging into a deep, deep crevice. From certain angles the crevice makes it look like the river simply disappears from view. Like magic. It is a breathtaking sight, whether in the winter snow, when it appears like a scene from Narnia, or in the summer when the vast amounts of spray sent up into the air catch the sun and create sharply focused rainbows. From certain angles, you can look directly into the crevice, a view that always sends shivers up my spine. All churning, angry white water, in a ferocious free fall.

The walk down to the falls has now been carefully laid with artificial pathways of plastic-that-looks-like-wood, which has removed some of the fun and terror of slip-sliding your way down to them. Gullfoss still gets its own back on you though; when the wind blows that cold spray at you, you get a free freezing cold shower. It is certainly refreshing. The moral of the story: even if it's a sunny day, bring a coat. You'll be grateful. Icelanders always carry at least a coat whenever and wherever they go outdoors.

For the best views, though, you need to clamber up a series of grey jagged rock plateaus, so you can get as close as you dare to the falls. The noise is deafening, and the rocks sometimes slippery, but it's always worth it. To get the idea, have a look at the cover of Manchester band Echo and the Bunnymen's *Porcupine* album, which was shot at Gullfoss. The combination of stunning Icelandic scenery and four darkly dressed dour Englishmen never looked so good.

Sigríður Tómasdóttir is often mentioned in the same breath as Gullfoss. Mainly because her father was a local farmer who owned the land and consequently the waterfall. He decided to lease the falls to a foreign company in the 1920s. The company attempted to use Gullfoss to produce hydro-electricity, but it failed – due to a lack of funds and not, as is commonly thought, because of Sigríður's protests and her threat that she would throw herself into the falls to save them. Sigríður is said to have marched to Reykjavík to make her point and there's no doubt that she was an active campaigner. But she didn't 'save' them – Gullfoss was eventually bought by the State and is now a nature reserve in its own right – and she certainly didn't fling herself into the rapids: she died in Hafnarfjörður in 1957 at the ripe old age of eighty-seven. I'm not sure about her strategy though; I don't think she quite thought her threat through. I mean, if you were the only person protesting for Gullfoss to be saved, and you were up against formidable companies and unforgiving officials, surely throwing yourself into a large waterfall with fatal consequences would be playing right into their hands? Have a think about it, Sigríður, please. There is a monument to Sigríður at Gullfoss though. Just look for the throng of tourists, it will be there somewhere.

Back on the coach, your next stop is likely to be Geysir. Geysir, it probably goes without saying, gave rise to the English word 'geyser' and is one of my favourite words to have made the Icelandic–English crossover. My other favourites are 'heck' and 'berserk', if you're interested. As the coach rumbles up the Haukadalur valley, you can't help but notice the plumes of steam rising into the air and, more than likely, a few other coaches outside the gift shop and information centre. Over the road, though, is where it all happens. The whole area is a geothermal park sitting on top of a bubbling and boiling witch's cauldron. Multi-coloured mud pots belching away, whistling steam vents, hot and cold springs, warm streams, and alien-looking plants can all be found here. On the lightly sloping red-grey land, there are several areas roped off and circles of people standing around with their mouths open. Head straight for Strokkur, 'the Churn', and join them. At your feet will be a light blue pool of water in a sunken hole in the ground. As you watch, the hole will begin to fill up, quickly reaching the surface. Here, the water seems to be in turmoil, thrashing around under pressure. You can see that the surface of the water starts to curve outwards and upwards, and you wait. Don't forget to keep breathing. The water keeps pushing at its 'lid', doming outwards, and then it does it. It explodes upwards in a tower of water, reaching 20 to 30 metres in height. It is amazing, stunning, like nothing you have ever seen before. Close your mouth and wait ten to fifteen minutes. It will do it all over again. It's brilliant, isn't it? I have spent hours watching this natural phenomenon, and I never get sick of it. It always makes me go 'Oooh' like a good fireworks show, and you can have lots of fun trying to capture the explosion on film.

The café there is awful though. Just don't bother; it sells paper trays of reheated French fries and rubbery chicken nuggets to the masses. It's thoroughly depressing, eating the awful food there, in front of a TV playing an English football match, surrounded by tourists from the world over. I don't mean to sound negative, or even superior.

I'm just saying; this is one of Iceland's greatest sights, if not one of the world's. I'd rather be out there watching it and eating a sausage roll than stuck in the café where it doesn't even feel like Iceland. It feels like Skegness.

Everyone used to come here to see 'Geysir', the actual one, but that has unfortunately been largely dormant since 1916. Whether its dormancy is perpetual or temporary no one knows. It's said that Geysir could thunderously thrust a spectacular jet of super-heated water and steam into the air as high as 80 metres, but now it just sits there, gurgling to itself. Its opening is 18 metres wide and its chamber is 20 metres deep, which goes to show just how powerful it must have been. Sadly, there are two possible reasons for its dormancy that are entirely the fault of human interference. The first is the continual throwing of rocks and other objects into Geysir, which may have damaged it. The other – which now sounds unbelievable – is that in the 1960s the Icelandic government permitted geologists to force an eruption, using soap. Only for special occasions, mind. I don't think that this was a good idea, do you? Geysir did briefly wake up in 2000, after a period of earthquake activity, but has gone back to sleep now. I just hope this means that no permanent damage has been done.

Around Geysir and Strokkur, you are free to wander. There are other smaller geysers, warm turquoise pools, hot springs and mud pots. Litli Geysir just sloshes around like a Jacuzzi gone mad. Two things will happen, without doubt. Firstly, you'll see someone who can't resist it any longer putting their fingers into some water then withdrawing them quickly with a scream or shout. Yes, it is bloody scalding. I can vouch for that. The ropes and warning signs are there for a reason. The second thing that's bound to happen is that you will return to Strokkur, for just one more eruption. It's a certainty. You won't be able not to.

On to Þingvellir, then. The name, once broken down, makes much more sense – *þing* means 'parliament' and *vellir* translates as 'meadows' or 'fields'. What this doesn't do though is illustrate just how important a role this site has in Iceland's history, politics, culture and geography. Scrap that; the world's geography.

Let's deal with the geography first. Þingvellir is in the south-westerly corner of the eponymous national park, which was founded in 1930. The park covers a surprisingly large chunk of Icelandic countryside and includes the Öxará river and Þingvallavatn, the largest lake in Iceland. Most people, though, focus on Þingvellir, and it's easy to see why. Often named as one of the most beautiful places in Iceland, and one of the few spots on earth where the mid-Atlantic ridge can be seen out of the ocean, Þingvellir is truly extraordinary. You can actually see the rift between the European and North American tectonic plates, and stand between the two. The geography student inside me gets very excited about this. I don't think you'd realise that you were standing in such an important fissure without being told, but once you know, it is pretty amazing, especially when you learn that due to tectonic movement the rift is growing at a rate of 1.5 centimetres a year. The valley floor is also sinking every year by a few millimetres – during 1789 it is said to have dropped 0.5 metres – further proof that everything you see around you there is on the move.

The ubiquitous visitor centre is there, along with

wooden walkways that freeze solid in the winter and become death traps. Einar took Nichola and me there, once in the depths of winter. I think it was early January and there was a light scattering of snow and an even lighter scattering of tourists, due to the time of year and a bitingly cold wind that kept most sane people in doors. He showed us around, and then took us for a precarious walk through the intercontinental divide and down into the valley itself. The valley is home to a hotel – I think this was shut; maybe it only opens in the summer, it felt ghostly quiet – and a rather quaint quintessentially Icelandic church. We crossed over the frozen tributaries of the Öxará river, which made creaking noises beneath our feet, and walked towards the church. Snow had started to fall again, and Nichola was concentrating really hard on finding a perfect snowflake. She was wearing a black jacket, and the cold quiet scene was punctuated with squeals of joy when she found one against the dark fabric. I've just read this back to myself, and she sounds like a simpleton. This isn't the case; the snowflakes were spectacular and I could see why she was getting excited. One was a perfectly formed star and I took a picture of it before it melted away. The church is a little beauty. Typical of churches in Iceland, it is a cream-coloured wooden structure with a single short wooden spire. It has three windows down each side, which we peered into, easily frosting the cold glass. Einar was justifiably proud to be showing off the place, especially to two ignorant English people too busy catching snowflakes.

Irrespective of this, Einar went on to give us a potted of history of Alþingi. In doing so, he was essentially giving us a lesson on the history of Iceland, so I listened up. Alþingi

('All-Thing') is the world's oldest parliament that is still in operation. The first Alþingi was convened at Þingvellir in AD 930, for two weeks during the summer, and went on to become an annual event. All thirty-six regional chieftains from across Iceland attended in order to form a nationwide meeting of the country's leaders. Also in attendance was pretty much everyone else, and huge Glastonbury-style tented cities grew up. The crowds turned up en masse to watch the sessions, hear new laws being passed, settle disputes, have a good natter, watch some executions and play some games. Probably Twister, we decided. That or Buckaroo. The elected Law Speaker would recite law from memory for everyone present, standing on the 'Law Rock', a natural platform and amphitheatre. These days, the Law Rock is marked with a flagpole, but – get this – the exact spot isn't really known. The marker is just an approximation. At least you can blame this on those pesky tectonic plates though, right?

Although Alþingi's influence would wax and wane over the coming centuries, it never disappeared. Alþingi is now based in Reykjavík, in a chunky, regal building made out of Icelandic stone, looking out over a grassy square, but Þingvellir still plays its role too. Vast crowds of Icelanders turned up at Þingvellir to hear the formation of the Icelandic Republic on 17th June 1944, while the ethos of free speech and democracy live on in its new home in Reykjavík.

The landscape is staggering. Þingvellir sits on a plain, which had a light dusting of the finest white snow when we visited with Einar. Through this we could see occasional scrub patches and odd, stunted pine trees. The bruise-coloured waters of lakes and streams stood out against the sugar-white snow. The plain gave way to a smudge of grey-white mountains that seemed to be too big, as if a child had drawn them in. The sky met the mountains, stretched far in every direction, and was heavy with yet more snow, threatening a white-out.

We took photographs of each other in front of the church, with the winter wonderland and the distant mountains providing the perfect backdrop. The snow had continued to fall and the light started to disappear, leaving a soft, pinkish-coloured sky and the reflective white ground to provide the only illumination. In silence we walked back to the car, with the only sound being snow squeaking under our feet.

In one of my many moments of madness, and despite my Icelandic pals' warnings, I had booked another excursion named something like 'Northern Lights Adventure' or 'Northern Lights Magical Mystery Tour'; I forget which. Disregarding the already considerable strain on my credit card, and the presence of thick cloud in every corner of the sky, I boarded the tour bus and joined the other foreign tourists, who were trying to look nonchalant but whose cameras and noses pressed against windows gave them away.

The guide, a healthy, happy-looking middle-aged woman, was chirpy enough and gave us some background on the elusive Aurora Borealis before cheering everyone up by mentioning that there had been a good show on the previous evening. I had spent lots of hard cash and what amounted to several days' worth of hours on similar trips and seen zip, so I was heartened to hear this. At the very least, we would get some hot chocolate, she told us.

It was difficult to get my bearings as the coach wove its way out of Reykjavík into the countryside to allow the best chance of a viewing. It was to my surprise then that we ended up at Þingvellir. We all tumbled out of the coach onto crunchy snow underfoot, pulling coats and scarves around us against the cold night. Faces pointing skyward, we stood in darkness and searched the sky. All that could be seen was a dense fuzz of cloud and the occasional snowflake falling softly to the ground. The guide, ever hopeful, got her patter up, stating that the cloud would part to reveal the most incredible light show. We strained our necks even further.

One girl, probably in her late teens, took a photo of herself and her friend, probably for use later on Face-twit, or some other social network. This prompted an immediate reaction from a tall, stern-looking German man, who, without hesitation or manners, shouted, 'Do you mind? Your flash is ruining it for all of us.' The girl looked somewhat taken aback, caught between surprise at his outburst and trying to work out exactly what she was spoiling. She needn't have worried though, as the coach driver chose that exact moment to put the coach's lights back on, and at full beam too. With a 'harrumph' from the German guy, and a suppressed giggle from the girl, we re-boarded and drove back to Reykjavík without seeing a single swirl of a Northern Light. The guide was right about one thing. The hot chocolate was very good.

✳✳✳

North of Þingvellir, but not featured on many Golden Circle (or Northern Lights) tours, is the village of Reykholt and the old homestead of Snorri Sturluson. Born in 1179, Snorri was bound to do well; his father's side of the family were mainly chieftains and his mother's side included Egill Skallagrímsson, star of the famous *Egils Saga*. Snorri, by chance, was not educated or raised by his parents, but by an influential Norwegian who happened to be related to the Norwegian royal family. This would be problematic for Snorri later on in his life, as we will see. I don't wish to jump too far ahead. Snorri, a busy lad, became a celebrated poet, author, historian and politician. He was elected not once but twice as Law Speaker at Alþingi. This is an unusual feat in itself. Snorri quickly gained chieftainship and was fortunate to inherit land. His marriages, however, did not work out, on account of him being a bit of a 'shagger', in today's parlance. He is alleged to have fathered several children by three different women, and maintained a childless relationship with a fourth. On moving to Reykholt, he made improvements to the farm and also commissioned the building of a new hot pool, Snorralaug.

Despite his luck with the ladies and the new hot pot (perhaps the two were not unrelated), things did not turn out well for Snorri. His initial alliance with and acceptance by the Norwegian royal family turned sour. He became embroiled in feuds in both Iceland and Norway and at one point had a thousand men chasing him through Iceland; he was only saved when a kindly cousin sent 800 men to assist. The Norwegian issue is what finished him off though. He was declared a traitor by the Norwegian king and chased from Norway. He was followed by an army of seventy men, who, at the direction of the king, stormed Reykholt, chasing Snorri into the basement where he met a grisly and gruesome end.

Somewhat ironically, Snorri's writings are now highly acclaimed in both Iceland and Norway, especially the *Heimskringla* – Sagas of the Old Norse Kings. His concepts and thoughts are recognised as having been well ahead of their time. So much so that a few years back, Iceland produced a postage stamp to commemorate Snorri. If I ever get a stamp produced of me, I'll know I've made it.

Reykholt is consequently a bit Snorri-themed, as you might imagine. It's apparently home to sixty people, though I didn't see any of them. I did check out Snorralaug, a 4-metre-wide hot pot set into the green turf and surrounded by a low wall. This is where Snorri is alleged to have bathed, relaxed and 'entertained guests'. Stop it now. The pool is fed from a nearby hot spring and was lukewarm to the touch. You can't bathe in it, but you can tell English people have been here. I am not aware of any other nation being so utterly obsessed with throwing coins into any open body of water on the pretence that it will bring good luck. Next time you go somewhere that has a fountain or ornamental pond, look out for the English. They'll be there, closing their eyes and rubbing a coin before tossing it in.

There is a restored, but closed, underground tunnel that leads to the basement where Snorri was murdered. The village also has a museum devoted to Snorri, a statue of Snorri, and a Snorri learning centre. It didn't appear to have a decent sandwich for sale anywhere though, so I headed back to the car.

❋❋❋

Inverness in the highlands of Scotland is not the most attractive town. I wouldn't say it's ugly, but it's not far off. Apart from the river, and a couple of restaurants, it didn't seem to have much going for it. That was, until I found the bookshop.

Not just any bookshop, one that might just be the best bookshop in Scotland, if not bigger land masses. Leakey's is housed in a former Gaelic church and retains all the old-world charm, including stonework and a timber altar. It's immense and filled entirely with second-hand books. They are on two floors and grouped roughly by topic, although the Dewey Decimal System clearly does not apply there, judging by the volumes on the floor, on chairs and on every other conceivable surface.

Staff were helpful, but otherwise unobtrusive. There was a wood-burning stove in the centre of the floor, and a zigzag of pipes took the warmth upstairs, where, if you were still not warm enough, you could buy bowls of homemade soup. The entire shop was enveloped in the smell of wood smoke and a broth bubbling away.

I browsed. Then I browsed some more. Time was ticking away, so I removed my watch and placed it in my pocket, in order to be untroubled by the passing of hours. I moved slowly from section to section, pausing to pull out volumes here and there, perusing the travel section with particular rapture, before being overwhelmed by the wall of orange-spined Penguin novels. I stopped for a while to read on a wooden chair.

I returned to the travel section and went through it shelf by shelf. I was looking for anything Iceland related. Scandinavia featured heavily. Norway. Finland. Tattered travel guides. Sweden, the Faroe Islands... getting closer... Iceland. Got it. Instantly I saw a smallish hardback book with a faded spine that was once red. It was called *Rivers of Iceland* by RN Stewart. I eased it out from the shelf and scuttled back to my reading chair, which was delightfully close to the wood burner.

The book smelt old. Not in a bad way, but of years passing by. The cover was worn and the pages were yellowing. It had the sort of smell and feel that could never be replicated by an e-book. It fitted pleasingly in my hand.

Inside, I learnt that the book was published in 1950 by the tourist bureau of Reykjavík. Now I was intrigued. Major General Stewart, it seemed, was quite the man. As well as being a ranking military officer, he had written books before on the subject of angling, and this wasn't even his first trip to Iceland. The book was about angling too, but I wasn't put off by that. I've experienced some 'tight lines' in my time.

Major General Stewart also talked about food – 'like all Scandinavian countries they are fond of sweet soups; rhubarb soup figures in the proportion of four to one over all the others, prune soup comes next. Personally I rather like them, but perhaps they are an acquired taste' – and language, which he 'makes very inadequate and entirely ungrammatical attempts to speak'. I knew how he felt.

The descriptions of lava fields, farms and life in 1950s Iceland rolled on. Stewart described pulling the plug on his bath in a Reykjavík hotel to find the water rushing out all over the floor, seemingly unconnected to any plumbing, and his 'bedroom slippers floating like boats'. There were illustrations of Icelandic scenes, and photographs of freshly caught fat salmon. I liked it.

I found out sometime later that a couple of years before, an Icelandic newspaper had become similarity intrigued by the book and had dispatched a reporter to Scotland to find out more. The reporter had unearthed a treasure trove of detailed notes, unpublished works and unseen photographs of the Major General's trips to Iceland.

I was quite taken with the book, and I carried it up to the counter to pay. The guy, partially obscured by towers of books, looked surprised. 'This shouldn't be on the shelves,' he said. 'It's quite rare; there only a few left in circulation.'

I explained that it definitely was on the shelves, that I had spent the past few hours reading it, and that, crucially, it would be coming with me. A tense period of negotiation followed. I won. Well, I got the book. We don't need to discuss the price, do we? The point is this. If someone, sixty-plus years from now, when I'm dead and buried, can read my book about Iceland and gain as much pleasure as I did from *Rivers of Iceland*, then it's a job well done. I tucked the book under my arm and headed out into the cold Scottish wind.

I had the book with me on my journey to Reykholt and around western Iceland. I enjoyed dipping into it every now and then, seeing what the old major had to say. Actually, he talked about the area with something less than fondness: 'I approach a lava field at night it seems to be the haunt of demonical spirits, not necessarily evil, but merely possessed of a fiendish amusement in placing difficulties in your way, well knowing they have a worse joke for you in a yard or two. The imaginative mind can fashion all sorts of monstrous shapes from lava under the cold light of the moon, and the undulating radiance of the Northern Lights gives light and movement to them.' Perhaps I didn't need to worry then, given that I had yet to see the Northern Lights. The old major had beaten me on that point.

About five kilometres on the 518 from Reykholt is Deildartunguhver, a hot spring. Not just any hot spring though, but Europe's largest. At peak flow, it churns out 180 litres of water per second. The temperature of the water is at boiling point. Not surprisingly, the plumes of steam are visible from some kilometres away, and you can see streams of hot water flowing over the nearby fields, their grass scalded and steam rising from them in the most peculiar manner. It's definitely worth a visit. Yes, the whole place has been commercialised by the power company that owns it, but it hasn't just been fenced off as out of bounds, as it might have been in other countries. Instead, you can get right up to the powerful springs that jet out of the ground. Dangerously close, in fact, and separated by only a flimsy 2-foot wooden railing.

The UK's health and safety geeks would have a field day here, I thought to myself as I leant out against said railing to get that perfect picture. I felt the droplets of water land on my arms, and, yes, I can verify that they were bloody hot. I got the picture though. The water is pumped to the nearby towns of Akranes, Borgarnes and Hvanneyri, through large steel pipes that are thought to be some of the longest such pipes in the world. Impressed? Me neither. I did like the fact that the deer fern grows there and nowhere else in Iceland, and that the neighbouring greenhouses were growing big, fat, juicy tomatoes and flogging them there, in a little stall. Overall, I liked the place. It felt good to be there; maybe it was just all the different colours that made it feel hyper real, like being in a cartoon, or a digitally enhanced photograph. Silver pipes, blue sky, green fauna, light green moss, dark green slime, bright red rocks, and perfectly, perfectly white steam.

Not far from Deildartunguhver I dropped in to see Icelandic hothouses at their best. I'd heard all about them, along with the associated myths. You will certainly have heard them too. Stuff like Iceland is Europe's largest banana producer. It's not. It's Spain, if you were wondering. Iceland still imports bananas.

This hothouse was owned and managed by Gunna, who, despite me rocking up unannounced, was kind enough to show me around, and to let me explore a little by myself. Gunna concentrates on producing flowers for the commercial market. These were amazing. In polythene tunnels, and there were several on the site, they resembled a rainforest in bloom, with flowers everywhere, in neat rows according to species or colour. The effect was of a felled rainbow, each row of brightly coloured flowers representing a part of the spectrum.

I wandered from hothouse to hothouse, looking

at tomatoes and chillies growing as if it was the Mediterranean, not 66 degrees north. The tomatoes hung from their vines. Gunna explained how they harnessed the heat from the steam, through some sort of heat exchange, but to be honest I was distracted by the bright colours and the delicious smells. The hothouses provoked a childhood memory of being in my granddad's greenhouse, picking tomatoes and eating them straight off the vine, or at least with a single pinch of salt first. I was also distracted by a sign that I'd spotted; it advertised eggs for sale to boil in the hot pots just over the road. I was tempted. It would sort out lunch, I thought, as I absently rubbed my stomach.

I was about to go, when a smaller, more cubic hothouse caught my eye. It was all alone, towards the rear of the site. I asked Gunna what was inside, and she invited me to 'go and see'. I slid the glass doors to one side and stepped once more into the humid air. The entire space was filled with a banana tree, complete with green bananas hanging from its branches. All around it snaked black pipes of the hissing steam that makes the very existence of banana trees in Iceland possible. I though that was pretty remarkable.

Taking R1 north out of Reykjavík to the north-west, you go through the town of Mosfellsbær before coming to an exciting (no, really!) 5700-metre-long tunnel which passes under Hvalfjörður (whale-fjord). Although you have to pay a small toll, I was happy to do this rather than spend half a day driving all the way round the coast to get to the other side of the fjord, which only feels like a stone's throw across the sea. The tunnel kind of takes you by surprise: rather than being on the level, it heads downwards at a fairly steep angle, to a depth of 165 metres, before climbing upwards at the same angle and shooting you out into the daylight at the other end. I quite enjoyed the experience. I am easily pleased, but I couldn't help thinking that they should have made the roof of the tunnel out of that special Perspex you find in aquariums, so you could see the sea and fish as you drive. I'd definitely pay a bit more for that.

I shot through Akranes – best known for football – and Borgarnes – best known for cows, and kept driving. If I'm honest, the landscape there wasn't all that inspiring. Mainly lava fields and the odd glimpse of a cold ocean – next landfall: Greenland. I stopped briefly at Brú, mainly for fuelling the car, and fuelling myself with that scalding hot black coffee that seems to keep Iceland running. There wasn't much there, apart from a huge petrol station, which seemed to be the centre of that particular universe.

Off to the east lay Langjökull (Long Glacier), which is Iceland's second largest glacier. It's the glacier you can see in the distance from the falls at Gullfoss, and covers an area that's fifty kilometres long and 15 to 20 kilometres wide. It is said to be retreating. Langjökull was featured in an ambitious and daring art project in 2010. This may have caught your attention on the news or the interweb. I know that it did mine. In November of that year, Bjargey Ólafsdóttir took part in the world's first global climate project. The aim of the campaign was to highlight the causes and effects of climate change through art. Not just any art though, art that could be seen from space and photographed by satellites. Called the 350 EARTH project, it featured eighteen locations across the globe, including the Thom Yorke (Radiohead lead singer) designed and endorsed UK installation 'King Canute' on Brighton Beach. I saw it, and it looked like a man standing on a gingerbread house.

Bjargey's design, in my opinion, was far superior and despite not being rock-star endorsed, it still caught the imagination of the media and general public alike. She created a massive polar bear on Langjökull's ice and snow. Using 10 litres of eco-friendly red dye, in 900 litres of water, Bjargey drew an outline of a lolloping bear, measuring a huge eighty by fifty metres. She was assisted by thirteen volunteers, you'll be glad to hear, and they used a grid system similar to those found on children's cereal packets to get the design on to the glacier. The effect was astonishing. Not only was the image striking, and enhanced by the extreme and extremely beautiful landscape in which it was set, but it got climate change mentioned in the international media, and most importantly it got people talking about the issues. While I'm not going to use this platform to support the campaign against climate change, or otherwise, I was impressed by Bjargey and her team's motivation and sheer determination to do something different to promote their cause. The 'Red Polar Bear' might be visible from space, but to me, it's the people that see it down here on earth that will make the decisions about climate change. I think Bjargey deserves some credit for that. If you get the chance to see the pictures, do so. They're astonishing.

I was heading for Sæberg, but en route something utterly gobsmacking happened. Something that I will not be able to shake from the recesses of my mind for the rest of my life. The vehicle in front was a small red minibus, about the size of a Ford Transit. It was tootling along the road at a sedate pace, not at all in any rush. I hadn't seen any vehicles for some time so it felt unusual to be following one for a change. After a few minutes it dawned on me that there was a face in the back window of the bus. Not just any face, but that of a cute white horse. Remarkably, the vehicle had been converted into a horse wagon by removing the seats. I'll never know how they managed to get the horse into to such a confined space, but it didn't look at all unhappy. In fact, it looked as though it was used to taking trips in a vehicle better designed for groups of school children than horses.

Icelandic horses have taken over the world. Not just because of those heart-warming photographs you see in the travel brochures (horse and foal, foal nuzzling mother, foreground of snow, background of frozen mountains, all big eyes and furry fetlocks), but because of their unique characteristics. It is thought that there are 100,000 Icelandic horses across the world now, compared to the still impressive 80,000 that remain in Iceland. How do they know this? Well, each Icelandic horse has to be registered and its lineage traceable back to Iceland. No certificate? Not a true Icelandic horse, sir.

Icelandic horses are small, rugged beasts, measuring somewhere between 12 and 13 hands. Hands? Me neither, sorry. It is the only breed of horse in Iceland, and fiercely protected. It has a thick, double insulated coat for those adverse Icelandic winters, and is relatively disease free. This is one of the reasons that there is an import ban on horses into Iceland, to protect the Icelandic species. Even horses reared in Iceland and shipped out to compete in competitions are not allowed back in; that's kind of sad, isn't it? You spend months, years even, training little Hnýsa to be the best show horse in the whole of Iceland, and decide she can compete in the World Championships. Let's say our fictional, yet high-achieving horse wins. She still can't return to her homeland. Seems kind of harsh, doesn't it?

There are a couple of reasons why Icelandic horses are really special, but before I explain, let me just say this. The preferred nomenclature is 'Icelandic horse', not 'pony'. I'm told that 'pony' might be deemed a little offensive, and there is also some suggestion that there is no actual Icelandic word for 'pony'. I find this hard to believe, given that there are over one hundred names for the colourations of Icelandic horses alone. Anyway, stick with horse, not pony.

Icelandic horses have extra gaits. The usual gaits for a horse are trot, canter and gallop. Icelandic horses have the near-unique *tölt*, which a smooth, fast yet comfortable ride, supposedly for travelling at speed over large expanses of terrain. It's said that the rider should be able to hold a glass of wine in one hand and reins in the other and not spill a drop. I don't condone drinking and riding, but you get the point. Some, not all, Icelandic horses have another gait. This is known as *skeið* or *flugskeið* – flying pace – and is somewhat faster, as the name suggests. Horses that can *tölt* and *flugskeið* are considered the best of the breed and are accordingly much sought after. Horses that can do both and travel by minibus are worth huge sums of money.

I finally reached Sæberg, which is little more than

a farmhouse on the edge of a fjord, set away from the village itself. I approached via a single-lane track, flanked on either side by pretty purple flowers, and parked in the over-large stone car park. The buildings nestled sweetly into lush green meadows that sloped down very gently into an expansive yet calm fjord. There were Icelandic horses in the fields and an ancient rusted tractor sat nearby, as a tribute to simpler times. The host arrived from seemingly nowhere, and, although she was exceedingly kind and took great care to show me all the available facilities, I couldn't wait to get back outside into the view. My ears pricked up when she mentioned a hot tub, and I was chuffed when I saw it outside, all blue, steaming and inviting. I dumped my kit in a clean, functional yet austere room and headed back outside to explore.

I drove north for a few kilometres to a bleak and desolate outcrop, which I had been told about at the farmhouse. The reason for the trip was simple: this was a designated seal sanctuary. Not one with tourist centres, glass screens and fluffy seal toys for sale, but an area of the fjord that's been set aside for the safe breeding and day to day living of local seals. I was a bit concerned that I wouldn't find it, it being another patch of sea, next to another lush meadow, next to the long, straight, dusty track I had been driving on for what seemed like miles. I needn't have worried; there was a huge warning sign showing a picture of a seal. I'm not sure of the exact statistics of seal-related road collisions in that remote corner of Iceland, but I doubt the sign did much to prevent them.

I parked up and strolled down a few metres of hillocky ground to the sea. At first I couldn't see anything, but then

I started spotting them. Or rather, they started spotting me. Their whiskery heads broke the surface as they popped up for a look, all kind eyes and inquisitive noses. Grey seals have the Latin name *Halichoerus grypus*, which means hook-nosed sea pig. This seems a little insulting. I think they are more like dogs that have spent too much time in the sea. I stood there transfixed as the plump of seals took turns in observing me before diving back down, presumably to report on their findings. The collective noun for seals – and I love these things – can be bob, colony, harem, herd, pod, rookery, spring, team, or, as you can see, my favourite: plump. A plump of hook-nosed sea pigs. Brilliant.

On the way back to the hostel, my thoughts turning to food and that hot tub, I stopped off at Hvammstangi. A sleepy village of around 500 people, it had clearly closed for the day, what with it being nearly 7pm and all. The supermarket was the only thing open and I stocked up on essentials. Then I noticed the strange stares I was getting from the village's teenage populace. I'd never experienced that level of unfriendliness in Iceland before, so it came as a bit of a shock. There were three of them, riding those diminutive BMX-style bikes favoured by insolent teenagers worldwide, and it was clear that they had recognised that I was English. They sat and stared, occasionally making mumbled comments to each other. It was not altogether great, and the bad feeling was exacerbated by the presence of Arctic terns. I took a look at the Seal Centre, which was also closed, so I settled instead for posing alongside a collection of wooden seals, before the uninviting atmosphere got to me and I left with haste.

It didn't feel like an Icelandic village; it felt a lot more rustic and, well, sub-Arctic than anywhere else I'd come across. It felt like an Inuit village in Greenland or Alaska, where the children are left to roam with dogs, machinery is left to rust where it stopped working and the general feeling is one of depression and foreboding. As I left the village though, I saw that someone had attempted to cheer the place up by building a couple of stone people from smooth spherical rocks placed on top of one another, painted in bright and funky colours. That reminded me of the Iceland that I knew and loved, and the little couple cheered me up no end.

Oddly though, it was a resident of Hvammstangi that lent me a helping hand. With a big issue. The Icelandic language. I've never been any good at languages, being typically English in this respect. French and German were thrust upon me in my early teens, but that was too little, too late. However, I'm not typically English in my attitude to this. In fact, I'm deeply ashamed of my inability to speak anything except my native English. I'm especially ashamed when my Icelandic friends ask me if I can speak any Icelandic.

At first, it was fine to apologise profusely and say that I couldn't. I mean it is an extremely difficult language to learn, isn't it? It's true to its Viking roots, and has an alphabet both different and similar to English. For example, the letter 'z' was abolished in 1973, and the letter 'þ' sounds roughly like 'th' in 'this'. The problem was this: once my trips to Iceland became more frequent, into double figures, it started to become difficult, downright embarrassing, to say that I couldn't manage anything further than 'thanks', 'yes' and 'no'. Oh, and 'pig', as taught to me by a five-year-old Icelandic girl.

I mean, I had tried to remedy this in the past. On one occasion, I walked into a bookshop in downtown Reykjavík and explained that I'd like to learn Icelandic. After pointing out, and there was a point there, that Icelanders generally speak English very well (as in why bother to learn?), the sales assistant eventually produced a cellophaned set of books and CDs. They looked somewhat intimidating, and he must have seen the expression on my face. 'Do you know of John Grant?' he asked. 'He played Iceland Airwaves last year.' I said that I had heard of the American singer/songwriter. 'Well, he came and bought these books too. After a few months, he was able to converse in Icelandic.' As sales patters go, it was a pretty good one. I bought the set, placed it under my arm and hurried out of the store to get stuck in.

Once back at my good friends' place, I opened it up. My mind was bent with talk of inflections, declensions, conjugated verbs and neologisms. I couldn't get my head around the different alphabet, let alone the rapid delivery or flexible word order. I needed help.

Help came from Helga Guðrún Hinriksdóttir, a teacher from Hvammstangi. I spotted her online offer to help out travellers and those new to Iceland with Icelandic. I knew I needed help, and gave Helga a shout to find out more.

Firstly, I wanted to know why she'd decided to offer mini Icelandic lessons.

'I always think "what if it was me",' she replied. 'I love learning languages and if I were travelling somewhere,

I would love to receive a private mini language lesson. I also think that this is a fantastic way of welcoming tourists to Iceland.'

Next, I asked why she thought Icelandic was seen as such a difficult language to learn.

'The grammar is very difficult. Not only do we conjugate everything (nouns, verbs and adjectives), but some letters also change during the conjugation – *mamma* becomes *mömmu*, for example. Then there's the question of the "exceptions to the rules" and, as I call it, the "just because", when there's no rule but merely a habit or a feeling.'

My eyes started to cross, and I felt a familiar feeling of apprehension rise up inside me. It was time to come clean.

I explained that I was petrified of learning Icelandic. What was Helga's best piece of advice for a scaredy cat like me?

'Talk to old people or to young children. They are usually very patient and they don't know English so neither of you can really switch to English when you're in trouble with words.'

That seemed fair enough. But was there any hope for me? Had she ever known a non-native speaker speak Icelandic flawlessly?

'Yes. I once had a student who was fourteen at the time and had moved to Iceland just three years before, and one could not hear she was not native. Her grammar was also fantastic. With adults, I know one German woman who speaks Icelandic almost perfectly.'

Helga went on to explain that take-up for her mini lessons had been slow until she started offering pancakes and coffee to go with her words of wisdom. I can see why this would be. I'm told that her Icelandic pancakes (*pönnukökur*) are divine, especially with blueberry jam. But that's just a distraction.

Ultimately, Helga gave me hope that with a little patience, a bit of help, some pancakes and coffee, and a lot of work, Icelandic could be learnt. I promised to get those books back out just as soon as I got back home.

Back at the hostel in Sæberg, I removed the covers from the hot pot and eased myself slowly into the naturally heated waters. The hot pot was sunk below ground level, so I had a unique view of the fjord filled with the cold Greenlandic sea. I closed my eyes and tried not to think of those evil Arctic terns, instead filling my head with exploding geysers, elusive Northern Lights, warrior Icelanders, perfect snowflakes, stone people, mastering Icelandic and splashing around with a plump of seals. I was wrinkled like a prune by the time I got out.

Chapter 10

A Creative Bunch

Iceland is a seriously creative place. Everyone is at it. Icelanders publish, read and sell more books per capita than any other country. Everyone has been in a band, or is in a band, and is probably making a film about being in a band in Iceland, or at the very least blogging about it. Art and design is everywhere you go, from the main streets of Reykjavík to the car park of Keflavík Airport. When you are there, this creative and innovative spirit creeps in under your skin. It starts with taking some arty photos, probably of, say, Esja, or Geysir, and before you've left you'll be vowing to buy a better camera and develop your own website.

Let me give you an example of this. In late 2011, a man was caught by Reykjavík police and fined for a traffic offence. Nothing unusual in this; the sort of thing that happens every minute of every day in every major city across the world. But in this case the driver was playing a fiddle while driving. He just couldn't wait to get home to start making music: he had to play and drive at the same time. Brings a whole new meaning to in-car entertainment, doesn't it?

Even children's TV isn't safe from the ever-creative Icelanders. *LazyTown* – if you are a mum or dad, you'll know it, maybe even be sick of it – originates from this little island. More specifically, it is the brainchild of Magnús Scheving. Magnús is apparently super creative. He trained as a carpenter and then built his own house, where he lives with his family. He once took a bet with a friend. They each chose a sport for one another. The only rule was that they shouldn't know anything about the sport beforehand. Magnús had aerobics selected for him. He took the European Aerobic Championship title in 1994. But that's not all. Magnús is Sportacus in *LazyTown*.

LazyTown has proved to be a winner all over the world. Sportacus and his sidekick Stephanie take on Robbie Rotten, who wants to keep *LazyTown* lazy. Sportacus eats 'Sports-Candy' – fruit and vegetables to you and me. *LazyTown* currently airs in over one hundred countries in numerous different languages. How about that for creativity? I must eat more Sports-Candy. Maybe that's the answer.

Hafdís Huld must surely eat Sports-Candy. I once caught up with Hafdís just before one of her gigs. No, I literally caught up with her as she dashed inside to warm up after a photo shoot in the chilly autumn weather. I introduced myself and, despite her obviously being busy, I was then ushered into her dressing room. Hafdís Huld Þrastardóttir is clearly untroubled by her success, and was easy to chat to. She is small in stature, and has sparkling blue eyes with a gentle blonde bob. On entering the dressing room she perched on a cheap plastic chair and pulled her knees up to her chest, hugging her own legs. The room was sparse, with no diva trappings, save for the blueberries – I knew it, the Sports-Candy! – and chocolates (oh) on the table. Celebrity does not exist in Icelandic culture. She speaks English with a strong Icelandic accent, which she played on to exude maximum charm. She has a streak of humour that cuts through most of what she says, often leaving her and anyone else in the vicinity with a fit of the giggles.

Hafdís is already a star in Iceland, having achieved three Number One singles. She rose to fame with dance pioneers GusGus and FC Kahuna, but her own brand of acoustic folk has been melting hearts all over the globe, leading to performances at Glastonbury, Secret Garden Party and the South by Southwest showcase in Texas. She has contributed songs to advertising campaigns by Icelandair, starred in them for BMW, and collaborated with luminaries such as Tricky.

I asked Hafdís whether she found it an advantage being a musician from Iceland, especially in the current climate where artists such as Sigur Rós and Björk were commercially and critically successful.

'Wherever I came from, I think I would shape my music and how I am, and I haven't experienced being born in Spain, or Japan or America, so I couldn't tell you. I think that it has shaped me, coming from Iceland, but I think my music is quite personal to me. I think it's all connected somehow. You can't help noting the energies and nature all around when you are in Iceland; of course it's going to influence you, whether it's direct or if you are aware of it or not.'

That's quite a confident answer.

'I think wherever I came from, I'd be OK. I'm not saying I'd switch. I'm very happy being from Iceland, and I like going back there after my tours. It feels like a nice little secret, going back there. It still feels so private and detached from everything else. It feels like a lovely little hiding place.'

I liked that notion of Iceland as a hideaway, a neat little bolthole to escape from all the madness in the world. I decided to ask a question which I knew had been asked a thousand times but still intrigued me.

'Icelanders, by their very nature, are a creative bunch,' I began. 'This is something I admire hugely. Everyone seems to be writing a book, or is in a band, knitting jumpers or creating art. So why do you think Icelanders are so creative?

'I get asked that quite a lot,' she replied. 'I don't know. My guess would be that we have a lot of very cold weather. If we had lots of sunshine, we would probably just be in the park. But with lots of cold weather and twenty hours of darkness in the middle of the winter, it makes sense to go inside and create something. It lifts your spirits, and other people's spirits around you. Making music is something you can do to candlelight with a cup of tea next to you.'

I spotted a chink in her logic. Considering her previous over-confident answer, surely now she was saying that Iceland was crucial to her music after all. 'So maybe if you had been born in Spain, for example, you wouldn't be here now?'

'I'd just have a gorgeous tan and be really good at beach volleyball.'

She had got me there. I felt myself start to blush, and looked at the floor.

Perhaps thankfully, we were interrupted by Hafdís' manager and I was politely yet firmly requested to leave.

Afterwards, the gig was a huge success. Hafdís alternated her sweet and quirky songs with intriguing and humorous banter. The combination was utterly beguiling. She played a song that sounded and felt familiar. 'I've got it all figured out,' sang Hafdís. I couldn't disagree with that. After all, she had told me so herself.

Iceland's inspiration and creativity can rub off on you too. William Morris, JRR Tolkien and WH Auden are all good examples, but to me there is no greater or more amusing example of this than the case of Bill Drummond. Drummond, now best known for his involvement in 80s and 90s bands such as Big In Japan and the KLF, and for the question of whether he burnt a million dollars in cash or not, first came to Iceland in the 70s. The story is that he travelled to Iceland with his sister on a fishing trawler, with plans to walk from the north of Iceland to the south. I don't know if he completed this feat, but it certainly kickstarted his association with Iceland. Fast-forward a couple of decades and Drummond, having seen success through a number of different guises, decides to fork out on a piece of art. Not just any piece of art, but 'A Smell of Sulphur in the Wind' by Turner Prize-winning artist Richard Long.

Drummond gets up one morning and decides that he is no longer enjoying the picture, which consists of a stone circle built by Long set against a mountain vista. In Iceland. He decides to sell the work for exactly the $20,000 that he paid for it. Consequently, he cuts the picture into 20,000 square, identical-sized pieces and attempts to sell them off for $1 each.

This is where Iceland re-enters the story. It's possible that Bill is subconsciously drawn back to Iceland without even knowing it. He plans to return to Iceland, locate what's left of Long's stone circle and bury the $20,000. That's right, bury $20,000. Imagine that. But it doesn't end there. Wanting to take things full circle, Bill decides to take a photograph of the location and hang that on his wall instead. Now, I'm not saying that Iceland is entirely to blame here – clearly Bill had a certain amount of input. He could have chosen anywhere in the world; but where else in the world would have had the attraction, or pull, or creativity to inspire such crazy behaviour?

Hafdís Huld, along with the obligatory Sigur Rós, Of Monsters and Men, Snorri Helgason, Borko, Rökkurró and Amiina provided the soundtrack to the eastern leg of my trip around Route 1. Foo Fighters, with all their Icelandic connections and before they disappeared up their own stadium-sized holes, also featured. Together they became the soundtrack to my journey, and I can no longer listen to their tracks without being transported back to this joyous little trip.

With the Mývatn area behind me, I re-joined Route 1 heading east. The road rose up into the mountains through alpine valleys and deserted farms before the tarmac stopped and I found myself on unpaved roads and got covered in dust every time other vehicles sped past. The road became more and more exposed, frequently twisting and turning to reveal sharp drops down to hidden valleys.

At one point, between Mývatn and Grímsstaðir, I pulled over to visit a mountain hut. These huts are located in isolated areas and are for emergency use only; it was easy to see how grateful you would be to find one, especially in the deepest winter snow and bitterest winds. The hut was painted orange, which I suppose would have helped it stand out in the winter wonderland, and was a square, flat-roofed affair, with a short covered chimney poking out from one side. It excited my adventurous side, and I couldn't wait to peek inside. I was overjoyed to find the hut open, and cautiously opened the door. Ignoring the smell of stale beer, and even staler air, I found a small bed, a cupboard with meagre supplies, and most reassuringly a fire set and ready for lighting. I thanked the warm June sunshine that I wasn't there in an emergency, and stepped back outside. The view from the hut was absolutely stunning, looking down a series of valleys from which the road would disappear and then reappear far in the distance. The sun glinted off vehicles far below us, making them look like shooting stars across the rocky, alpine-esque scenery.

This little emergency hut, providing shelter in the face of whatever weather is thrown at it, is the responsibility of ICE-SAR – Iceland Search and Rescue Association. ICE-SAR can trace its roots to the Westman Island Rescue Team in 1918, but has changed quite a bit since. Oh, and they've achieved a great deal too. ICE-SAR were the first international team to arrive on the scene after the earthquake in Haiti in 2010, and they have acquired a safety-training vessel, and for that matter, the first rescue helicopter in Iceland (operated in conjunction with the government funded Coastguard). They have dealt with some volcanoes going off, or something, too. I forget the details.

ICE-SAR is a modern, all-singing, all-dancing search

and rescue organisation. Although singing and dancing are frowned upon during actual rescue missions. Not only do they have all the kit – snowmobiles, super jeeps, mobile communication centres, ships, lifeboats, dog teams, quad bikes, hovercrafts, snow groomers (me neither!), mountain bikes, kayaks, anything you can think of – they also have some of the most highly trained and specialist search and rescue teams in the world. And there is something else. ICE-SAR members wear a red and blue uniform that is not dissimilar to that of Spiderman. Except it doesn't shoot webs.

As well as looking out for us landlubbers, ICE-SAR also takes maritime safety very seriously. In addition to the previously mentioned ship, it has fourteen other vessels around Iceland's coast, thirty-five RIBs (rigid inflatable boats) and ninety inflatable boats. It runs a compulsory maritime safety course for sailors, which has dramatically cut the number of Icelandic lives lost at sea.

ICE-SAR's biggest achievement, though, if you are asking me, is the way it has harnessed the altruism and skills of Icelanders across the country to save lives. Whether it's daring rescues of hapless tourists from deep glacial crevasses, changing tyres in the West Fjords, educating others in accident prevention or running youth groups, ICE-SAR does all of this with volunteers.

ICE-SAR has ninety-nine search and rescue teams dotted right across Iceland (you'd think they would make it 100, wouldn't you?) and an amazing amount of volunteers who offer their services, skills and knowledge to get Icelanders and foreigners out of sticky situations. I think this is quite a feat; roughly 10% of the country's population are willing to perform such a crucial role, for no pay. This is surely something to be commended. I can't think of many other countries where this would happen.

There are many reasons for people to sign up to ICE-SAR – getting to drive a big truck while wearing shades, being involved in training exercises, camaraderie, access to Gucci kit, but above all, Icelanders seem to have an inbuilt need to help each other. Maybe it's after centuries of living on a harsh, inhospitable island isolated from the rest of the world, maybe it's because they just want to be self-sufficient in every possible way. Whatever the reason, I'm glad that they are there. Next time you drive past a little orange hut, I hope that you are too.

I eventually 'peaked out', as real mountaineers say, and began to travel southwards, downhill towards Egilsstaðir. After travelling so far through the Icelandic wilderness, I was looking forward to arriving at Egilsstaðir, the so called capital of the east. I was sorely disappointed. Perhaps I was drawn in by the radio suddenly picking up a signal again, or at least the dream of a hot pizza and a cold drink. I made a beeline for the filling station, which doubled as the local diner. In sharp contrast to the rest of the town, the place was buzzing. The forecourt was jammed with outsized trucks and the very finest agricultural vehicles. Their drivers were perched along the counter, chowing down on lunches of burgers, fish and meat stew. The rest of the diner was also full, with most of the town's 2200 inhabitants preferring to dine out, it seemed. There was a sense that everyone knew everyone else, and while it wasn't unfriendly, it was clear that I wasn't one of the locals. There was certainly an element of the Wild West there, and it felt like I had entered a saloon. People didn't quite stop eating, and there wasn't a piano player to stop playing anyway, but they definitely noted my arrival. I ordered the fastest of fast food, gobbled it down, refuelled the vehicle and shot off. I probably left some rubber on the forecourt.

Back on the road to nowhere, I spotted a reindeer, and then another, and then another. I stopped the car, grabbed my camera, and walked slowly towards them. Without even acknowledging me, they walked slowly away. I walked towards them this time crouched low. They walked away. And so began the slowest ever game of hide and seek. They stayed just out of range of my camera's zoom, but I was thrilled just to see them. I wanted to see more of them but either they were naturally wary, or else it was hunting season.

I did some research and gave Clint a call. I had spoken to Clint on the phone, and on arrival, he was on it again. Clint seemed to be on the phone an awful lot, clearly a busy man. He called for Pete, who came to meet us. Clint snatched a few seconds from his phone conversation to explain to Pete that I wanted to see the reindeer. We were on the flat, fertile plains of Cheshire, England rather than in eastern Iceland, and the reindeer were in a large enclosure. Though we weren't far from Chester, with its footballers' wives and soap stars, all I could see was green grass and trees covered in light pink blossom. A breeze blew a few wispy clouds around in the sky.

Pete led me into the enclosure and then rattled a bucket of food. The reindeer appeared out of nowhere and quickly jostled for prime position. There was clearly a pecking order, or should I say, nuzzling order in place, as the leaders of the herd forcibly pushed their way to the front to get their food first. The smaller deer, yearlings and females were left at the back while the males came forward to grab a mouthful from my outstretched hands. Their gentle, warm mouths scooped the food from my palms, reminding me of feeding horses with sugar cubes as a little kid. The reindeer were not at all shy; they jostled and pushed me too, trying to gain my attention. If that failed, they used their hooves in a pawing motion to attack my legs. That certainly worked, I thought, as a bull animal painfully raked a hoof down my calf muscle.

Clint, clearly a big-hearted man, had bought some of the herd, and the other animals had been rescued. The intention was to diversify from his fishery business and create a petting zoo. It didn't work out.

'It didn't feel right, all these lovely reindeer here, and then kids would turn up and try and feed them jelly babies,' Clint explained. 'I shut it after two weeks.'

I knew what he meant. Even though it was moulting season and the reindeer were exchanging their old coats for new, they were still lovely-looking creatures. Their fur was dense and warm, ranging from white to chocolate brown. Reindeers have two layers of fur: a warm, woolly undercoat, and a longer, coarser outer coat. They have big, friendly eyes, narrow but powerful legs and large feet that adapt to the season; in winter, the feet shrink back, exposing more of the sharp hooves for digging through the snow and ice to the edible lichen and mosses beneath. Their knees also click, so they can hear where other members of the herd are; especially useful in dense, Arctic blizzards. Not so much in Cheshire. And they even have special noses that heat the air they inhale before it hits their lungs – like, I suppose, a car heater.

What really got me, though, were the antlers. Reindeer are unusual in that both males and females have antlers, which are renewed every year. The antlers on these boys and girls were already growing to epic proportions, just like you see in the films. They were covered in a thick, luxurious fur that was almost velvet in texture. They didn't look real, as if they were too perfect to have been made by nature. Pete explained that they were ultra sensitive. I reached out and with the tip of one finger touched an antler of a deer standing nearby. He looked absolutely startled, and shivered all over, like a child tasting lemon for the first time. Sensitive was clearly an understatement.

One of the reindeer was different to all the rest. She hung about at the back of the herd and seemed to lack the confidence to come forward for food, even when the others had had their fill. She was white-furred, with almost albino features. Where her antlers should have been, though, were two rounded red lumps of flesh. Clint told me that she had been bought by a local farmer, who had been told to make sure she knew 'who was boss'. This had meant, to the farmer, tying this beautiful creature to a concrete block and then hitting her with a stick. She became so frightened, so scared, that she flipped herself over, landing on her antlers and breaking them off. Clint had been told of her plight, and, thankfully, had been able to rescue her from the farmer. I won't repeat what he said he'd do to the farmer if he ever caught up with him, but part of me agreed. How anyone could treat that creature with such cruelty and brutality was beyond me.

I thanked Clint and Pete for their time and they seemed pleased that I had come to visit them. They seemed genuinely excited and enthusiastic about reindeer, and I could see that they took pride in looking after their little herd. As I walked out of the enclosure, I spotted a sleigh, all done up with Christmas decorations at the back of a wooden shed. I'd forgotten that reindeer were also magical creatures, able to take Santa across the skies at Christmas, delivering presents to all the good little boys and girls waiting eagerly below. Pete saw me looking.

'We use them for Christmas,' he said, pointing at the sleighs and somewhat stating the obvious. 'We have done schools, weddings and hospital wards – the kids love it.' I pictured the looks of wonder and amazement as a real, live reindeer pulled a sleigh into a children's hospital ward and delivered Christmas presents from its sacks. I think that is brilliant: two fully grown men from the north of England spreading Christmas cheer and lighting up children's lives by using a small but magical herd of reindeer.

In Iceland there is a herd of about 3000 reindeer, most of whom live in the east. They are not native creatures, although they are obviously able to cope in Arctic conditions. The first and second attempts at creating the Icelandic herd failed though, so maybe it's not as easy as I thought. The reindeer there now are all descendants from the third herd, which was transported to Iceland in the 1850s. They are now sought after by hunters, and hunting licences are hard to come by. Hunting, by the way, is essential to keep the herd to a manageable size as they have no natural predators in Iceland; and to stop them eating all the jelly babies. No, not really.

However elegant, beautiful and charming these creatures are, there is one thing that you will be told in Iceland. Reindeer meat is exquisite. Icelanders love it, and I can see why. I have tried reindeer meat a few times now – in Alaska as a life-saving breakfast sausage after a night on the Alaskan Amber beer; as a burger in a restaurant that was trying out 'unusual' meats and failing to impress – but what really stands out is a Christmas party in Reykjavík. That was my first taste, and, understandably, I was a little apprehensive about eating Prancer, Vixen and their mates. I needn't have been though. The lean meat was succulent, slightly gamey, slightly smoky, slightly like its venison cousin, but entirely fantastic. It tasted rich, smooth and tangy. I went back for some more. Don't tell Clint and Pete though. I don't think they'd like it.

I travelled on towards Djúpivogur, in the south-east corner of the country. My destination was the hotel at Berunes, near to the village of Breiðdalsvík. 'Hotel' doesn't really do this place justice. It is a collection of farm buildings, complete with its own church and graveyard. The main building, which was clearly the farmhouse in a former life, has been kept in a traditional manner, with wooden furniture and photos on the walls of generations past. Having read the last few sentences, you would be forgiven for thinking this was a creepy, isolated place with a church on its doorstep and the ghosts of ancestors walking the rooms. You'd be wrong though. The overall effect was like staying at a not-often-seen auntie's house. I was made to feel very welcome from the very moment the car crunched its way up the gravel driveway. The Icelandic owner popped out to meet me, followed by a clutch of chickens. She didn't speak a word of English, but was clearly very practised at making everyone and anyone feel welcome in spite of any language barrier. I was the first guest to arrive, so I was taken from room to room and asked to choose which one I wanted to sleep in. I initially chose an attic room, but after realising that I would probably kill myself on the steep wooden ladder in the middle of the night, I opted for one on the ground floor with wooden walls and a window looking out on the quaint church.

After briefly sitting on the bed, looking at the walls, it was back to the car to explore the area. Essentially Berunes is handily positioned on a fjord that contains no other visible buildings, and between two other fjords with the same dearth of facilities. Outstanding natural beauty, yes. Somewhere for a sandwich, no. I pointed the car towards Breiðdalsvík, where, after a good few kilometres, I eventually ended up. After a near miss with a most unsanitary-looking café and the rear of a filthy filling station, I headed towards the swimming pool, which seemed the most sensible thing to do. Not only for a swim, but to meet some local people who might know a thing or two about where to eat out.

The pool was housed in an ultra-modern Scando-style wooden building that would leave all the municipal leisure centres in the UK reeling in their own 70s-style, concrete-fasciaed, toe-nails-in-the-shower filth. It was the sort of building that had undoubtedly been designed by an Icelandic team on their iPads during a team-building session. It was sleek and trendy yet friendly and welcoming. For a small town of 273, they have done remarkably well.

A strange yet wonderfully Icelandic thing happened. The manager, having heard my English tones, left his office and entered the reception area. There was no one else around, I noticed, as he bellowed, 'Welcome! Welcome to my house!'

'House' was pronounced as the Icelandic '*hús*', and I was reminded of a Scottish guy I used to work with, who pronounced it in the same way. I checked behind me again, but no, he really was talking to me. I missed his name, but he proceeded to pump my hand. He was somewhat more rotund than you'd expect from a leisure centre manager, but was wearing the T-shirt, shorts and flip-flop combo of someone that might have to submit to lifesaving duties at any moment, but has thankfully never had to put such skills to the test.

He promptly took me on a tour of the leisure centre, and showed me everything. The gym. The sports hall. The store cupboard. The pool. The hot pot. He talked non-stop in a mixture of English and Icelandic, which combined with his accent and sheer enthusiasm made it difficult to understand every word. The meaning was clear though. I was very welcome there, and was welcome to use any of the facilities. I explained that the thought of lifting weights made me queasy on the best of days, and I was more physically suited to lolling around hot pots. I was taken aback by the guy's friendliness though, and his overwhelming pride in his job and his small section of his small town. I'm not sure that you would experience this anywhere else in the world these days, least of all in the

UK. In the UK, you might get told off for running near the pool if you were lucky; otherwise you might be grunted at as you had the cheek to ask to go swimming, thereby ruining any chance the teenage lifeguarding team had of simultaneously getting off with each other and watching television.

After I'd carried out the said lolling about in the hot pot, and even had a refreshing swim in the outdoor pool, the local school obviously opened its gates and a dozen gangly youths arrived. Not that they were badly behaved, I had just got used to the serenity and peace of having the place to myself. The sort of serenity and peace that doesn't last long with a game of water polo taking place, or repeated attempts at diving onto the back of an inflatable crocodile. I just kept slipping off.

There was a handball court in the centre too. Handball is not a well known sport in the UK. I wasn't even really aware of it until I was swept along to a televised match in Iceland. I think it was Iceland vs. Sweden in some sort of European championships.

The reasons I'm vague on the details? I was too busy trying to keep up with the fast-paced game while at the same time having it explained to me by various Icelanders, who had to keep breaking off to cheer. Or drink beer. Or drink beer and cheer. The whole room was crammed with Icelanders cheering on their team; it was infectious. I was soon whooping and cheering along with the best of them.

Later I got to see the Iceland vs. Belarus match at the Laugardalshöll sports arena in Reykjavík. The atmosphere was amazing. The crowd went absolutely wild when the Icelandic team came out, and shouted until they were hoarse every time they scored, which was a lot. The game shuttled back and forth with such ferocity, my neck ached from trying to keep up. It was fantastic. I'm not really into watching sports, with the exception of cricket, but this I could get into.

Handball is not Iceland's national sport – that is actually *glíma*, a form of wrestling – but it might as well be. It's estimated that when the national team got to the final match of the Beijing Olympics, 80% of the nation were watching them.

A similar number of Icelanders were undoubtedly glued to their screens for the London 2012 Olympics, especially for their game against the host nation. By a stroke of luck, I managed to get a ticket for the Iceland vs. Team GB match. It was pure luck, thanks mainly to a ticketing system seemingly devised by the same people who developed the National Lottery. Einar sent me an Icelandic shirt to wear for the occasion.

Handball exploded in popularity in the UK during the 2012 Olympics, with more and more fans becoming engaged as the contest went on. To find out a bit more, I grilled Ciaran Williams, a Team GB player, about playing in Iceland, playing against Iceland and the rise of handball.

'I know that you play handball professionally,' I began. 'How is the Icelandic team viewed?'

'The Icelandic team is fantastic! I love the way they play, with a strong, aggressive defence and a very quick counter-attacking style. For a country with such a small population to produce such a constant stream of top-class players is testament to the country's development programme and approach to sport.'

'Have you ever played handball in Iceland? How did that go?'

'I had a trial with Selfoss a couple of years ago, but that didn't work out due to financial problems. I would love to play in Iceland one day though, as it's a beautiful country – I have visited four times now.'

'I watched the Olympic match between Team GB and Iceland. The first half was pretty close, but the second belonged to Iceland. What happened?'

'We played a great first half, and tried to match them for counter attacks and strong defence. Unfortunately in the second half we couldn't maintain the same level of play. Their experience and also squad depth proved the difference. After the game, Óli Stefánsson was one of the first to congratulate us and told me we were on the right path, which is a huge confidence boost for us going forward, that people recognise we are getting stronger and better. To hear this from one of the greatest players of all time was a huge boost.'

I hope that handball does take off in the UK. I really enjoyed my afternoon at the Copper Box watching this fast and thrilling sport. I nearly understand all the rules and nuances. My Icelandic friends continue to explain them to me in any case. Likewise, if handball does take off in the UK, we might just have to turn to our neighbours in Iceland for a few tips.

As I made my way out of the Breiðdalsvík leisure centre, I saw that the manager had positioned himself near the door, to literally wave me off. After complimenting him on his 'house', and thanking him for his hospitality, I asked him if there was somewhere that I could get something to eat in town. He was visibly torn between inviting me back to his place for dinner and recommending a restaurant a few kilometres out of town on Route 1.

My point here is this: Icelanders seem to be fiercely proud of their heritage and country, and although they may appear – excuse the pun – frosty and aloof when you first meet them (as, for example, in 'saloon town', Egilsstaðir), this more often than not melts to reveal a warm, welcoming heart. They are willing to help you in any which way they can. One of my close friends, at my suggestion, took a weekend trip to Reykjavík with his pregnant wife. They chose to travel in January, and unfortunately decided on a short self-drive trip to the south coast, in a two-wheel-drive car. That part was not at my suggestion, I should add. Perhaps not surprisingly, they hit difficulties on a cold, snowy road, and found themselves stuck in a bleak and remote location. With no houses in sight, and front-wheel-drive unable to cope with that level of snow and ice, they settled in for a long wait. After a few minutes though, an Icelandic farmer appeared in a super-sized truck. Without saying anything, he silently attached a tow-rope to my friends' car and pulled them back onto the road. Without a word, he untied his rope, gave a friendly wave, and disappeared off into the snowy wilderness. If that was not an example of true Icelandic altruism, I don't know what is. It made a remarkable impact on my friend, who will tell this story at the drop of a hat.

Maybe it was me at Egilsstaðir. Maybe I mistimed the visit, or misunderstood the relevant etiquette. Maybe it was my haste to get fed. Whatever the reason, perhaps the contrast between the welcoming manner of the Icelanders

I had experienced at the youth hostel and the leisure centre, and the style the rest of the Western world now finds acceptable had become too stark. I'm not asking for a false, Midwestern US 'have a nice day, y'all' approach, but I certainly have grown to admire and appreciate the sheer friendliness and gregarious nature of the average Icelander.

To take this theory a step further, I think that there is a tangible link here to the Icelandic natural inclination towards creativity. I agree with Hafdís Huld that the long dark winters are almost certainly responsible in part for the evenings of music, art and writing, and the obligatory hot chocolate. But I can't help thinking that actually this creativity is an expression of the desire to share, to be welcoming, to nurture friendships and be part of a family and a community. Most creative pursuits involve some sort of sharing; whether it's writing a book to share knowledge or a story, performing music for the pleasure of those around you, being involved in a film for others to watch, or making a meal for friends and family, it fuels the warmth and open-hearted nature of the national psyche. This is what is being done. And I like that. I like it a lot.

Chapter 11

Dauðalogn

Snæfellsnes must be trying to keep its secrets and beauty hidden under a bushel. That's what I thought when the car first ground to a halt and I stepped out into what appeared to be some form of sinking mud, which quickly enveloped my boots; even the car had started to submerge under its own weight. I also thought, what exactly is a bushel? I didn't, actually, but if you are interested, it's an old-fashioned measure of dry goods, such as corn.

I had stopped off to see the English House, mainly because of its name, I suppose. It's actually a Norwegian building that was transported to Snæfellsnes some years ago and got its name from its owners, a couple of English gentry who bought the house and surrounding land to use in the summer. The salmon fishing is supposed to be fantastic there, but my intentions were thwarted by the viscous, sticky mud and I retreated, imagining myself growing a handle-bar moustache, wearing a pin-striped suit and bowler hat, and casting my lines into the cold, glacial river in search of a fat, fresh salmon or a sleek Arctic char. I bet old Major Stewart stopped by there. I thought that maybe I'd have a ghillie too, to retrieve my fish, but decided that was perhaps a dream too far, and anyway my socks were wet as well now, so I'd better get back into the car and stop fantasising.

Snæfellsnes is a peninsula that protrudes from the west coast of Iceland and is often called 'Iceland in miniature'. This rather endearing description owes a lot to Snæfellsjökull, a glacier seated on a volcanic peak at the far end of the peninsula that on the map looks not unlike an omelette in a frying pan. The Snæfellsjökull – Snow-Mountain Glacier – has achieved global celebrity, having been the starting point for Jules Verne's *Journey to the Centre of the Earth*, and, more locally, it was the subject of Halldór Laxness' *Under the Glacier*. Snæfellsjökull can even be seen all the way from Reykjavík on a clear day.

I had a very strange, yet oddly comedic, Geography teacher at my secondary school. Actually there were two of them, a Morecambe and Wise of the classroom if you will. Anyway, the one teacher was very excitable about glacial erosion and lava formations. I'm not sure if he had ever visited Iceland, but he would have been in his element here, and especially at Gerðuberg, where Iceland's tallest basalt columns can be found. If you are not sure what I mean by basalt columns, think of the Giant's Causeway in Northern Ireland. These giant grey columns have formed rows and stand up so straight, it's as if they are man-made. Even though they were shrouded in fog when I visited, they still made an impressive sight. Around the base were cubes of fallen columns, and I was tempted to see if I could push a standing column over myself. Instead, I made my way back to the car.

Arnarstapi sits in the south-west of the peninsula, in a small bay that consists of steep basalt cliffs over which spraying white waterfalls cascade directly into the sea.

It is really just a collection of summerhouses and remote detached buildings with too much space between them to give any sense of social cohesion. Stranded and rusting snowmobiles added to this sense of desolation, and I tried hard to imagine the place on a summer's day, with its vista of Snæfellsjökull rising up behind it and the sea swelling gently at the cliffs beneath the little houses. Today was very different though. Snæfellsjökull was wearing a cape of thick dense cloud that obscured her summit and most of her flanks. In the village, the wind was whipping up the sea and making the light drizzle fly horizontally through the air so that it covered my clothing and hair in a thick dew that slowly but surely soaked me through. I made my way down to the harbour, which looked pretty modern and had some facility for landing and processing fish. I have no knowledge of this industry, but the smell, large plastic boxes and the tarmac covered in bloody puddles and fish scales give it away. I peered into the windows of the buildings, but it appeared mostly deserted, except for one larger gentleman who was trying not to see me, hiding behind his computer and trying not to make eye contact.

I was joined by a black and white sheepdog. He was a friendly fellow, with a black tail that curled up onto his back, in the style of most Icelandic sheepdogs, including my old friend Mosi. He was clearly itching for someone to play with, and repeatedly brought me stones that he dropped at my feet with a baleful look. I spent a good few minutes throwing them for him, and he dutifully returned them. He must have been bored stiff there. There wasn't anyone else in sight, save for Computer Guy, and it was January, which meant he still had several months to wait until the tourists arrived to give him some respite, and, doubtlessly, some of their ham sandwiches too. I took care not to toss the stones too far though; I didn't want him tumbling over the cliffs to the frothy sea below. The coast there was spectacular, with lava formations rising up out of the sea like giant stepping stones. Some were topped with green tufts of vegetation and white gulls hunkering down to get out of the fierce wind. And I didn't blame them, the wind seemed to whip across the sea and head straight for your face. I was pleased that they were leaving me alone too, as I remembered watching a TV documentary about gulls that had started to attack people and I recalled those other fulmars which are actually sick on you as a defence mechanism.

I made my way down to the beach, which was enclosed by towering lava formations made shiny by the wind and rain, and looked out to sea. To my right, over the smooth, rounded dark stones, was a sea cave. The entrance was several metres high, and the sea repeatedly crashed through it, causing white froth to spray high in the air, in dramatic contrast to the flat black stone. The cave appears in many an Icelandic tourist brochure, and one Icelandic band (For a Minor Reflection, the band I saw at Airwaves; not the one with the monkey) has even filmed a music video in that exact spot. I knew that there was another, even more famous and pictured geological wonder just down the coastal path towards Hellnar – a rock arch called Gatklettur – but my hands and face were freezing, and I needed a hot chocolate or else I might have collapsed. So I trudged back to the car, tossing a few more stones for the hound on the way, and even momentarily stopping to apologise to him for leaving him there in that cold, wet, windswept place.

On leaving Arnarstapi, you can't help but notice the huge stone statue of Bárður, created by Ragnar Kjartansson. This is the setting for another Icelandic saga. Bárður was – allegedly – an ogre or Shrek-like character and is said to have lived at nearby Djúpalón, with his daughters. Following a dispute over his eldest daughter being set afloat to Greenland, Bárður took revenge on his two nephews, Rauðfeldur and Sölvi. Rauðfeldur found himself shoved into a ravine while Sölvi was flung off a high cliff. Rauðfeldsgjá is now the name of the narrow ravine, and Sölvahamar the name of the cliff where Sölvi had an enforced flying lesson.

Out of shame or anger, Bárður sloped off into Snæfellsjökull, where he is believed to have remained; legend has it that he now protects the glacier. He certainly sounds pretty formidable, and the sculpture was equally impressive, made out of local stone, and towering over me – I could have just about squeezed through the giant's legs. He seemed to have a happy face though, so I wonder if there was a happy ending to the story that I'm not aware of.

After a credit card-bending hot chocolate and doughnut, I ventured a few kilometres further out on the peninsula to Djúpalónssandur and Dritvík. These two beaches are extraordinarily beautiful, albeit not in a typically beach-like way. Their beauty is not of blue seas, white sands and palm trees. Instead it is all about intensity and colour. A bustling aquamarine sea turned over waves that burst into flashes of white foam that travelled up the perfectly black beach. At the top of the beach were outcrops that had been worn into different formations by the powerful forces of nature; lava, wind and sea have created jagged caves, sharp cliffs and narrow chasms. The constant changes have resulted in a beach that is entirely black in colour and made from stones that have worn themselves into perfectly rounded shapes. They made a satisfying crunching sound as I walked on them, like stepping on glass marbles.

It was my intention to stop and take photographs, but I couldn't. I was overwhelmed by the beauty of the place, and the snaps that I took didn't seem to do it justice. I felt like I was on the edge of the continent; that nothing existed beyond that point. I gazed at the sea repeatedly hitting the black beach. That white on black, white on black, white on black, combined with the sound of stones and sand being dragged back into the ocean was simply hypnotic and I did well to regain my senses before the waves became a little too close for comfort. I stepped back before getting a shoe full of water for the second time in a day.

Drítvík is a little further around the coast, and despite my best intentions and a well-paced walk, I only just made it before the daylight failed. It was January and it would be dark by about 3pm. I wanted to see the lifting stones there: four stones of varying weights, which establish whether you are strong enough to be a fisherman. Disappointingly, I couldn't find them. I've since been told that that smallest stone – the Bungler – has been broken by one too many tourists. Bloody tourists, eh.

There weren't many tourists where I was staying for the night, at Hotel Búðir on the south coast of the peninsula. The hotel is probably buzzing in summer, but that night there appeared to be very few guests and the price seemed to have been adjusted as a result, meaning a very affordable night and, even better, dinner and breakfast included. The hotel is situated on an estuary and is alone apart from a diminutive Icelandic church to keep it company. The hotel burnt down in 2001 and had to be rebuilt, but had kept most of its charm and style. The framed pictures of local birds and fish were a nice touch, as was the antique telescope that gazed out of a large window towards Snæfellsjökull. But the glacier remained hidden from view as the wind had failed to chase the cloud away from its snowy peak.

My room was absolute bliss, with a bed that seemed to have been made entirely out of marshmallow, an en suite that resembled the very best of Scandinavian style architecture (no toilet-roll dollies there!) and a traditional wooden window that perfectly framed a view of the river running into the cold sea. I could see why Halldór Laxness had been a frequent guest; it must have been very inspiring to hole up there and just keep writing. I hoped some of his literary magic might rub off on me. As for holing up, I was tempted to do the same.

Hungry from all that walking and sea air, I was looking forward to dinner and I was not disappointed. The food was outstanding, and was very local and very well cooked and presented. I was served a melt-in-the mouth pork belly, carrot purée and beetroot liquorice starter, followed by a wholesome monkfish, potato purée and cauliflower foam main. I was overjoyed with the monkfish; the waiter told me that it had been caught that morning in Arnarstapi and its firm, perfectly white flesh couldn't have tasted any fresher. Dessert was a warm chocolate cake, Icelandic vanilla ice cream, coffee mousse and blueberry paint. I was in heaven. It was delicious, one of the best meals I had ever eaten. I washed the lot down with a splendid Icelandic beer, and then took a walk outside. The sky had begun to clear, but neither the Northern Lights nor Snæfellsjökull were visible; concealing themselves from me once again. I would have felt a little let down had I not got a gut full of the best Icelandic food and a head just a little fuzzy from that excellent beer. It was time to hit my marshmallow bed.

I awoke to find that it was 10am and that I had slept right through the night, save for a terrible few moments when I'd completely forgotten where I was – this happens to me a lot when travelling – and again when I was woken by what I could only assume was the yipping of an Arctic fox directly outside my bedroom window. That doesn't happen quite so much. I availed myself of the breakfast, which was served buffet style and included meats, breads, fruit, yoghurts, fish and pastries. It was very good, so I went up several times to fill my plate, and felt truly English as a result, but knowing that my mother would be proud of me.

Outside, light was just seeping through the dark sky, giving a ghostly pale-blue cast to everything. Nothing was moving. It was best described as *Dauðalogn* ('dead calm'). I sneaked out of the hotel and walked the short twisting path to the church. It's a traditional wooden structure with a short wooden spire, on top of which sits a plain cross. The church looked at home there, but would make a fine addition to any Midwestern US village. The sun had started to rise, and a sliver of pinkish glow was reflected on the white door of the church. It didn't feel at all eerie, and I felt at peace there. I liked the sound of the sea and the birds nearby. I don't want to dwell on gloomy topics, but I wouldn't mind being buried there. I was thinking this as I weaved through the graves, all of which were well tended and some of which even had electric Christmas lights on them. Like I say, it just seemed a pleasant, simple, friendly place to be for the rest of eternity.

But Búðir wasn't finished with me yet. As I looked back towards the hotel, I could see that Snæfellsjökull had started to show herself. Her lower flanks, crisscrossed with ravines of white snow, were now visible, giving way to a crisp, perfectly white glacial topping. It looked like icing on a wedding cake. I don't know whether it was the scenery, the location or the harsh sea breeze, but there was a tear in my eye. I really wouldn't mind being buried here.

Back on the road, I retraced my steps to the junction of the 567, which led down to Djúpalónssandur and Dritvík. I was tempted to return and find the lifting stones, just to prove I wasn't a bungler, but decided not to and kept going. I was pleased, then, to discover that Hellissandur, the first seaside village I arrived at, had a replica set of stones. The museum was all closed up for the long winter season, but there was a delightful note on the gates stating that people were more than welcome to look around the grounds. Which I did. There was a charming statue of a fisherman holding out a fish to what I assumed was his son, which was a tribute 'to all those lost at sea'. The backdrop of Snæfellsjökull made this all the more poignant, and I – a confirmed landlubber – struggled to even comprehend what it would be like to leave your wife and children and head out into the cold, rough Greenlandic sea, knowing that you might never return. I was in a dark mood that day, but my mood lightened on seeing some traditional turf houses, a collection of whale bones (massive), and of course the lifting stones. I gave them a try. I'm keeping the results to myself though. I'm not a bungler, let's leave it at that.

Hellissandur has another claim to fame, which is quite something for a town of only 400 people. It has the tallest structure in Western Europe. How cool is that? It's a 412-metre-high mast that seemed to go on forever into the white, cloudy sky. The mast is kept in place by several steel guy lines and is so tall that it would loom over the Eiffel Tower, at a paltry 324 metres. The mast was originally built by the US military to transmit a now-defunct navigation system for ships and aircraft, but is used these days by the Icelandic National Broadcasting Service for long-wave radio transmissions.

Next along the coast was Rif, which looked so bleak, desolate and empty that I didn't even stop, instead preferring to push on to Ólafsvík. Ólafsvík is a well-known fishing port on the north coast of the peninsula, and due to its location was one of the first towns to become a fishing port under Danish rule. It is a pretty little town, with the ubiquitous coloured roofs, and sea views, but what makes it even more special are the mountains behind it. They seem to have been painted on by an overzealous landscape painter, who, as if not happy with his work, then added an impressive waterfall right in the town, near the medical practice. The falls tumble down to a small stream, which in turn burbles through the streets before reaching the sea.

I wandered up to the waterfall and admired the view

as the town stretched out before me. Something caught my eye. Ólafsvík has a most peculiar church. Although clearly modern, it is built from a series of steep-sided prisms and painted white. The bells rather than being inside the steeple are positioned in another, separate prism, one on top of the other. It was certainly eye-catching, although I was concerned that its modern style might quickly go out of fashion and leave the town wishing they had plumped for something more traditional. Ólafsvík is also a place to come to in summer, I was told, as many whale-watching tours set off from there. As it was January, however, and just as cold as the day before, I was back in the car fairly quickly.

After a quick meal in Grundarfjörður, which consisted of a cheese burger slathered in cocktail sauce and chips covered in paprika, I headed towards Bjarnarhöfn. I tried to think of HP brown sauce and vinegar on chips in a vain effort to divert my thoughts from what I knew was coming. Even the awesome Kirkjufell – Church Mountain – failed to distract me, despite being a mightily impressive mountain actually protruding out of the sea on its own small peninsula in front of the town.

Hildibrandur Bjarnason could soon be something of a star. He generates media coverage, and has appeared on television, the internet, and in the newspapers. He has his own website, and the motivation and business acumen that might just bring significant success. Not that he has much competition, mind. Hildibrandur Bjarnason produces *h*ákarl, a near national Icelandic dish of fermented shark, from his small farm in Bjarnarhöfn.

Bjarnarhöfn is an isolated farm between Grundarfjörður and Stykkishólmur. It is demarked by a metal shark sign at the side of the road. The farm lies some five kilometres beyond this, along a single-track road and through metal gates. It looks like a typical Icelandic farm: a clutch of small white buildings with red roofs. A church stands nearby, and the main farmhouse enjoys views over a rounded yet intricate coast of deep blue sea dotted with small tuft-like islands. The backdrop matches this, with its snow-streaked dark grey mountains and green mosses and grasses. But I digress. Perhaps on purpose.

Well, *hákarl* has a fearsome reputation, but let's start with the facts. *Hákarl* is produced from Greenlandic shark, which is a prehistoric shark that hasn't physiologically changed for aeons. It's also highly poisonous, thanks to the high levels of uric acid and trimethylamine oxide that it uses as an effective antifreeze against the chilly waters of Greenland and Iceland. The effects of eating the shark in its 'fresh' state range from similar to being extremely drunk to, well, death. Arctic sled dogs that ate the meat accidentally have been recorded as having been unable to stand due to the impact on their nervous systems. The only way to make the shark edible is to process it, which is exactly what Hildibrandur Bjarnason does, and does so well.

January is a great time for *hákarl*. Not only is it the month of Husband's Day (Bóndadagur), meaning that I should get a gift from Nichola (don't worry, there is Konudagur – Wife's Day – too), but it is also the start of the season in which Þorrablót mid-winter feasts are held across the country. *Hákarl* is a fixture of both celebrations. This time of year is also traditionally when Greenlandic sharks are taken from the sea and the whole process begins.

As I arrived at Bjarnarhöfn, the smell of shark hung in the air. It was a thick, cloying smell, which, combined with the usual smells of a farmyard, made for a heady concoction. My head was full of tales of Gordon Ramsay having been unable to keep the stuff down due to its pungency, and Icelanders being divided on whether *hákarl* is a true delicacy or truly grotesque. My stomach, in response to both the smell and my intense trepidation, was already shrinking in size and warning of its fragility.

I was met by Hildibrandur and, not far behind, his elderly Icelandic sheepdog and a sprightly-looking cat. We shook hands and I noted that Hildibrandur, although not a youngster, had a healthy complexion and the good strong grip of a man who has worked all of his life. The shark must be good for you then, right?

Hildibrandur led me into a barn which had been converted into his private 'shark museum'. The exhibits had all come from his family, been donated by friends, or, in the case of the dried shark heads, been prepared by Hildibrandur himself. There was a boat, several displays of farming and fishing equipment and a menagerie of arthritic-looking stuffed wildlife. Ignoring all of this, Hildibrandur led me to a wall of photographs. One of them depicted a whole Greenlandic shark hanging from the front of a tractor and looking absolutely huge. Greenlandic sharks can live up to 200 years and can reach weights of up to 1000 kilograms. They are similar in size to the great white, but not as sleek-looking. Not as pretty as Spielberg's Jaws.

Hildibrandur explained that the sharks are no longer specifically hunted, but do frequently get caught by fishing trawlers. When they do, he gets the call. Once at the farm, the shark is skinned and the large slabs of meat are removed and sliced into more manageable chunks. There are no bones in the meat, only a form of cartilage, which presumably makes the whole butchery process much easier. Judging by the head and skin remnants I found outside later, not much goes to waste; I expected to have nightmarish visions of this for some time. Intriguingly, Hildibrandur told me that a by-product from the shark is a fatty oil which in Victorian times was used to light city streets.

Hildibrandur went on to explain that the shark meat is then boxed up for a period of six weeks. The more traditional method is to bury it on a gravelled hillside, but Hildibrandur's technique allows him to keep a closer eye on the whole process. There was no mention of the old wives' tale about urinating on the shark while it's on the ground, and as the whole preparation process was clearly professional and a matter of personal pride to my host, I didn't mention it either. The shark is then taken outside and hung up for four months. There was a wooden building outside which had been especially converted for this purpose. It had a roof, but the bottom half was open to the fresh air, and the top half was protected only by wooden slats. Here, the outer shark meat takes on an orangey-amber hue, although the smell remains impossibly pungent and caused me to physically recoil as I approached the building.

Hildibrandur revealed that the Greenlandic shark has never been known to be diseased, and that it is free from cancers and the like. As a result, it's become more popular and parents in Reykjavík are now keen to feed it to their children as a new health food, especially in the face of increasing threats from swine flu and other communicable diseases.

The time had come then. Hildibrandur disappeared into a back room, and I knew why. I had so far been fascinated by the whole process, and had become so enthralled with the historical, cultural and practical aspects of *hákarl* production that I had temporarily forgotten that I would have to try some. Now, as Hildibrandur returned with a small dish containing cubes of *hákarl*, I started to panic. Hildibrandur added to the pressure by proclaiming 'Seize the day!', before stabbing a cube of shark meat and swallowing it whole. His face broke into a huge smile. The implication was clear: the challenge was on.

I placed a smallish piece of white meat on to my cocktail stick. This white meat is called '*skyr*-shark' after the white yoghurt-like dessert I love so much. As I examined the sinewy, shiny cube of meat, I wished wholeheartedly that it was real white *skyr* instead. The smell coming off it was repugnant, and I knew if I didn't do it then, I never would. My throat felt closed. My stomach was in knots. I placed the cube of meat in my mouth and bit down. My mouth was filled with the most intense fish flavour. And something more. My whole being was centred on the taste in my mouth; it took all my focus, all my attention. The consistency was surprisingly soft, less chewy than I'd expected, but it was the taste that was unforgettable, incomparable. It didn't taste like anything else I'd ever tried. Was I able to swallow it? That's between Hildibrandur and me.

✳✳✳

Between Grundarfjörður and Stykkishólmur, things went berserk. Not really, but I just wanted to use that word. It's one of my favourite words, and it is particularly relevant here. Berserkjahraun lava field, while not much to look at, gives rise to both one of my favourite words and one of my favourite stories about Iceland.

Berserkers were proper scary, proper crazy Norse warriors who would fight like a man possessed, seemingly going into a trance or rage that enabled them to continue battling to the death – either their own or that of their opponent, whichever came first. A downside to this was that they were often – understandably – shunned by the local community, and in some Nordic countries even outlawed. A local Icelandic chap, though, decided to employ two berserkers (they probably used a dodgy CV, or at least omitted the word 'berserker') to clear a path through the lava field to his farm. Things went awry, however, when one of the berserkers fell in love with the farmer's daughter. The farmer is said to have killed him – not sure how, if the berserker was that formidable, but anyway – and you are supposed to still be able to see his burial mound next to the path carved through the lava field.

This wasn't the last time that the building of roads caused trouble in this area. Route 56, the road into Stykkishólmur, had to be moved from its original mountain pass to its current location after stories that the spirit of an old troll was causing difficulties for drivers on the road, who reported feeling the presence of another being in their

225

vehicles. To be fair, turning around to see an old troll sitting in the back seat would put you off a bit, although I'm not sure that there are many countries in the world where this would have caused the whole road to be shifted as a result. You can't argue with trolls though, can you?

Next on my list, and I had been looking forward to this substantially more than eating fermented shark, was a family-run brewery in Stykkishólmur. On arrival, I was met by Ragna and her son-in-law Einar. Ragna invited me in, and, most obligingly, the whole factory came to a grinding halt to welcome its visitor. Ragna quickly opened up some of their recent brews, starting with Jökull Bjór (Glacier Beer), a regular beer and the brewery's first. It was fantastic. Without going all Oz Clarke about it, it tasted like beer should taste: clean and refreshing but with a bitter tang, and even a faint taste of something else, like liquorice or lemon.

Einar then took me around the small brewery, explaining the brewing process in detail, and describing some of the perks of the job. 'Every morning at eight, I have to taste the beer to see what stage it's at,' he said. Sounded like a good job to me.

I was introduced to the master brewer, who looked uncannily like Sideshow Bob from the Simpsons, with a shock of tasselled ginger hair on top of his head, and a slim, perpetually slouched body. Like the hops and malt, he had been imported from Germany. Hops and malt can't be produced in Iceland, but the third and final ingredient certainly can. Their water was crisp, fresh and from a mountaintop a few hundred metres away, where lava fields filtered it naturally so that it arrived at the brewery in a pure, unadulterated state. It was what gave their beer an edge; it made for an impeccably clean, refreshing brew. A good 'session' beer, as they say, and in this case I think they were right. The quality of the water and the purity of the ingredients makes for easy drinking and – this is the bonus – much less of a hangover, what with the absence of all those chemicals that the enormo-breweries tend to add.

Unlike the enormo-breweries, which have placed profit and efficiency over taste and quality, the beer there was properly stored and allowed to mature for up to five weeks before being bottled. Some factories have reduced this crucial part of the process to only a matter of days, and use chemicals instead. It makes a mockery of 'lager' meaning 'to store' in German, and as I discussed this with Einar, I saw that Sideshow Bob was nodding along enthusiastically.

Einar explained that the brewery had started operations in 2007, and despite some unusual, uniquely Icelandic challenges, had continued to grow. First off, all alcohol had to be shipped to Reykjavík to be proofed before being distributed – which meant that the brewery couldn't supply locals with beer without, perversely and expensively, shipping it back from Reykjavík. Thankfully this madness had stopped in the past couple of years, Einar told me. However, he was still stymied by Icelandic law, which prohibits the advertising of alcohol in the Icelandic media. The same law does not apply to foreign, imported magazines though, which almost always contain large glossy ads for the major alcohol brand leaders.

Ragna popped back behind the bar to crack open a couple of other bottles, to which I had no objections. She let me taste their Þorrablót beer – designed especially for the mid-winter season – and the Jökulhlaup ('Glacial Flood') brew. Both were slightly darker, but equally good. I could have stayed all day. The little brewery, a fairly recent concept in Iceland, and still one of only a handful, seemed like a delightful place to work. I jokingly asked Einar whether he had any positions open. He led me to several vast plastic containers, each containing several thousand bottles of Jökull Bjór.

'The labelling machine broke down yesterday,' he said. 'All these bottles need labels glueing on by hand.'

Maybe not then. On the way out, Einar and Ragna had a couple more surprises for me. The first was a section box of bottled beers to take with me, which was exceedingly kind of them. The second, I wasn't sure how to take.

'You've been eating shark, haven't you?' said Ragna, in that direct, no-messing manner that many Icelanders have. I felt my face flush, and I started to feel embarrassed.

'Don't worry,' she said, 'you smell like a real Icelander now.' I smiled and decided to take that as a compliment. Although I did consider destroying all my clothes in a blazing fire.

I concluded that a walk in the fresh air around Stykkishólmur might help loosen the smells trapped in my clothing, and I was delighted with what I found. Stykkishólmur was perfectly sized; it had all the facilities – swimming pool, coffee shops, restaurants, funky-shaped church – but in the most idyllic setting. It seemed to have got the balance just right between a self-sufficient, bustling town and a quiet idyll between the sea and the mountains. The ferry to the West Fjords leaves from the small, heart-shaped harbour, and maybe that helps keep the balance in check – enough purpose and business to keep the town alive, to keep things interesting, but a location that stops the whole world from descending on it.

Standing at the edge of the harbour, looking out at the ocean and Súgandisey, an outcrop that protects the town and is topped with its own brightly coloured lighthouse, I realised that Stykkishólmur was a very special little place, and I vowed to return there some day. Heck, I might even live there in my old age.

Chapter 12

Sea Monsters of the West Fjords

Even as I boarded the ferry to the West Fjords, I couldn't shake a sense of anxiety, even dread. I wasn't sure where the feeling had come from, but as the ferry slowly loaded its cargo of cars, people and chattels from the quayside in Stykkishólmur, it worked its way to my stomach and burrowed in there. The sky and sea were competing to see which could reach a deeper shade of blue, and the summer sun was so warm that I removed my jacket, but in my head, things had already clouded over. This was compounded by the ferry announcing its departure with a frankly unnecessary blast of the foghorn, and an equally unwelcome blast of diesel fumes from its engines.

Slowly, we edged out of Stykkishólmur, leaving the pretty harbour in a trail of white foam on a thankfully tranquil blue sea. The blue sky was divided into segments by the pristine white rails and tall mast of the ferry. The harbour was busy with fishermen unloading their catches, and I couldn't help thinking that I should eat more fish. Maybe I'd have some for tea.

The ferry, for reasons unknown, takes two and a half hours – including one short stop – to cover the reasonably short distance between Snæfellsnes and the West Fjords. I haven't worked it out – I am fundamentally lazy – but I bet you could drive it quicker. This wasn't the point though, and I tried to sit back, relax and enjoy the stunning vistas that passed before me, but the strong black coffee seemed to be making me more anxious, if anything. Even a trio of flying puffins spotted through the window failed to cheer me up. I couldn't work out why this was. Was I worried by the West Fjords tales of isolation, wilderness and deafening silence? Was I afraid that the West Fjords might have been over-hyped and that I was set to be disappointed? My mind felt like the search mode on a car radio.

The only stop en route was the island of Flatey. As we chugged into the small harbour, I left the confines of the cafeteria to have a quick peek. The island looked tiny, albeit pleasant enough in the August sunshine. Sheets were blowing dry on washing lines, and the ever-present white Icelandic church looked particularly calm and peaceful. On the harbour side, though, there was a hubbub of activity. The arrival of the ferry was quite clearly the highlight of the day – I don't expect that there is much on TV there – and people were all milling around the quayside. The postman was handing out mail directly to a crowd of local residents, while an elderly chap in a grubby *lopapeysa* was, somewhat suspiciously, passing a full yellow Bónus bag to a passenger in such a furtive manner that it could only be 'a deal going down', as they say on the mean streets of Flatey.

I wasn't aware of it at the time, but Lay Low, real name Lovísa Elísabet Sigrúnardóttir, had discovered Flatey as being somewhere truly special. So special, she devoted an album of songs and a video to the little island in the middle of Breiðafjördur Bay.

Lay Low is a multi-instrumentalist, born in London to a Sri Lankan father and an Icelandic mother. Her website sums up her vocal talents as 'a rich chocolate sound with a sweet cinnamon rasp and a sip of whisky to take the edge off', which is a lovely description if you ask me. It's when she pairs her voice with a simply strummed acoustic guitar, though, that the magic really happens.

Under the 'Lay Low' moniker, Lovísa has released several albums, including the Americana-tinged *Please Don't Hate Me*; *Farewell Good Night's Sleep*; and *Brostinn Strengur* (Broken String). Iceland remains very much in Lovísa's thoughts. *Brostinn Strengur* used Icelandic poems for lyrics and was nominated for five Icelandic music awards.

When I caught up with her for a chat, I asked, 'How important is Iceland to your music?'

'It is very important. In Iceland I started playing music and in Iceland I get inspiration; in Iceland I have friends who play in my band, in Iceland I listen to a lot of great music, and in Iceland I grew up and live. So I would say it is very important.'

'And Flatey? Where did that come from?'

'It is a beautiful and very quiet island, and after a unanimous decision by me, the director and the producer, it was just meant to be.'

Lovísa isn't the only one to have been inspired by Flatey. Halldór Laxness was a fan, I'm told, and more recently, Baltasar Kormákur set his film *White Night Wedding* there. Baltasar has a history with the place; his father painted the unusual altarpiece in the island's church.

Perhaps I'd got it wrong them. I should have stepped

off that ferry. Judging by Lay Low's album of quiet, gentle songs, punctuated only by the rasps of stray cockerels, and her video of an island of simple and stark beauty, I should have. Maybe next time I'll stop by. Until then, I'll seek solace in Lay Low's beautiful records.

At Brjánslækur there was a queue of traffic waiting for us to disembark before they could board. There was nothing there other than the jetty, and the impression was one of escape, as if people were trying to flee some unseen disaster, albeit on a super-slow ferry.

Once on the open road, I headed west towards Breiðavík on the tip of the West Fjords (duck fans: on the beak). Nearby Látrabjarg was meant to be a birdwatcher's paradise. I do not approve of the word 'twitcher', which is far too sinister if you ask me. Látrabjarg is also allegedly the most westerly point in Europe.

Anyway, my mood was not at all lightened by the state of the roads, which were often little more than farm tracks (I had, in my brilliance, only a two-wheel drive with a hairdryer engine), and the downright depressing sights that greeted me between Brjánslækur and Breiðavík. The first of these was a rusting but complete shipwreck that had come ashore in 1981. Unusually, no one had done anything with it, other than erect a plaque stating that it was a shipwreck from 1981. I took a look around it, and it made me feel quite sad, this former soldier of the seas being left in the middle of nowhere to rust away. She stood proud on the beach but was slowly turning to a tatterdemalion; her paint all but gone, her deck rotten, and her hull starting to turn brittle in the salty, wet air. It was an arresting sight, but I could not help but think that it should be recovered from the pristine fjord and laid to rest somewhere else, somewhere where both the boat and the landscape would be shown respect.

Further along the ever-winding road there was a more intentional display at a small museum. Two doomed and now decrepit planes sat on the roadside, in what I am sure was a prized exhibit. They too were rusting and out of place in the northern wilderness.

As if to confirm my dark mood, I noticed a run-down and ramshackle roadside shack with boarded-up windows and a dilapidated roof. Metal farming tools lay rusting at its base. On one of the boarded windows, someone had scrawled in thick paint: 'Special Offer – 3 nights for the price of 2'. I chuckled to myself at the black humour.

Eventually I reached Breiðavík, which was nothing more than a series of farm buildings and accommodation – oh, and a church – just off the expansive and unusual yellow-sand beach. On booking in at the guest house, I was ushered to a room that had the thinnest, narrowest bed I had ever seen. Sleeping in a straight line would be the only option. I was also told that the 'menu' that night would comprise only one dish, and that was catfish. I couldn't think of a more unappealing fish, and after trying to reach Látrabjarg by car and failing (due to a lack of road surface and sense of direction), and then walking down to the beach to try and cheer myself up (this was unsuccessful), I went to bed feeling grumpy and hungry. I was all too aware that I couldn't even turn over without falling flat on the floor.

In the morning, things did not improve immediately. Someone had painted two beautiful murals of puffins on the gable wall of the guest house, as a kind of Icelandic homage to Banksy, but they turned out to be the only puffins I would see that day. I was told that the puffins had left Látrabjarg for the year. This was confirmed when I later saw a sign for puffins on the side of the road. Someone had written the word 'No' next to the picture and put a cross through it. Helpful, if nothing else. I still felt anxious and not completely at ease. I decided to forget about Látrabjarg and pointed the car towards Patreksfjörður.

The sun was shining, and I couldn't see a single cloud in the sky. Highly unusual for Iceland. I started to feel a little happier and even had a little sing to myself, in the style of Jónsi from Sigur Rós. The high jinks didn't last, however. At Patreksfjörður I went to the only petrol station, and found that it was not working. Or my card wasn't working. One or the other. I desperately needed fuel, but there was no one there to assist, just an unhelpful little machine. What had happened to all those petrol station attendants anyway? In a fit of rage, I drove off with the petrol cap wide open. Then I had to pull over to take a call from my bank in the UK, who informed me that my credit card had been used fraudulently in a petrol station in Patreksfjörður in Iceland. I closed my eyes and counted to ten. In Icelandic. So far, the West Fjords had not been kind to me. Breiðavík had felt like the end of the world last night, not the end of Europe; and now this. Ten was not enough, I thought, as I stomped out of the car to put the petrol cap back on. I felt like doing a Basil Fawlty and hitting the car with a small tree.

Not happy, I drove doggedly towards Bíldudalur. The town appeared to be closed for business, or even evacuated.

Not one of its 175 residents was to be seen. Nothing was moving, except for a lone oystercatcher wandering up and down the road. The wind was blowing in from Arnarfjörður, the fjord that surrounds the town on three sides, its grey-brown sides bearing down on the place and threatening to shove it into the cold sea.

Another slice of dark humour: someone had highlighted all the cracks and imperfections in the road with white paint, in preparation for repair works. With the town completely devoid of tarmac on both sides, surely this was a joke? Even the oystercatcher appeared bemused.

The reason for being in Bíldudalur was the Sea Monster Museum. This intriguing little exhibition concentrates on the sea monsters of Arnarfjörður and is based on locally garnered accounts and eyewitness testimonials of the strange, possibly mythical creatures that reside in the fjord. The museum could have been completely crass and the object of ridicule, but it has been created with so much enthusiasm that it more than pulls it off; it does a wonderful job of presenting information in an interesting and intriguing manner, even for a sceptic like me.

The exhibition started with tales of sea monsters found all over the globe. There was an unintentionally funny moment in one video when, over footage of the strange and decomposing form of a supposed sea monster being landed on a trawler, the commentator straightfacedly stated, 'The captain ordered it to be thrown overboard due to the stench.'

The main room of the museum concentrated on Icelandic sea monsters, of course. As you will already be aware, the top four sea monsters in Iceland are as follows:

The *hafmaður*, or seaman (insert your own joke here). The *faxaskrímsli*, which is pretty much an ugly, oversized sea horse formerly known as the 'red comb'; it is covered in mussels (and presumably muscles) and I was told at the museum poses a 'real threat' – I doubt that somehow. Then there's the *fjörulalli*, or shore laddie, a Scottish-sounding wee beastie which looks like a sheep that's fallen in the drink; either that or a fat, woolly seal. Although *fjörulalli* are vegetarian, they allegedly and somewhat bizarrely have a perverted penchant for pregnant ladies. Finally there is *skeljaskrímsli* – the shell monster; dinosaur-like in form but hippopotamus-sized, this chap is not that different to the stereotypical view of the Loch Ness monster, if you ask me.

These four were the stars of the show and featured in several of the exhibits; there were also descriptions of them by people who had allegedly seen them. There was something about these real, decent people's accounts of sightings that made me think there might just be something in it. Hearing a no-nonsense farmer from the harsh environment of the West Fjords recount what he had seen – a shore laddie, whatever – had a much greater impact on me than it would have if I'd got the story from an actor or a madman.

One such story was that of Guðlaugur Egilsson, a sheep farmer who lived on the edge of Arnarfjörður at Litlu-Eyri. One day, Guðlaugur saw a shore laddie. It had a thick cloak of seaweed and shells and short stubby legs. It rattled as it lumbered along. Guðlaugur says it had the eyes and mouth of a sheep, but a tail that was a metre long. The shore laddie had the audacity to try and push our hero into the sea, but in the blink of an eye, Guðlaugur jumped over the diminutive beast and ran for home. The shore laddie was thought to have made its way back to the sea. It's not confirmed, but I bet Guðlaugur went for a stiff drink and a lie down.

A less fruitful story was that of Valdimar Ottósson, who rigged up a system to try and capture a sea monster on film at Krosseyri, a place noted for its sea monster activity; however, the first thing he captured was not a sea monster but a neighbouring farmer who had taken a shine to his equipment.

Other exhibits in the museum included a model of a deformed calf born in Otradalur in the 1930s. It had two heads and four legs, and I quote: 'a sea monster is believed to have had its way with the calf's mother'. I had to stifle a chuckle at the language used there. There was also a model of a 'little seahorse' found at Arnarfjörður in 1827. This 'baby sea monster' had flippers at the front but appeared equine at the rear, complete with hooves. I have to say that I though it rather cute, and saw no reason why it had been placed behind toughened safety glass, unless to stop visitors taking him home.

On the way out, I asked the delightful lady at the counter if she believed in sea monsters. She replied, 'I wouldn't say that I didn't believe in them.' That might be a double negative, but I knew what she meant – given the number of sightings and accounts, it was hard to dismiss their existence entirely. I wouldn't mind the baby one being around anyway. It was properly cute.

Beyond Bíldudalur, the rough mountain tracks that passed for roads around there ground across desert-like terrain, through rough rock slides and detoured around lengthy fjords. At the blind head of one mountain route, I came across two rams standing stock still at either side of the road, facing the oncoming traffic. One had two horns. The other had three, one of which twisted and spiralled out of control. Both looked decidedly evil as I passed them, as if I had crossed into their territory. They didn't even move as I drove by, other than to blink their eyelids over their mad, bulging eyes. If I get sent to hell, that pair will be at the gates, I'm sure of it.

Not far from Bíldudalur, I came across a natural hot pot and pool at Reykjafjarðarlaug. It had a man-made pool at the roadside end of it, built in 1975, but this looked less than inviting, on account of the murky sediment that had built up on its blue concrete bottom. Much more inviting was the natural hot pot just up the hill. Located at the end of a geothermal stream, it was encircled by lustrous green undergrowth and pale, weather-bleached wooden planks, on which you could sit and dangle your feet. The stream had long been dammed at one end, which created this magical pool.

Steam swirled invitingly from it, like a cup of coffee on a cold winter's morning. It was complete wilderness there – the only building in sight was a wooden structure which I presumed was the changing facility. I would be able to sit in the pool for hours, just unwinding and looking at the fjord vista in front of me. I was reaching for my shorts and a towel – I couldn't bloody wait to be honest – when I heard a shout. I turned back towards the pool and noticed that there was a French couple in the hot pot. Well, he was half in/half out of the pool – and he was inordinately hairy. She was dipping a single toe in and was wearing a revealing bathing suit. For the sake of my mother, who is bound to read this book, I should tell you that I didn't know where to look. 'The water is too hot,' the bloke said, by which point my eyes had refocused on him. His head was sweating. His whole head. His body, visible beneath the hair, was turning not so much red but purple. I told him he was brave – this went straight to his Gallic head, coming from an Englishman – and thought that actually he might just be stupid. I dipped in a tentative finger – it was absolutely boiling – and came to the conclusion that he was stupid, and that she was clearly wasting her time with him. It was a shame though, I was really looking forward to a dip, and as natural hot pots go, Reykjafjarðarlaug was a cracker.

On again. I stopped off at Dynjandi, a waterfall, or rather a family of waterfalls known as the 'Thundering One'. I can confirm that they do indeed live up to their name, and although they lacked the immediacy and power of, say, Dettifoss, they were impressive, especially big daddy waterfall at the top, which fell in a white foaming triangle of water of the sort that would usually be seen in a fairy-tale book.

My next stop was Flateyri, a small fishing village located in the north-western fjords. It has a population of 350, and on first glance it didn't seem to have a whole lot going on either. But that's not why I'd come. Perhaps it was morbid, perhaps it was respectful, but I'd come to visit Flateyri because of the events of 26th October 1993, when twenty-nine houses were crushed and twenty local people lost their lives to an avalanche in the town. I remember reading about this tragic incident in a newspaper when I was at school, and it had come back to me again recently when I saw the 2003 film *Nói Albinói* (not actually based on Flateyri, but on an avalanche disaster in an unnamed Icelandic village; there's also an unrequited love story and an albino teenager).

There was a respectful stone memorial to the victims in front of the church, on which I was saddened to read that one of the victims was one-year-old Rebekka Haraldsdóttir. The biggest single reminder of the tragedy though was the omnipresent avalanche defences that now cast their own shadow over the town. Built in a V-formation on the fierce slopes above Flateyri, they're designed to angle any avalanches away from the town and into the sea. A constant reminder of the forces of nature, I would have thought. As I left Flateyri, I was pleased to see that the residents hadn't completely lost themselves in the melancholy that could so easily envelop the place; someone had made a miniature harbour next to the avalanche defences, complete with six detailed miniature boats tethered to six miniature brightly coloured buoys. I liked it a lot.

I spent the night in the so-called capital of the West Fjords, Ísafjörður. After foolishly going to the wrong guest house, I had a wander around the town, which seemed to have all the major services but little in the way of character or soul. It rests on a spit of land that edges out into a fjord, and is accessible by one of three road tunnels, and by air or sea. And it's cold. It was August, but I still felt cold – this was the furthest north I'd been for a while. Nonetheless,

I was surprised to see that even the spindly trees in the town centre had had woollen scarves tied around their trunks. This turned out to be part of a movement that is increasing in popularity around the globe but was relatively new to me. Yarn bombing – also known as yarn storming, guerrilla knitting and graffiti knitting. And that's pretty much what it is: the graffiti of public places, using nothing more offensive than colourful wool.

Things have really started to kick off – should that be cast off? – in the yarn-bombing world: see the *New York Times* coverage, its own International Yarn-Bombing Day (June 1st, if you are interested), and even how-to-manuals, and it's caught on in Iceland too. Icelanders are avid knitters anyway, and you'll often see girls and women clicking away, on buses, supermarkets and cafés. I think it's really nice. You could argue that the knitting of the world-record-bothering longest scarf in Reykjavík is too mainstream to be counted as yarn bombing, but the wool-covered bike in Laugavegur, Reykjavík is a prime example (and not the mental health issue I once thought it was). My other favourite example in Iceland is the knitted breasts that got attached to street lights in the capital in order to raise awareness about breast cancer. I'm not even joking.

I like this whole yarn-bombing thing. It's never offensive, unlike its spray-paint precursor. I think there should be more of it; it is a delightful show of warmth and humour. It was certainly put to good use in Ísafjörður, where the town centre trees were protected from the biting wind by beautifully knitted multi-coloured woollen scarves.

It still felt like I was getting the cold shoulder from the

town though. The streets were empty, and the shops either closed or closing. The buildings were mainly 1960s blocks of austere concrete, and everything felt, at best, unwelcoming. Perhaps the town's isolated location exacerbates this (one of those road tunnels is 9000 metres long, by the way, and took four years to build), but I couldn't imagine what it would be like in the depths of winter, when the steep fjords prevent even the few hours of sunlight from penetrating the town. In January, Ísafjörður residents celebrate the return of the sunlight with 'sun coffee' (sólarkaffi) and pancakes. I think I'd need something stronger. Like amphetamines.

The town does have its own music festival, though – the proudly named 'I Never Went South' (Aldrei fór ég suður) festival – and it's also the home of the European Championships of Swamp Soccer. You can see the pitches, or swamps, as you enter the town. But as neither were happening during my time there, I was a bit snookered.

I found a fantastic little handiwork shop though, the sort that sells local crafts and produce. I was rather taken by a woollen article that took me a while to figure out, but once I did, it appealed to my inner romantic. The heart-shaped pocket of striped Icelandic knit, already warm to the touch, had two sleeves at the top and was actually a couple's glove, allowing couples to hold hands while walking along on the coldest, crispest days. I couldn't help but buy one. I was pretty sure it would pay for itself one day, if you know what I mean.

In the absence of someone to share my glove with, it threatened to be a pretty slow night in Ísafjörður, but I had a scrap of paper in my shirt pocket that might just change that. On it was just one word, scrawled in spindly, blue biro: 'Tjöruhúsið'. This was allegedly the best place for fish in the West Fjords and seeing as I had time to kill and a dangerous case of borborygmi, I decided to hunt it out.

I was directed out of the town centre towards the West Fjord Heritage Museum – which I later found was full of nothing but fishing tools and, bizarrely, accordions, and seemed to have situated itself on a fish processing/industrial site on the very outskirts of town. I checked the piece of paper. It didn't help, on account of there being no name on the outside of the wooden building. I thought that this was the place though. It was part of the museum complex, which consisted of three long wooden buildings. In fact, it looked like a long wooden shed, and even the door appeared to have been secured by a plank and nails rather than more conventional means. There was no one outside, but I heard laughter coming from inside. I opened the door, minding not to snag myself on the nails, but instead banged my head in a comedic yet painful way, and went in.

Inside, the lighting was low but warm and I could make out three long tables running the length of the room. Everything was made out of wood, and the floor creaked as I stepped forwards. A waiter, or at least I assumed he was a waiter, gave me the briefest of instructions by way of a welcome – 'Fish buffet, sit where you like, soup for starters' – before disappearing again. I barely heard him anyway over the sound of plates being scraped clean, laughter in different languages, corks being popped and glasses filled. Life, at last.

I did as I was told and grabbed a seat next to the door, then tried to work out exactly what the system was.

It seemed like a bit of a free for all, with a crowd gathering around a table at the far end of the room and then returning with full plates. I decided that I should do the same and headed for the steaming cauldron of soup.

'What sort of a soup is it?' I asked a nearby waitress.

In a snap, without malice or amusement, she replied, 'Fish.'

Of course. Silly me. I had some – it was delicious – but I was careful not to overfill on bread; I wanted to leave room for the fish. I'm glad that I did: Greenlandic halibut, monkfish, plaice, cod, our old friend the catfish, trout and lobster were all here. I'm told that the menu changes on a daily basis, dependant as it is on the catches hauled into the nearby harbour that day. The fish are prepared on site by the chef, in the smallest, most basic of kitchens, and served in the very pots and dishes that they were cooked in. The results, though, are simply divine.

I went for the halibut and the plaice with creamy mashed potato and a mixed salad. The halibut had been cooked in a rich tomato and herb sauce, and was amazing. The plaice was simply pan-fried but was also delicious. I quickly finished my plate before heading up to the table for some more. Halibut and plaice. Creamy mash. Salad. Creamy mash. Plaice. Halibut. Creamy mash. Halibut. I could have tried everything; should have tried everything, but it was too good to experiment with. Halibut.

I think I found a very special place there. It was certainly the best fish I'd had in a long time, if not ever. The ingredients were fresh, local and cooked to perfection, but also the atmosphere – after those evil sheep, ghost towns, pitted roads and rusting shipwrecks – was a lively gulp of fresh air. The restaurant might just be the beating heart of the West Fjords. Its friendly, warm ambience made me smile. I felt rejuvenated. Ready to tackle the West Fjords head on. Ready to start my travels again. I probably should have gone easier on the beer.

Ester Rut Unnsteinsdóttir is the director at the Arctic Fox Centre in Súðavík. She had a dilemma. A local farmer had shot and killed a pair of Arctic foxes. A Bambi-esque scenario ensued: unfortunately they were the parents of two small, no tiny, cubs. The farmer, all heart, brought the cubs to the centre and asked if Ester would become their adoptive mother. The other option? They too would be killed. Ester was in a spin; taking on the cubs would be against the centre's environmental and ecological policies and yet seeing the cubs go to their deaths would be too much for her to bear. She took the cubs in, on the strict proviso that once big enough, they would be released into the wild.

Ester told me all this while serving me the most delicious homemade waffles, rhubarb jam and whipped cream. 'One was big and the other small,' she said, 'so we called them "More" and "Less".' Ester is a very engaging person, full of stories, and she clearly takes a lot of pleasure in showing visitors around her interesting little centre dedicated to the Arctic fox. 'It's the only one in the world,' she said proudly, before pointing to a framed letter on the wall in which none other than David Attenborough apologises for not being able to attend the opening ceremony in 2007. I was impressed. Not as much as I was with the waffles though, but Ester doesn't need to know that.

The Arctic, white, polar or snow fox, depending on who you ask, is Iceland's only native land mammal and resides worldwide at this northern latitude. It is a clever little critter and has adapted well to the freezing temperatures and ever-changing diet. Unlike its red woodland cousin, the Arctic fox has developed thick, luxurious fur, special heat-exchange paws and some good old fat on his bones to keep him warm in temperatures of down to minus 58 degrees Celsius. He has an excellent sense of smell. He has furry paws to allow ice-walking, and he changes the colour of his coat to match the seasons, turning either a pristine white or a rarer blue-white in the snowy winter. He also has a bushy tail for warmth and, no doubt, showing off with.

The Arctic fox will eat pretty much anything: fish, carrion, and eggs are all on the menu. In difficult times he will even scavenge other animals' faeces. You've gone right off him now, haven't you? Fantastic Mr. Fox has some other less repulsive tricks though. He gathers and hides food during good, bountiful times and will come back for it during leaner days. He can tunnel into the snow to catch prey or to make a wind-free shelter to snooze in. That's pretty neat, and makes up for his dark secret. We all have faults, don't we?

Iceland's Arctic fox population has increased significantly over the last few decades and is now estimated to be approximately 10,000. There is some concern about this, no doubt fuelled by ornithologists holding up the remains of birds taken by Arctic foxes as exhibit A, and sheep farmers reporting lambs being snatched from their fields. The flipside is that they have increased in number, but so have the colonies of birds and the clever foxes are just taking advantage of this. Apparently, Iceland is a world-beating-sized nesting site for the great skua, and the Arctic foxes like nothing more than skua for breakfast, dinner and tea. I would have loved to have seen more of these wily critters, but then they are wily for a reason, I suppose. They certainly don't hang around for photo opportunities.

Ester told me and the other guests the story of how she and others had rebuilt the centre using mainly original materials – it looked like hard graft – and mentioned that she was preparing for a blueberry festival that weekend. On cue, her husband walked in with a teetering stack of plastic tubs, taller than Ester herself, each tub full to the brim with blueberries. The blueberry festival was to include acoustic music, picking the berries, a sponsored run and all manner of blueberry-themed goods baked by Ester herself. After the waffles, I was sorely tempted to stay on for it.

One of Ester's particular concerns was the plight of Arctic foxes in the area. There is a higher than usual density of foxes in Súðavík, and due to the presence of the road between the coast, which is where foxes search for food, and the mountains, where they live, there are a number of fatal fox vs. car collisions every year. Ester had designed a road sign depicting a silhouetted fox on a yellow background. She sells the design on T-shirts, aprons, stickers and so forth but was also lobbying for the signs to be put up around fox habitats across Iceland. I thought it was an excellent idea and felt compelled to at least buy a T-shirt from her to help the cause.

I went outside to have a look at More and Less. They were adorable bundles of fluff, quick and dainty on their feet, with darting eyes and sharp little noses. They had thick, dense fur and dashed about their surroundings like a pair of overgrown chinchillas. Ester had made a good decision. I was smitten with the pair and spent close to an hour watching them and taking photographs. Then I had an idea and returned inside to ask Ester about it. Would she mind if I went into their enclosure to take some closer photographs? I used this book as an excuse. I was expecting her to refuse – on the grounds of the foxes becoming too used to human contact, scent contamination, or health and safety – but I asked anyway.

'No,' she replied.

'Why not?'

'They have been shitting everywhere.'

'OK.' Fair enough.

As I left, Ester and her husband were still making preparations for the blueberry festival. He was running the Icelandic flag up the pole while she explained to me where to find the very best, plumpest blueberries. 'You need a slight slope,' she said, 'where the snow would stay the longest in winter.' Just out of town, I pulled over at a likely location, just as Ester had described, but next to a crystal-clear stream. I got out of the car, jumped the stream and found blueberries growing all around my feet. It was clearly 'Pick Your Own' time in blueberry country. I bent down and ate mouthful after mouthful of the plump, juicy, tasty berries. They were scrumptious. After a few minutes of this decidedly piggish behaviour, I was reminded of something else Ester had told me. She said that at that time of year, the local ravens gorge themselves on blueberries so much that they leave bright blue streaks of guano all over the town. I hoped the same wouldn't happen to me and got back into the car.

Once back in the UK, I was told that blueberries don't actually grow in Iceland. What I had seen and podged on were blue berries that were actually bilberries or bog bilberries. Somehow, 'bog bilberry festival' didn't sound half as appealing. The rhubarb in Ester's jam, though, was indeed UK-style rhubarb. Rhubarb is very popular in Iceland. It's one of the only fruits to grow that far north and has found its way into a good few Icelandic recipes. Ester's rhubarb jam was hard to beat, and reminded me of childhood rhubarb crumbles after Sunday lunches.

Being constantly on the lookout now for both Arctic foxes and a menagerie of sea monsters made the drive to Djúpavík long and slow. This was not helped by some seriously winding and treacherous roads around a series of ever-lengthening fjords, and – get this – at least forty kilometres of the journey was on a perilous single-lane dirt/dust track. The trip was not wasted though. Not only did I have several pounds of weight shaken from my body, I also enjoyed some of the most spectacular views in the West Fjords and indeed Iceland. A crisp blue sky was met by dramatic green mountains still dotted with last year's snow and striped with cascading waterfalls. Drangajökull, the West Fjords' only glacier (and the only one in Iceland not currently retreating, glacier fans!), peeped out from behind the peaks it has yet to crack, tongues of blue, white and grey appearing on the hazy horizon.

At one point, between two barren patches of Arctic desert on a high plateau, I caught sight of something moving from the corner of my left eye. As I turned to face it, I couldn't believe my eyes or my luck. It was a white-tailed eagle. These are immense birds; in fact they are the biggest bird of prey in Iceland. The have a wingspan of up to 2.5 metres and have been protected in Iceland since the 1930s, after having been ruthlessly hunted to near extinction. I'm told that they have made a successful return, both here and across Europe. One was recently sighted over an Asda supermarket in the UK, and petrified shoppers dived for cover. This one had a massive span of dark chocolate-brown wings, a sharply pointed head tipped with a yellow, mean beak. He had defined, evil talons that could clearly rip a hole in any mammal or fish. The giveaway, though, was the eponymous punk-rock white tail. The wings swooshed up and down in fluid motion as he effortlessly soared into the blue sky. It was a stunning vision; an awesome – in the true sense, not the overused American frat boy sense – bird of prey. I realised I had unconsciously been holding my breath, and slowly exhaled.

I stopped briefly in Hólmavík, and wished that I hadn't. The reason: the worst ever museum I've been to. It was called the Museum of Sorcery and Witchcraft, but may as well have been called the Museum of Tosh and Hogwash. It was full of plastic ravens, rubber 'necro pants' (don't ask!) and fake broomsticks. There was a glass case supposedly containing an invisible boy. That's right, it was empty. I felt cheated and disappointed by the place. So much so, I considered writing to the Minister for Culture and Tourism back in Reykjavík to complain. But at least I managed to stretch my legs and refuel both the car and myself.

The tarmac also ended there. The road to Djúpavík was nothing but a track. A sign suggested I pull over and put chains on my tyres. I didn't have any chains, and when I checked earlier, unlike the picture on the sign, my tyres had small floral patterns on them.

The 'track' snaked around so many mountains and fjords that I became completely disorientated. Perhaps more worrying was that some of the track was on cliff edges without any form of barrier. I drove with teeth clenched and knuckles white. Ominously, the sun had disappeared and a ferocious wind had started, buffeting the car in a most unsettling manner. They were not my exact words at the time, you'll understand.

Even the road signs had a symbol that I'd not seen before – a house with a cross through it. As in 'No One Lives Here Any More'. My phone signal had died completely by this point – very unusual for Iceland – and I found myself imagining the start of a horror movie. I mean, it would take forever for them to find my broken, dismembered body, wouldn't it?

The landscape changed again. The cliffs began alternating with bays full of white driftwood skeletons that would have taken four or five years to arrive from far-flung places such as Siberia. The twisted piles of bleached wood loomed in and out of the cloud and fog as I drove slowly past. Just around this next corner, I thought to myself, but it never quite was. Maybe the Museum of Sorcery and Codswallop had affected me more than I thought.

Djúpavík lies on the east coast of the West Fjords in the region of Strandir. It has several houses, an eponymous hotel and the remnants of a herring factory. In fact, it could be said that Djúpavík was once the herring fishing capital of Iceland. It has gone through a turbulent pattern of boom and bust, mainly due to the fishing and subsequent overfishing of the species that it relied so heavily upon.

I don't have any interest in herring – no, really – so my motivation for travelling to Djúpavík was different from most. Sigur Rós played there on the same 2006 tour of Iceland that I saw. Their movie, *Heima*, includes some of the most spectacular concert footage I have ever seen, and it was filmed in Djúpavík, a little, remote, isolated village on the edge of the edge of nowhere.

Slowly, Djúpavík revealed itself out of the gloom and murk. There were several large white buildings, a clutch of red roofed houses, three cylindrical grey fish storage tanks, a large (possibly unstable) concrete tower and the rusted hull of a beached and broken trawler. Am I selling it to you?

If I'm honest, even my heart dropped. It seemed so completely desolate, so utterly isolated, so hopelessly damned. I pulled up in front of the hotel and fought hard with myself not just to release the handbrake, pull a three-pointer and leave again.

The hotel used to be the accommodation for the female factory workers and it sits in the centre of the 'village', if that's the correct nomenclature. The village itself sits at the end of a long, spindly fjord, Reykjarfjörður, which seems to channel the wind straight into the face of the hotel. Above Djúpavík loom towering, behemoth mountains, from which a waterfall noisily cascades, providing the place with a never-ending soundtrack of whistling wind and crashing water. There were three boats in the harbour, not including the wreck, and someone had hung a line of fish out to dry across one end of the harbour. A broken and dilapidated pier end stood out at sea, now used by only gulls. They clearly liked their rotting perch, and gathered there in squawking numbers.

I went inside, heaving my bag behind me. My thoughts were focused on getting some food, and maybe even a beer, before going to bed, getting some sleep and then an early start and escape in the morning. What actually occurred was far, far better. I'm pleased for your sake as well as mine.

I was welcomed like a long-lost friend by Claus (it was his eighth summer working there; no obvious signs of mental health issues) and one of the owners, Eva, plus the hotel's resident dog, Freyja. Even more welcoming was the meal of local pan-fried cod, with rice and salad, a huge slice of orange cheesecake and – as previously hoped for – a very fine and cold Icelandic beer. It was not restaurant cooking, by any means, but very, very good home cooking. And there is nothing wrong with that.

There were only two other guests in the hotel, but that didn't really matter. I was made to feel 'at home' not just by Claus and Eva, but by the surroundings and furnishings. The shared bathrooms, the creaking floorboards upstairs, having to remove your shoes once inside, and the cat statue on the shelf above my bed.

Claus was a revelation. A German by nationality, he had made the move to Iceland and now spent his winters working as a postman in the city, his summers up in Djúpavík and any other time he had indulging himself in his passion for photography. He even had an exhibition of his work there in Djúpavík, in one of the disused factory buildings, which he was keen to show off.

Freyja and I snooped around the old buildings, trying to get a sense of what it might have been like here during the boom years. The wind howled, whipping up both the sea and Freyja's hair. The factory buildings were in various states of disrepair. Some had tarpaulins rigged up to protect the items underneath; others were more complete and still had 'Djúpavík' stamps on the walls. The fish storage tanks were huge, and my voice echoed around their vastness. I could see why Sigur Rós chose to perform in one of them; they were quite extraordinary spaces. Accessible only through tiny portholes, they had a single support in the middle, and circular, concentric rings of pipes on the floor. One was completely intact; the others had let in some water. Freyja looked vaguely alarmed at my intense interest in the buildings; either that or the wind was starting to bother her.

Claus told me that Eva and her husband Ásbjörn had been there for twenty-five years and had been restoring the factory buildings. I dread to think what they were like before then. I applauded their efforts, but seeing the size of the challenge, the work done and the work still to do, I hoped that it wasn't all just a folly.

Later on, Eva was keen to tell me about living in Djúpavík and the challenge of getting hold of essentials for the hotel, especially during the harsh, cold winters. Gjögur Airport is nearby, in an abandoned village – international airport code GRJ, if you'd like to book a flight – but there are only flights there twice a week, and that's weather and paying passengers permitting. A supply truck supposedly turns up weekly, but this too is infrequent and unreliable. Eva had started to phone guests a few days ahead of their stay and request the items she needed in return for a discount. I really like the idea of prospective guests checking in with a box of tomatoes and some bleach.

Eva also told me all about Sigur Rós playing there in 2006. She said that there were about 200 people there, and that it was a magical experience. Later, I got to see the band's entry in the guestbook. With a blush and a smile, Eva told me that there is a photograph of her and the band ('a lovely bunch of boys') in the *Heima* DVD booklet. I've checked. There is too.

I received a text message from Einar, just before I went to bed, on the single bar of connectivity that my mobile phone had traced. 'Might be a chance of Northern Lights tonight,' it read. I looked out of my bedroom window. The wind was spattering rain spots onto the glass with force, from heavy, laden clouds. I could just about make out the hire car, parked a few metres away, and I could hear the sea being ragged around. Not a chance, Einar. No way. I pulled the curtains closed and crawled into my cosy bed.

Just before I left the next day, Claus told me about a snooping writer that had come to 'review' the hotel a few weeks earlier. He had been found interviewing guests, making notes and poking around in private residential parts of the hotel. Claus was so offended by his behaviour that he threatened to throw the writer out. At this point in the story, Claus became agitated and red faced and he strained and stumbled over his words.

'I just wanted him to know that you can't quantify Djúpavík with checklists and scores. There is so much more here than that. It's a special place.'

I agree, Claus. It's a wonderfully special place. Utterly beautiful, completely different and consistently beguiling. The same could be said of the West Fjords as a whole. The stunning vistas, its 'special' kind of quiet, the flora and fauna, and the warmth and kindness of the people that live there. I'd come back, I thought to myself. I'd come back tomorrow. I was smitten with the place.

I didn't tell Claus that I was also a writer. I hurriedly paid my bill and dashed to the car.

Chapter 13

Blink and Save

'Bloody awesome,' Davina exclaimed in her high-pitched, hoarse whine.

'It's bloody awesome, isn't it?' she asked again, before I bobbed away from her, took a deep breath and submerged myself once more in the pristine, peaceful environment. I had to agree, it was 'bloody awesome', but somehow shouting this at the top of one's voice seemed disrespectful. I swam down and away from her, although I was tempted to 'Shush!' at her with a finger against my lips as if we were in a church or a library. I pulled myself gracefully into the perfectly blue underworld.

Perhaps not unsurprisingly, I had chosen to spend my thirtieth birthday in Iceland. More specifically, I had chosen to spend it diving in the depths of Silfra, part of Þingvallavatn, near the site of the ancient parliament. Silfra is a narrow, submerged channel between the European and American tectonic plates. It runs to several tens of metres deep and is widening by an estimated 2 centimetres a year. It is said to be one of the world's top dive sites. Not because of multi-coloured Disney-esque fish or strange coral formations, but because of the clarity of the water.

First, though, I met Davina, a twenty-five-year-old from Australia. She was 'backpacking' around Europe, from her base in London, and had clearly travelled to Iceland to 'tick some things off her list'. She was loud, brash and not at all the sort of person that I would choose to spend any time with. I was not given the choice. She was my dive partner for the day, and together we would dive. Which film had the tagline 'In space, no one can hear you scream'? Well, the same applies underwater, I found.

We were kitted out with dry suits, which go over regular clothes and are designed to keep water out and warmth in, as opposed to wet suits, which keep a thin layer of water next to your skin, which gradually warms. I was thoroughly grateful for this technology as there was a layer of frost on the ground and the glacial water remains at a steady 0 degrees Celsius. The gloves, though, were wet-suit neoprene, so I could feel exactly how cold the water was. And it was cold. So cold, in fact, that as I entered the water I involuntarily gasped, as my hands and face went numb.

Perhaps not so gracefully, considering my relative inexperience, load of diving kit and the multi-coloured nature of my garb, I launched myself into the water. Any physical discomfort – the mind-numbing cold, the claustrophobia from wearing a rubber suit with all the air removed – were quickly forgotten.

The water down there was unbelievably clear and clean. There wasn't a bit of murk or taint to it. The bottom of the chasm could be seen as clearly as the water next to my mask. The bubbles caused by my breathing and movements hurtled past me like meteorites in reverse. The further you looked out into the channel, the more intense the blue colour became. It was less like swimming, more like flying in the sky of a perfect summer's day. The sort of summer's day you used to have as a child, when it was OK to play outside in your shorts and not get home to your mum before 9pm, arriving filthy kneed.

There was nothing filthy down there; the water was clearer than any I'd seen before, having been exhaustively filtered as it trickled thorough lava fields on its way from its source within nearby Langjökull. You wouldn't think water could get to a new level of cleanliness, would you? It can. I've seen and tasted it. I've dived through it.

At one point, the channel opened up into a deep, wide chasm. It was as if someone had suddenly switched on widescreen and high definition at the same time. I'm told that this is nicknamed 'the Cathedral', and I could see why. I will never forget the feeling of being completely enveloped by that pristine, perfect place of natural wonder. I kept blinking, as if to store the incredible images to my internal hard drive forever. Blink. Save. Blink. Save.

We swam on, Davina and I. Geometrically perfect half-metre rocks had fallen to the bottom of the channel here and there, and between them pooled water that appeared even more blue than the blue water that surrounded them. The channel expanded and contracted, creating shallows where my knees brushed the rocks, and then deep chasms. It was a study in blue. It was a paint colour chart. It was a perfect slice of unparalleled beauty, the best that nature has to offer. Maybe that's what was taking my breath away, not the cold.

I felt completely at ease. I'm not religious, so I'm not going to pontificate about this being a new start, a rebirth, or anything like that, but it felt good. It felt especially good to be doing this on my birthday, my thirtieth birthday.

It seemed to be washing all my anxieties away. Instead of feeling stressed about what life might throw at me, I was OK. Instead of feeling concerned about whether I'd achieved enough in my life so far... oh, look at those beautiful bubbles. It felt, if this isn't too much, magical. The bubbles shot off towards the surface, streaking the deep blue vista with spherical comets of silver.

There is only one musician in Iceland who could soundtrack such beauty. Ólafur Arnalds. Ólafur produces a strain of music that is unique and original. It mixes neo-classical with electronica and ambient. It's inimitable and intriguing. If I were to produce a film of my underwater voyage in Silfra, Ólafur Arnalds would be the man to score it.

Ólafur has made numerous albums, including *Found Songs* and *Living Room Songs*, which were released track by track over his own social media. He has toured with Sigur Rós, worked with Amiina, Jóhann Jóhannsson and even dance genius Aphex Twin. All that, and he was only born in 1987.

I saw Ólafur play an extraordinary set at Airwaves in 2012, at Kex, a hostel and intimate music venue in Reykjavík. I sat on the floor like a school child as Ólafur, accompanied by violin and cello, performed his beautiful compositions, fusing classical and gentle electronic beats, while the sun shined on a snowy Esja across the bay. It was achingly, achingly exquisite. The audience listened to Ólafur work his magic in hushed awe.

Just before the concert, I had met Ólafur for a chat at the Bankastræti branch of Kaffitár, a well-known chain of Reykjavík coffee shops. He is quietly spoken and his answers were gentle but often accompanied by a laugh.

He considered his replies carefully, between sips of coffee, and reminded me that he had to collect a member of his band from the airport in a short while.

I started, to groans from Ólafur, with the usual question: Iceland and your music, is there a connection there?

'My usual answer?' he said. 'It's important where you come from, because that makes you who you are, but I don't think it has any more effect than living anywhere else, it just has a different, unique effect, because this is a unique place. It's very important, but I don't like to overplay it.'

I agree. Iceland is unique. Perhaps what Ólafur fails to see is just how much Iceland does affect his music, and that of his contemporaries. To me, the music from Iceland could not have come from anywhere else. It's more than just 'inspired by' – that throwaway line from cheap film soundtracks. Iceland weaves through his music like a glacial stream meanders through the cracked lava landscape.

'Do you enjoy playing in Iceland?'

'Yes, but I don't do a lot of it though. I get very nervous here, because I can feel my friends judging me. Outside of Iceland I don't really know the people. If my mum is watching, it can be a problem.'

I asked if there were any plans for more projects like *Living Room Songs*. I told him that during 2011 when he was releasing *Living Room Songs* track by track it used to be the highlight of my day to go home and see which song he had uploaded.

'There will definitely be more of those, I love doing those. I'll continue that series. *Found Songs*, *Living Room Songs* and then *Something Songs*. I have some ideas. I would really love to travel around Iceland for a week, recording a song in each town, using local musicians. So maybe in Akureyri we could use the Northern Symphony, and then in wherever Mugison is from, get him to play.'

I hurriedly made an offer to carry his bags, to which, again, he just laughed. I decided to buy him another coffee. After all, I needed to stay in his good books. A tour of Iceland with Ólafur Arnalds would be a dream come true.

Back in Silfra, Davina and I floated into a wide, shallow lagoon. Our experience had come to an end. I resisted the urge to swim back the way I'd come, like a psychotic salmon, and instead clambered out onto the cold lava ground. We schlepped back to the van, squelching water out of our gloves as we went. I had had the most fantastic start to my birthday, and I don't mean the buffet breakfast.

On the way back to Reykjavík, Davina bored me rigid with her tales of travel to places I had no interest in. She yapped on, without even waiting for answers. I don't mean to sound unkind or rude, but I really didn't want to hear her travel plans for Prague, or how she hoped her ex would transport her around London. I consoled myself by wiping the condensation from the window and watching the Icelandic countryside race by.

I'm not saying I'm any better than Davina, don't get me wrong. I don't class myself as anything other than a frequent visitor to Iceland. Yes, I've fallen in love with the place. I've seen plenty of it, and I still have plenty more to see. The interior remains to be explored, Einar promises to show me the secrets of the fjords in the east, and I have a vague plan about catching a series of boats from the UK to Iceland. There is a whole language to be learnt, and I haven't seen an elf. To the Icelanders I'm still an *útlendingur* – a foreigner – and probably always will be. The difference between me and Davina? I've spent time trying to get to know the people and places of Iceland; to experience more than just what is available to the average tourist on a weekend trip. This might seem an ironic thing to say on a trip such as the one to Silfra, but I mean it. The best times in Iceland arrive unexpectedly, not on pre-booked tours. I hope I have shown that to be the case.

Who would want to go to Prague anyway, I thought, as the Icelandic weather lived up to its reputation, lowered a cloud and emitted a steady stream of drizzle. Nothing could dampen my spirits though: I was in Iceland. And I had a reservation at one of Reykjavík's best restaurants.

Dill is based in the Nordic House. It is a very special restaurant; the sort of place reserved for celebrations of some magnitude. A thirtieth birthday fits the bill nicely, and I chose to not look at the prices on the menu. Today was not about expense. Today was my thirtieth birthday, and I was going to mark it in style.

Nichola and I were the first to arrive. With coats safely stored away, we were shown to our table with the hushed tones usually reserved for cathedrals and libraries (and deep blue chasms). Having done my research, I chose a seat with a view of the window. The lights of Reykjavík glimmered and glowed, and the city looked fantastic. Some of the illuminations were reflected in Tjörnin, and they moved slightly and disappeared with every slight ripple across the lake's near-frozen surface. The lakeside church Fríkirkjan stood proud by the shore, smaller than Hallgrímskirkja, its better-known cousin on the hill, but nonetheless proud. It was a truly Icelandic vista; it could not, should not be duplicated anywhere in the world. I knew that given half the chance, and aided by quantities of Icelandic beer, I'd soon be asking to move there again. Nichola, again, would have to spell out the impracticalities of simply dropping our lives and responsibilities at home, and I'd be left with latent promises of moving there one day. One day.

The promised bottle of Gæðingur beer was temporarily delayed, on account of champagne having been ordered. Daníel and Inga had arrived; I'm not sure if the two events were entirely coincidental. Daníel quickly raised a glass to me, and asked about my day so far. I didn't tell him about the Silfra dive as I wanted to keep that for Einar to hear; he already thought of me as a mad Englishman, and going lake diving in a dry suit in January would just confirm that for him. Instead, I diverted the conversation to comedy, and a show called *The Night Shift*, which is set in an Icelandic petrol station during, well, the night shift. I'd seen a couple of episodes, and Daníel was keen to hear my opinion. I told him that I was a fan, and that the series drew heavily on English comedy series, from *Fawlty Towers* to *The Office*. I said that I liked the character of the ginger-haired petrol station manager, played by a man who had also written some of the scripts for the series.

'That's Jón Gnarr,' he said. 'He is the mayor of Reykjavík now.'

I hadn't made the connection. When I did, I spat my champagne out halfway across the table. Only in Iceland, surely?

The restaurant was almost entirely in white, with

white curtains and white linen tablecloths and, at the far end, an open area through which you could see into the kitchen, as was the fashion. Two chefs, also dressed in pristine white, were busy chopping and preparing food in subdued, practised fashion.

Einar and Klara arrived, and the group was complete. Klara had made me a birthday cake earlier in the week. It was even decorated with *Sesame Street* characters, which proved that she really had done her research. Anything Jim Henson-related, and I am a five-year-old again. There was even a Cookie Monster and an Elmo. She smiled at me, and raised a glass of champagne in my direction. Einar commented that if we were drinking champagne, I must be paying. I knew that he was only joking, but I felt for my wallet through my trouser pocket to make sure that it was still there. I was pleased that the group was back together; I felt comfortable there, with my old friends.

The food started to arrive. First up was an amuse-bouche that contained raw scallops from the Faroe Islands and an espuma of broccoli. I wasn't sure about it, but it was clearly of a high standard and set us up for the meal to come. What I was really not sure about though were the scallops. From the Faroes? Why? I knew for a fact that Iceland had some of the best seafood in Europe, if not the world. Surely they could find something a bit more local, I thought; I realised later that I may have paid the scallops' airfare to Iceland. First class.

The starter passed in a blur of champagne, jokes and laughter. Mainly at my expense, I must add, but I didn't mind. I told Einar about the dive. He told me that I was mad. I already knew that.

Main course was lamb, served on a potato cake with seasonal vegetables and lamb's tongue. Nichola had already visibly blanched at the several mentions of lamb's tongue, but it turned out to be excellent. The tongue had been cubed and scattered liberally over the plate. The lamb fillet – mine and Nichola's well done, everyone else's still bleating – was also divine. It melted in the mouth, and was superbly complemented by the baby carrots and sprouts. It felt at once homely and celebratory. It was a meal fit for a banquet, and at the same time it wasn't that far from what a British mum might cook for a Sunday lunch. It was a finely balanced act, and one the chefs had pulled off superbly.

Inga then took us all by surprise. 'When I was young,' she said, 'the lamb's tongue was always my favourite part.' I looked at her, but she appeared to be serious. If this statement had come from Einar, or, to a lesser extent, Daníel, I would have thought no more about it. But from Inga, that sweet and unassuming Icelandic girl? The one with the cute *lopapeysa*-style gloves? I just couldn't see her relishing a dish made from the little pink tongues of half a dozen gambolling lambs. The effect was devastating, like learning that your best friend was into swinging, or something like that. I was speechless, and, of course, the source of much ridicule and laughter from the other Icelandic guests.

Before dessert, something truly unexpected happened. Actually, scrap that, two things happened. The first doesn't seem much as I describe it here and now, but it seemed incredibly kind at the time. At one point during our now somewhat inebriated conversation, Einar described how he had once worked on a fishing boat off Iceland's east coast and had made what seemed like a fortune to a seventeen-year-old lad. I asked what fish he was catching, but neither my extremely poor Icelandic nor his excellent English could produce the English name for the fish. Even after a barrage of fish names came at us from all corners of the table, we could not come to an understanding. The waiter took it upon himself to find his personal laptop and carry out a bit of light research, whereupon he returned to the table with a picture of the fish in question. All of this was done without asking, and done in such a pleasing, helpful manner, that I couldn't help but be bowled over. I can't think of anywhere else in the world where customer service is so good. It was a capelin, by the way, a fish I have never heard of either.

The second act was even nicer, and might have brought me to tears had this not been socially unacceptable, even in these softer times. Daníel, Inga, Einar and Klara had bought me a gift for my birthday. I know that doesn't sound much, but I had not expected it, and, to be honest, gifts from friends and family had dwindled to the socks and handkerchiefs variety. This was nothing of the sort. It was a fantastic little book on Icelandic delicacies, with some awesome photographs of the food and the places it came from. It even had recipes, should I feel brave enough to give them a go. Einar flipped the book open to a page he wanted to show me. His expression was both proud and mischievous. I looked down at the open book before me. It was Hildibrandur and his shark, served, as ever, with a grin than ran from ear to ear.

While the beer was flowing, and in a break between

the sumptuous courses, I was handed a second present. This one was different though. It had been chosen with particular care and thoughtfulness. It was a beautifully packaged jigsaw puzzle of a stunning image of Hvítserkur, a spectacular arched sea stack in northern Iceland. I'm not usually into that sort of stuff, but this really caught my imagination. A clear product of yet more ingenious Icelandic creativity; I wanted to find out more.

The two Icelanders behind Puzzled by Iceland are Þóra Eggertsdóttir and Guðrún Heimisdóttir. They describe themselves as 'two blue-eyed, blonde-haired moms' and came up with the idea of starting a company while they were both on eighteen months' maternity leave from work. Each has two children, and wanted to do something other than change nappies. Which is fair enough, I can't argue with that.

Perhaps unusually, though, they didn't have any idea what they wanted to do, other than start a company of some sort. Inspiration often comes from the strangest places. In this case inspiration came from the Swedish royal family. Guðrún came across a puzzle featuring a photograph of the Swedish monarchy. This triggered the realisation that in Iceland you couldn't buy a puzzle of, say, the Icelandic president. This was somewhat 'tongue in cheek'; any such puzzle would be a comedic novelty, but nothing more. Slowly, the concept changed and evolved into what is now Puzzled by Iceland.

Since its inception in August 2010, Puzzled by Iceland has been producing bespoke, beautifully designed and manufactured puzzles of the most alluring and dramatic Icelandic scenes and wildlife. They are packaged in neat little boxes and come with an information leaflet. Even the information leaflet about my Hvítserkur sea stack filled me with delight: 'Some say it looks like a rhino drinking from the sea, others say it looks like a dinosaur.' The prospect of whiling away cold winter evenings by completing puzzles with your nearest and dearest as you drink hot chocolate and the very worst Icelandic weather rages outside seems almost impossibly cosy and romantic.

I can see why the puzzles have become so popular: regardless of whether they depict tourist hotspots, lesser-known sights or Icelandic fauna, the images are visually stunning. Northern Lights flashing over the Öxarárfoss waterfall in Þingvellir. The cutest puffin caught in a close-up. A white Icelandic horse against distant snow-capped mountains. The neon-streaked landscapes of Þeistareykir in north Iceland. At once evocative of Iceland's natural rugged charm and beauty, each piece of puzzle clicking into place leads you to the next, and on until the gorgeous image is complete once again.

The final course, the dessert, arrived. It was a triumph of caramel, toffee and *skyr*. It was delicious and dreamy, and easily the best course of the day. The night continued. Einar and Klara eventually made their excuses and left in a flurry of kisses and handshakes. Nichola and I went to a bar 'downtown', as they say in Reykjavík, accompanied by Daníel and Inga.

Already tipsy, we exchanged stories about our home countries along with rounds of the improbably named Polar Beer, each of us trying to outdo the last, attempting to prove which was the greater nation. Although the discussion degenerated into fits of laughter and half-hearted bravado, Daníel may have just come out on top, with a cracker of a story.

During the harsh winter of 2010, he told us, several European airports were forced to close on account of 'inclement weather' – in reality, a few centimetres of snow. In Paris, an Icelandair plane was due to return to Keflavík. With the airport closed and all flights grounded because of the snow – and, more likely, a health and safety executive – ground crews refused to work and no planes left that day. Or so they thought. The Icelandair pilots took matters into their own hands. Quite literally. They each grabbed a shovel and dug the plane out of the snow and onto the runway, then successfully took off and returned to Iceland. Their efforts were duly noted; not only was the flight the only one to leave that day, but the Icelandic president was aboard and mentioned the pilots' endeavours in a parliamentary speech. If I was Icelandic, I too would be proud of those two chaps. I mean, you would never see that from British Airways, would you? Instead, though, it was in part viewed as something that an Icelander should do, in the same way that every Icelander should be able to drive in any conditions, especially on cliff edges, and also be able to barbeque at any time of year. It's as if it's part of the national psyche. I thought it was pretty impressive all the same and I told Daníel so. He was taken aback by this, and I thought I saw a gulp of pride in his throat, either that or the Polar Beer was getting to him.

The night slowly started to wind down. Even in Reykjavík it's difficult – but not impossible – to keep partying forever on a Wednesday night, especially when your friends have to work the next day. In the modern workplace, even in Iceland, there is no room for hangovers. The melancholy slowly crept in as the alcohol took its toll, and the conversation gradually petered out.

I got thinking though. It must be a good feeling to be proud of your country. All of the Icelanders I have met are immensely proud of their culture, heritage and country. Not in an American, fake-patriotism way, but in a genuine way. I think that now, after all my travels and experiences in Iceland, I can see why. Iceland is an extraordinary country. I don't know anywhere else like it, from its bubbling cauldrons, explosive volcanoes and secret hot pools, to the occasional visiting polar bear, skittish Arctic fox and ubiquitous puffin. From the deserts of the interior and their violent paint-stripping sandstorms to the cold white glaciers and the new landforms being created daily before then getting covered in purple lupins.

Equally extraordinary is the small community of people that lives on her and calls her home. I don't know why I've started using the feminine pronoun to describe Iceland, as if she were a boat, but the sentiment is certainly true. The people of Iceland are also out of the ordinary. Maybe it's the Viking heritage, the harsh environment or the long winters, but they are something special. From Hafdís Huld and her blueberry fetish, Ester and her foxes, to Sibba and her hidden folk. From Sóley, Snorri, Lay Low and Ólafur Arnalds, to Lily and Fox. From Hildibrandur and his shark, Siggi in New York with his *skyr*, to the girl in the Mickey Mouse T-shirt selling her family farm's ice cream. I feel lucky to have met them and shared their world, if only for a short time.

The real stars, though, are the Icelanders who have

welcomed me into their homes and lives, have taken great care to show me the best of their country and to make sure that I watch the Eurovision Song Contest every single year. Einar, Klara, Daníel and Inga have made Nichola and I feel that they are so much more than friends, more like our very own Icelandic family. When we got married, Einar and Klara sent us a *lopapeysa* each. They are still very much in use every winter; pulling one on makes me feel warm inside and out. (Wasn't that a porridge advert in the 80s? Oh, never mind.) For this I am deeply grateful to them all, and I feel extremely lucky to have met them. Without them, none of my Icelandic adventures, experiences or hangovers would have happened. This book certainly wouldn't have been possible. We are a lot like the Famous Five. Except there are six of us.

Nichola and I wandered through the dark, cold streets to our hotel. When I was at school, I was once forced to join a special spelling class, much to my chagrin. I was only allowed to re-join my original class after I had announced to the teacher the difference between 'wander' and 'wonder'. Tonight, though, both words applied, as both of us were deep in thought and, well, 'going via an indirect route at no set pace'.

I didn't know when I'd be able to return to Iceland. Nichola was pregnant with our child, and soon I'd have a little person to look after. My priorities would be sure to shift, and I'd been told that babies didn't come cheap. We idly chatted about names, but we both know that the name had already been chosen. We had even been calling the bump by the name, and we already knew it was a girl.

Back at the hotel, now several thousand krónur

lighter and quite tipsy, I held the boxed jigsaw puzzle in my hands and looked at the photograph of Hvítserkur on the front. The jagged white and black rock loomed out of the light blue sea against a green-blue sky. Arches in the rock revealed the Icelandic landscape behind. The picture was just stunning. A puzzle, so simple, yet so ingenious. It felt like I was taking a piece of Iceland home with me. Or several hundred pieces. I was really chuffed with that gift, I have to say. It was really thoughtful of them and it reminded me that Icelanders, once you break through that tough, icy exterior, are some of the kindest, nicest people you could ever hope to meet. That evening, with that small group of friends, will stay with me forever. I'm sure of that.

A few years ago, through my work, I was dispatched to see a post-mortem examination. The experience will stay with me for a long, long time to come. Not simply because I will never, ever be able to wipe from my mind the image of the intricate insides of a human being, nor because the whole procedure was done in such a professional, business-like manner, nor even because a small part of me, deep down, kept repeating, 'Don't believe it, it's not real' (it didn't look like it was, it looked like a B-rated horror movie). No, what will stay with me forever is the pathologist approaching me with a human brain in his rubber-gloved hand. As he placed it on the table before me and started to cut through the lobes with his scalpel, he paused momentarily. He looked up at me through his plastic safety goggles and the screen of Perspex between us and said, 'Think of all the memories and knowledge contained in here.' He then returned to dissecting the organ in front of him, precision-slicing through the wobbly matter. And I did think of all the memories in there. I kept thinking of them over and over again. All that I can hope for is that when I go, my brain will be full of love, happy memories and that cathedral of blue, in a frozen lake, in the middle of frozen Iceland.

One year later, on my thirty-first birthday, the road between Keflavík and Reykjavík was closed. Due to snow. This almost never happens. Flights in and out of Keflavík had been suspended. No one was digging the planes out this time around. The ring road was also shut, but this is less unusual. A snowplough had got stuck in Reykjavík, and an ICE-SAR volunteer had been assaulted by an irate motorist who thought he should be able to get through a road closed for his own safety. Snow, delayed by several years of warm winters, had arrived properly in Reykjavík.

The snow had been falling, not continuously, but without thaw, since November, three months earlier. Snow had fallen, snow on snow, snow on snow, as the old Christmas carol goes. Icelanders have a number of words for snow; this was definitely *hundslappadrífa* – flakes as large as a dog's paws.

Around Reykjavík it was piled in huge mounds, lining every road and making you feel like an insect between the furrows of a ploughed field. Public spaces had been cleared, but eventually the mounds of snow had run out of places to be pushed. Each car park had its own mountain range of churned snow.

Snow was sitting on everything. It had covered the

ground completely, and buildings and street furniture had either been obscured or had gained a white topping of a good few inches. Low street lights had been swallowed by the encroaching drifts, giving the place an eerily orange glow, like from a torch placed behind a human finger. At Tjörnin, school children were playing football on the solidly frozen lake, wearing fluorescent orange bibs and aiming for plastic-cone goals.

The sky had emptied itself and the glowing pink clouds had disappeared, for now at least. Without the snow-laden clouds keeping temperatures constant, like an eider-feather duvet over the country, the mercury plummeted. As darkness approached, the sky was completely clear, even in Reykjavík, which for once wasn't the 'Smoky Bay' after which it was named.

I had received a phone call from Einar. This was it. This was the one. If there was one day on which I was going to see the NL, it was today. NL. Our code for Aurora Borealis. We had long since given up calling it by its more common moniker. Eight years' experience had proved that using its full name was the first step to definitely not seeing the NL. Einar had arranged for a friend, one with a 4x4 beast of a truck, to collect the two of us from downtown Reykjavík and I was instructed to wear my thickest, warmest clothes. Not a problem.

Þórir arrived with a swoosh of chunky winter tyres through deep, fluffy snow. He was wearing a thick down jacket and sat far from the steering wheel, in a position familiar to boy racers in supermarket car parks the world over. His 4x4 was pretty beaten up, and seemed to be already full, despite Þórir being the only occupant.

I pushed detritus from the seat and climbed aboard. Einar did the same in the rear.

The roads were snow covered and slippery in the city; outside it they were downright treacherous. Þórir pointed out his house and a lane that cut though the thick snow. 'That's not actually the road,' he said. 'The snow plough couldn't find it, so he made a new one.'

We headed out of Reykjavík and towards Þingvellir, leaving the light pollution behind us, in the form of a fuzzy orange glow that slowly but surely disappeared from view. The first rule of NL hunting: get out of the city. Any NL will be obscured by the city's lights.

The second rule of NL hunting: it has to be cold and clear. I checked the digital display in Þórir's truck. It said minus 15. It was cold outside, so it was a good thing that Þórir had cranked up the heating to a toe-warming maximum. I leant forward and craned my neck to look at the skies; yep, they were perfectly clear, not a wisp of cloud. I rubbed my hands together in anticipation.

The truck barely noticed the snow on the ground, unlike the abandoned, snow-bound vehicles that stood scattered across both verges, with no sign of their drivers, and the group of tourists staring out disappointedly from the inside of their steamed-up, wheel-spinning minibus. We bounced further out of the city on roads raised above the landscape in order to stop snow building up on them, yellow markers on either side demarking our route. 'The snow should blow off the highest points,' Þórir told me. I had never realised that before. The strategy was only partly successful though, as the further we went, the more snow there was on the road, blown across it in huge drifts.

This was dry, light snow and the wind had no problem pushing it around and whistling it into streamlined banks, not dissimilar to dunes on a beach.

I had left Nichola and Lily, our seven-month-old daughter, back in Reykjavík. It would have been too dangerous for them. Yes, I would have loved them to see the NL, but I couldn't, and wouldn't risk it. Lily was happy just trying to catch snowflakes anyway.

We headed towards the mountains; other traffic, even cars with the locally popular extra rooftop insulation, had long since disappeared. Only our headlights shone out, reflecting off the steep snowy mountainsides, beneath a crescent moon that loomed in the dark, clear sky above.

Eventually the drifts became too much, the road ran out and Þórir pulled over and stopped. I hopped out of the truck. Without the engine noise, all I could hear was the wind whistling over the frozen landscape and the soft squeaking of snow being compacted under my boots.

Þórir called my name. I struggled with the zip on my coat, then cautiously waddled through the snow to his side of the vehicle. Einar and Þórir were standing stock still, both staring at the same point on the horizon. I followed their gaze.

'Is that… is that…?' I stammered. 'Is that what I think it is?'

'Yes,' said Einar.

'Yes,' said Þórir.

I saw the Northern Lights for the first time. A bright streak of green cut through the black sky from the horizon.

My heart started to pound. My breathing stopped. My mouth opened involuntarily. I stopped shivering. I heard the blood rushing through my ear holes. This was it.

The Northern Lights – *norðurljós* – lit up the horizon; a thick smudge of bright green light the colour of copper flames illuminated the space where the snowy mountains and the black night met. Einar pointed out that tendrils of the lights were coming off and arcing up and over our heads. These were more difficult to spot than the lights on the horizon, but they were there nonetheless. They were just difficult to distinguish against the bright, twinkling stars set in the deep black sky.

My eyes returned to the horizon, where the constantly moving green lights were beginning to shimmer and shake. They zigzagged and reformed. They circled and swirled. They disappeared and reappeared.

I stood and watched for I don't know how long. Occasionally, I turned to celebrate with Einar and Þórir by way of back slaps or slightly embarrassing high-fives. They told me stories of previous Northern Lights shows they had seen, speaking in low voices, never turning away from the display.

My face had frozen, but I couldn't speak anyway. I stood there mesmerised by the fluorescent strands dancing in the sky before me. It didn't feel real. It felt like a dream, but it wasn't. I was finally seeing the Northern Lights. In Iceland. It had taken eight years. Countless trips. Credit card bending to breaking point. A whole book.

It was worth it, I thought to myself. Definitely. On my thirty-first too. I climbed back into the truck and all three of us drove wordlessly back to Reykjavík. I blinked and saved. Blinked and saved.

Further Listening

Amiina, *Puzzle* (2011)
Björk, *Biophilia* (2011)
Björk, *Debut* (1999)
Borko, *Born to be Free* (2012)
Cheek Mountain Thief, *Cheek Mountain Thief* (2012)
Dikta, *Get It Together* (2011)
Dikta, *Trust Me* (2012)
FM Belfast, *Don't Want To Sleep* (2011)
For a Minor Reflection, *EP* (2012)
For a Minor Reflection, *Reistu þig við, sólin er komin á loft* (2007)
GusGus, *Arabian Horse* (2011)
Hafdís Huld, *Dirty Paper Cup* (2008)
Hafdís Huld, *Synchronized Swimmers* (2010)
Jónsi, *Go* (2010)
Jónsi, *GO LIVE* (2011)
Jónsi & Alex, *Riceboy Sleeps* (2009)
Lay Low, *Farewell Good Night's Sleep* (2009)
Múm, *Finally We Are No One* (2006)
Of Monsters and Men, *My Head is an Animal* (2012)
Ólafur Arnalds, *Found Songs* (2009)
Ólafur Arnalds, *Living Room Songs* (2011)
Pascal Pinon, *Twosomeness* (2013)
Retro Stefson, *Retro Stefson* (2013)
Rökkurró, *Í Annan Heim* (2010)
Rökkurró, *Það kólnar í kvöld* (2007)

Seabear, *The Ghost That Carried Us Away* (2008)

Sigur Rós, *( )* (2002)

Sigur Rós, *Ágætis Byrjun* (1999)

Sigur Rós, *Takk* (2009)

Sigur Rós, *Valtari* (2012)

Sin Fang, *Flowers* (2013)

Sin Fang, *Summer Echoes* (2011)

Snorri Helgason, *Winter Sun* (2011)

Sóley, *We Sink* (2011)

Svavar Knútur, *Amma* (2012)

Further Reading

Nanna Árnadóttir, *Zombie Iceland* (OkeiBækur, 2011)

Quentin Bates, *Cold Comfort* (Robinson, 2012)

Hallgrímur Helgason, *101 Reykjavik* (Faber and Faber, 2002)

Hallgrímur Helgason, *The Hitman's Guide to Housecleaning* (Amazon Crossing, 2012)

Arnaldur Indriðason, *Hypothermia* (Vintage Press, 2010)

Arnaldur Indriðason, *Jar City* (Vintage Press, 2000)

Halldór Laxness, *Independent People* (Vintage Classic, 1946)

Tim Moore, *Frost On My Moustache* (Abacus, 2000)

Sarah Moss, *Names for the Sea: Strangers in Iceland* (Granta Publications, 2012)

Zane Radcliffe, *The Killer's Guide To Iceland* (Black Swan, 2005)

Sjón, *The Blue Fox* (Telegram Books, 2008)

Paul Sullivan, *Waking up in Iceland* (Sanctuary, 2003)

Acknowledgements

This book is dedicated to Nichola and Lily, for their endless patience and support, allowing me to 'pop' to Iceland at the drop of a hat, and just being so loving.

Mum, Dad and my sister Lisa showed support in very different ways but always picking up the pieces when it went wrong. Mum with devastating honesty, Lisa with practical support and Dad, although not credited in the text, accompanied me on trips to the Westman Islands and the West Fjords.

None of this would have been possible without my Icelandic 'family', whose kindness and generosity have been fundamental to this whole project, along with some of the finest meals I have ever tasted. Einar Guðberg Jónsson, Klara Kristjánsdóttir, Daníel Scheving and Inga Jasonardóttir, I raise a toast to you all. Einar deserves particular credit for suggesting this whole malarkey in the first place, and for barbequing in extreme conditions.

Lucy Ridout has been the best ever editor, adding professionalism and making sense of my otherwise scrambled words. Eygló Svala Arnarsdóttir and Quentin Bates have been my expert proofreaders, and provided encouragement and advice throughout.

Other thanks go to – in no particular order – Zoë Robert (and all at *Iceland Review*), Snorri Helgason, Lovísa Elísabet Sigrúnardóttir (Lay Low), Þorleifur Þór Jónsson and Mosi the dog, Sóley Stefánsdóttir,

Mike Lindsay (Cheek Mountain Thief), Hildur Kristín Stefánsdóttir (Lily and Fox), Nanna Árnadóttir, Anna Anderson (*The Reykjavík Grapevine*), Ani Simon-Kennedy (Bicephaly Pictures), Hreinn Pállson, Auður Ólafsdóttir (iheartreykjavik.net), Ásta Andrésdóttir, Ólöf S. Baldursdóttir (ICE-SAR), Ciaran Williams, Þóra Eggertsdóttir and Guðrún Heimisdóttir (Puzzled by Iceland), Halla Ingólfsdóttir, James and Sarah Littlewood, Eva Björk Guðjónsdóttir (Air Iceland), all at Icelandair, Eyrún Hafsteinsdóttir (Embassy of Iceland, London), Florian Zimmer (Morr Music), Sigga and all at BB44 Guesthouse, Inga Kristjánsdóttir at Tiny Iceland, Chloé Mulcahey, Helga Guðrún Hinriksdóttir, Mark Ollard (Iceblah), Claus Sterneck, Andrew Haddon, Sigurbjörg Karlsdóttir, Kamilla Ingibergsdóttir and all at Iceland Airwaves, Maria Wilkinson, Alex Hardie, Jade Smalley (for flapjacks), Emma Godfrey-Ford, Liz Herdson, Carmel McNamara, Kristen Hall, Roopa Cheema, Nick Miners, Pascal Pinon, Ólafur Arnalds, Siggi Hilmarsson (Siggi's Skyr), Agnar Sverrisson (and all at Texture, London), Hafdís Huld, Cliff and Pete at Tarvin Sands Reindeer Centre in Cheshire, Hotel Búðir, Hildibrandur Bjarnason, Mjöður Brugghús (now sadly out of business), Icelandic Phallological Museum, Sigur Rós, Amiina, Icelandic Sea Monster Museum in Bíldudalur, Jón Gnarr, Eliza Newman, Kjartan Lárusson on behalf of ITB, Nick Hill (map illustration), Kit Foster (cover design), Helen Hart & Sarah Newman at SilverWood Books, Ester Rut Unnsteinsdóttir and all at the Arctic Fox Centre in Súðavík, Noel Metcalfe (who I still miss), and Þórir Ingvarsson for showing me the Northern Lights.

A note of thanks to *Iceland Review*; some passages in *Iceland, Defrosted* have previously been published online in my columns on Daily Life, Iceland Review Online.

My sincere apologies to anyone who deserves a thank you but does not appear on this page. It's not intentional!

Kickstarter

In December 2012, *Iceland, Defrosted* was launched as a Kickstarter project, with the objective of crowd-sourcing funds to publish the book in print and e-book form. The project was highly successful, with 122 backers from across the globe pledging 179% of the required funding. I would like to thank all of the backers, as without them, *Iceland, Defrosted* would remain forever on my hard drive.

An extra thank you to the following kind and generous backers: Einar Guðberg Jónsson, Ally Kingdon, Daníel Scheving, James Littlewood, Sarah Hart, Ian Cumberland, Jude Storton, Katharine K Wiley, Søren Snehøj Nielsen, Mark Pinto, Wayne Budgen, and last but not least, Lisa Hancox. This book would not be here without you. *Takk fyrir.*

Glossary

Alþingi – the parliament of Iceland

bjór – beer

brennivín – a spirit made from fermented potato mash

Dettifoss – a waterfall in north Iceland

Einstök – a type of Icelandic beer

Esja – a mountain outside Reykjavík

Eyjafjallajökull – an infamous south Iceland volcano/glacier

foss – waterfall

Gæðingur – a type of Icelandic beer

Geysir – the original geyser

Gullfoss – a waterfall north-east of Reykjavík

hákarl – fermented shark

Hallgrímskirkja – a church in Reykjavík

Harpa – an architecturally striking concert hall in Reykjavík

Heima – a Sigur Rós film

huldufólk – hidden folk

ICE-SAR – Iceland Search and Rescue

jökull – glacier

Jökulsárlón – a glacial lagoon in south Iceland

Jónsi – the lead singer of Sigur Rós

kaffi – coffee

kleinur – Icelandic twisted donuts

kreppa – financial crisis

Langjökull – a glacier in west/central Iceland

laufabrauð – thin 'leaf bread', served at Christmas

Laugardalslaug – a swimming pool complex in Reykjavík
lopapeysa – traditional Icelandic woollen jumper
Mýrdalsjökull – a glacier in south Iceland
nammi namm – yummy yummy
pylsur – Icelandic hot dogs
skyr – a yoghurt-like dairy product
Snæfellsjökull – a glacier in west Iceland
stræti – street
Sundhöllin – a swimming pool in Reykjavík
takk – thanks
takk fyrir – thanks for
Vatnajökull – a glacier in east Iceland (largest in Europe)
Þorrablót – a mid-winter feast

Printed by BoD™ in Norderstedt, Germany